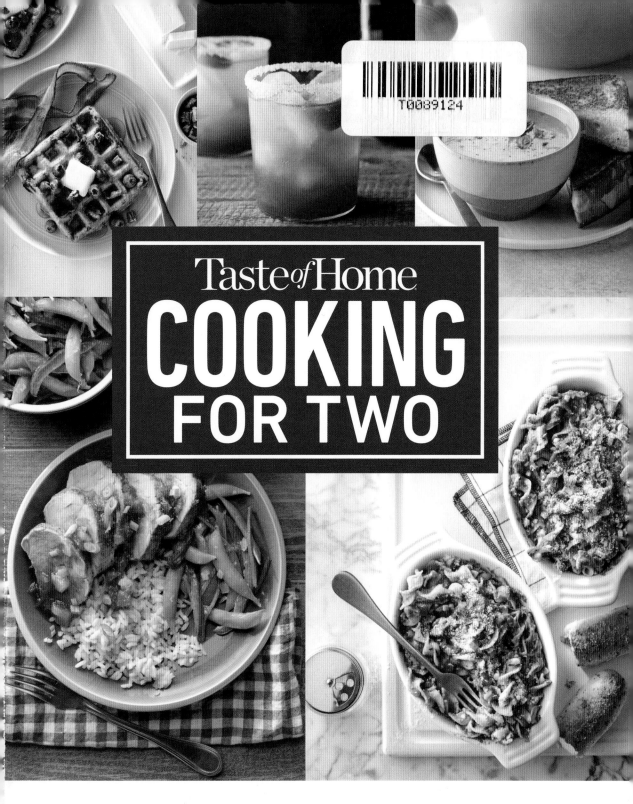

Taste *of* Home
COOKING
FOR TWO

TASTE OF HOME BOOKS • RDA ENTHUSIAST BRANDS, LLC • MILWAUKEE, WI

© 2022 RDA Enthusiast Brands, LLC.
1610 N. 2nd St., Suite 102, Milwaukee, WI 53212-3906
All rights reserved. Taste of Home is a registered
trademark of RDA Enthusiast Brands, LLC.

Visit us at **tasteofhome.com** for other Taste of Home
books and products.

International Standard Book Number:
978-1-62145-771-8

Executive Editor: Mark Hagen
Senior Art Director: Raeann Thompson
Editor: Hazel Wheaton
Art Director: Courtney Lovetere
Deputy Editor, Copy Desk: Dulcie Shoener
Copy Editor: Elizabeth Pollock Bruch
Contributing Designer: Jennifer Ruetz

Cover
Photographer: Dan Roberts
Set Stylist: Stacey Genaw
Food Stylist: Josh Rink

Pictured on front cover: Sesame Chicken Stir-Fry, p. 102
Pictured on spine: Lime Coconut Smoothie Bowl, p. 55
Pictured on back cover: Orange Rosemary Carrots, p. 205;
Four-Cheese Stuffed Shells, p. 161; Chocolate Peanut Butter
Shakes, p. 15; Cheese-Stuffed Burgers, p. 74; Cauliflower
Broccoli Cheese Soup, p. 69

INSTANT POT is a trademark of Double Insight Inc.
This publication has not been authorized, sponsored
or otherwise approved by Double Insight Inc.

Printed in China
1 3 5 7 9 10 8 6 4 2

Grilled Pepper Jack
Chicken Sandwiches, p. 90

FABULOUS FOOD JUST RIGHT FOR TWO!

Love to cook but don't love all of the leftovers? Tired of wasting time, effort and money cooking large-yield dishes that eventually end up languishing in the fridge? Or maybe you long for the comforting casseroles, snacks, soups and sweet treats that please a crowd but don't make sense for small households.

Whether you're an empty nester or a newlywed, or you're simply cooking for a pair, *Taste of Home Cooking for Two* has the answers! This all-new collection of small-serving recipes helps you whip up the mouthwatering favorites you crave in just the right quantities.

Each of the 317 incredible dishes in this collection is sized right for one, two or three diners. From dips and spreads to entrees and desserts, the perfect dish is always at hand.

You'll also enjoy...

• A complete set of nutrition facts with every recipe, and diabetic exchanges where applicable.

• Timelines for prepping and cooking, and step-by-step directions to help you plan meals effortlessly.

• Reader reviews and no-fuss tips from the pros at the Taste of Home Test Kitchen.

Best of all, special icons highlight dishes that help you make the most of your time. Look for recipes that use today's most convenient gadgets—the air fryer 🍤 and Instant Pot® 🍲. Also, look for the clock icon 🕐 for dishes that take 30 minutes or less, from raw ingredients to ready to serve, so you can quickly spot the recipes you need when your time is tightest.

With full-color photos, fast weeknight staples, delicious appetizers and snacks, fabulous sides, tempting desserts and so much more, *Taste of Home Cooking for Two* is your guide to quick, easy specialties sized just right for your home.

TABLE OF CONTENTS

MORE WAYS TO CONNECT WITH US: 🇫 🐦 📷 📌

SNACKS

Make tonight appetizer night! You won't have to fill the fridge with loads of leftovers. These special apps, snacks and drinks give you just the right amount of deliciousness.

CHOCOLATE CINNAMON TOAST

Looking for a fun snack? Toast cinnamon bread in a skillet and top it with chocolate and fresh fruit. Add a dollop of whipped cream to each slice to make it extra indulgent.
—Jeanne Ambrose, Milwaukee, WI

TAKES: 10 MIN. • **MAKES:** 1 PIECE

- 1   slice cinnamon bread
- 1   tsp. butter, softened
- 2   Tbsp. 60% cacao bittersweet chocolate baking chips
    Optional: Sliced banana and strawberries

Spread both sides of bread with butter. In a small skillet, toast the bread over medium-high heat for 2-3 minutes on each side, topping with chocolate chips after turning. Remove from heat; spread melted chocolate evenly over toast. Top with fruit if desired.

1 piece: 235 cal., 13g fat (8g sat. fat), 10mg chol., 131mg sod., 29g carb. (19g sugars, 3g fiber), 4g pro.

HOMEMADE CHOCOLATE SHORTBREAD

This recipe has been in my files for a long time, probably since I first learned to bake. I make these year-round with variations—adding a thin coat of icing to make them even richer, or making them into a sandwich cookie with frosting in the middle.
—Sarah Bueckert, Austin, MB

PREP: 10 MIN. • **BAKE:** 20 MIN. + COOLING
MAKES: 1 DOZEN

- ¼   cup butter, softened
- ¼   tsp. vanilla extract
- ½   cup all-purpose flour
- ¼   cup confectioners' sugar
- 1   to 2 Tbsp. baking cocoa

1. Preheat oven to 300°. In a small bowl, cream the butter until light and fluffy, 3-4 minutes. Beat in vanilla. Combine the flour, sugar and cocoa; add to the creamed mixture. Beat until dough holds together, about 3 minutes.
2. Pat into a 9x4-in. rectangle. Cut into 2x1½-in. strips. Place strips 1 in. apart on ungreased baking sheets. Prick with a fork.
3. Bake until set, 20-25 minutes. Cool on pans for 5 minutes before removing from pan to a wire rack to cool completely.

1 cookie: 64 cal., 4g fat (2g sat. fat), 10mg chol., 31mg sod., 7g carb. (2g sugars, 0 fiber), 1g pro.

TEST KITCHEN TIP

Unless a particular recipe says otherwise, always let your cookies cool on the pan for at least 1 minute before moving them to a rack—it helps them set up and keep from crumbling.

PEANUTTY POPCORN BALLS

These tasty, salty-sweet gourmet treats make a lovely surprise tucked into the toe of a Christmas stocking, but they're delicious any time of year and just as welcome tucked into a lunchbox!
—Candace Harris, Walker, MN

TAKES: 25 MIN.
MAKES: 2 POPCORN BALLS

- 2 cups popped popcorn
- ½ cup salted peanuts
- 2 Tbsp. brown sugar
- 2 Tbsp. light corn syrup
- 1 Tbsp. creamy peanut butter
  Dash salt

1. In a large bowl, combine the popcorn and peanuts; set aside. In a small microwave-safe bowl, combine the brown sugar, corn syrup, peanut butter and salt. Microwave, uncovered, on high for 30-45 seconds or until bubbly; stir. Pour over popcorn mixture; mix well.
2. When it is cool enough to handle, quickly divide the mixture and shape it into two 2½-in. balls. Let stand at room temperature until firm; wrap securely.

1 popcorn ball: 421 cal., 25g fat (4g sat. fat), 0 chol., 394mg sod., 44g carb. (26g sugars, 5g fiber), 12g pro.

RICH HOT CHOCOLATE

Each February, my friends and I gather for an outdoor show called Mittenfest. We skip the Bloody Marys and fill our thermoses with this hot cocoa instead.
—Gina Nistico, Denver, CO

TAKES: 15 MIN. • **MAKES:** 2 SERVINGS

- ⅔ cup heavy whipping cream
- 1 cup 2% milk
- 4 oz. dark chocolate candy bar, chopped
- 3 Tbsp. sugar
  Vanilla rum, optional
  Sweetened heavy whipping cream, whipped, optional

In a small saucepan, heat heavy cream, milk, chocolate and sugar over medium heat just until the mixture comes to a simmer, stirring constantly.

Remove from the heat; stir until smooth. If desired, add rum. Pour into 2 mugs; top with sweetened whipped cream if desired.

1 cup: 653 cal., 49g fat (32g sat. fat), 107mg chol., 79mg sod., 60g carb. (56g sugars, 4g fiber), 9g pro.

Pumpkin-Spice Cocoa: Heat ⅔ cup heavy cream, 1 cup milk, ½ cup white baking chips, 2 Tbsp. canned pumpkin and 1 tsp. pumpkin pie spice over medium heat just until mixture comes to a simmer, stirring constantly. Remove from heat; stir until smooth. If desired, add 3 oz. RumChata liqueur.

Toasted Coconut Cocoa: Heat 1 can coconut milk, ½ cup milk , ⅔ cup chocolate chips and 2 Tbsp. sugar over medium heat just until mixture comes to a simmer, stirring constantly. Remove from heat; stir until smooth. If desired, add 3 oz. Malibu rum.

Spicy Cinnamon Cocoa: Heat ⅔ cup heavy cream, 1 cup milk, ⅔ cup chocolate chips, 2 Tbsp. sugar, 1 tsp. ground cinnamon and ⅛ tsp. cayenne pepper over medium heat just until mixture comes to a simmer, stirring constantly. Remove from the heat; stir until smooth. If desired, add 3 oz. cinnamon whiskey.

Chocolate-Orange Cocoa: Heat ⅔ cup heavy cream, 1 cup milk, ⅔ cup chocolate chips, 2 Tbsp. sugar and 1 tsp. grated orange zest over medium heat just until mixture comes to a simmer, stirring constantly. Remove from heat; stir until smooth. If desired, add 3 oz. Cointreau liqueur.

4½ tsp. lemon juice
4½ tsp. reduced-sodium
    soy sauce
  1 Tbsp. canola oil
    Dash garlic powder
    Dash pepper
¾ lb. sea scallops
  2 small green peppers,
    cut into 1½-in. pieces
  1 cup cherry tomatoes

1. In a small bowl, combine first 5 ingredients to make a marinade. Pour 2 Tbsp. marinade into a bowl or shallow dish. Add the scallops and turn to coat them. Cover and refrigerate for 20 minutes. Cover and refrigerate the remaining marinade to use for basting.
2. Meanwhile, in a large saucepan, bring 3 cups water to a boil. Add the peppers; cover and boil for 2 minutes. Drain and immediately place peppers in ice water. Drain and pat dry.
3. Drain scallops, discarding the marinade. On 4 metal or soaked wooden skewers, alternately thread the tomatoes, scallops and blanched peppers.
4. On a lightly greased grill rack, grill the kabobs, covered, over medium heat, or broil 4 in. from the heat, for 3-5 minutes on each side or until the scallops are firm and opaque, basting occasionally with reserved marinade.
2 kabobs: 235 cal., 7g fat (1g sat. fat), 56mg chol., 616mg sod., 12g carb. (4g sugars, 2g fiber), 30g pro.
Diabetic exchanges: 4 lean meat, 2 vegetable, 1 fat.

TEST KITCHEN TIP

Do not leave the scallops in the marinade longer than 30 minutes, or the acid in the lemon juice will start to break down their texture and your scallops may be mushy.

SCALLOP KABOBS

I'm always on the lookout for recipes that are lower in fat and heart-healthy, too. These kabobs fill the bill. I like to serve them with a fruit salad and a light dessert.
—Edie DeSpain, Logan, UT

PREP: 25 MIN. + MARINATING
GRILL: 10 MIN. • **MAKES:** 4 KABOBS

ONION PITA PIZZA

For an appealing appetizer or snack, try this twist on pizza. The flavorful blue cheese and onion on the crispy pita crust are sure to hit the spot, along with your favorite summer beverage.
—Mary Lou Wayman, Salt Lake City, UT

PREP: 25 MIN. • **BAKE:** 15 MIN.
MAKES: 2 SERVINGS

- 1 large onion, thinly sliced
- 1 Tbsp. butter
- 1 pita bread (6 in.)
- ⅔ cup 1% cottage cheese
- 2 Tbsp. crumbled blue cheese
- 2 Tbsp. chopped walnuts, toasted

1. In a small skillet, cook the onion slices in butter over low heat until golden, 20-25 minutes, stirring occasionally. Place pita bread on an ungreased baking sheet and bake at 350° for 8-10 minutes or until lightly browned.
2. In a food processor, combine cottage cheese and blue cheese; cover and process until blended. Spread over the pita bread; top with onion. Sprinkle with walnuts. Bake 3-5 minutes longer or until heated through. Cut into wedges.

½ pizza: 293 cal., 14g fat (6g sat. fat), 25mg chol., 645mg sod., 26g carb. (7g sugars, 2g fiber), 17g pro.

REFRESHING TOMATO BRUSCHETTA

This recipe is best when made with sun-warmed tomatoes and basil fresh from the garden. My husband and I love this so much, we can make a meal of it alone!
—Greta Igl, Menomonee Falls, WI

TAKES: 20 MIN. • **MAKES:** 2 SERVINGS

- 3 tsp. olive oil, divided
- 4 slices French bread (½ in. thick)
- 1 garlic clove, cut in half lengthwise
- ¾ cup chopped seeded tomato
- 1 Tbsp. minced fresh basil
- ½ tsp. minced fresh parsley
- ½ tsp. red wine vinegar
- ⅛ tsp. salt
- ⅛ tsp. pepper

1. Preheat oven to 350°. Brush ½ tsp. oil over 1 side of each slice of bread. Place bread slices, with the oiled side up, on a baking sheet. Bake for 5-7 minutes or until lightly browned. Rub the cut side of garlic over the bread.
2. Meanwhile, in a small bowl, combine the tomato, basil, parsley, vinegar, salt, pepper and remaining 1 tsp. oil. Spoon onto the bread; serve immediately.

2 pieces: 155 cal., 8g fat (1g sat. fat), 0 chol., 327mg sod., 19g carb. (2g sugars, 2g fiber), 3g pro.
Diabetic exchanges: 1½ fat, 1 starch.

LAYERED ITALIAN SODA

Italian sodas are fun, and your gang will love them. Try making the sodas with different flavoring syrups, or topping each glass with a dollop of whipped cream and a cherry.
—Taste of Home Test Kitchen

TAKES: 5 MIN. • **MAKES:** 2 SERVINGS

- ¼ cup black currant or blackberry flavoring syrup
- ½ cup orange juice
- 1⅓ cups carbonated water, chilled

Place 2 Tbsp. syrup in each of 2 tall glasses. Layer each glass with ¼ cup orange juice and ⅔ cup carbonated water, slowly pouring each down the inside of the tilted glass to keep layers separated. Serve immediately.

Note: This recipe was tested with Torani brand flavoring syrup. Look for it in the coffee section of the grocery store.

1 cup: 118 cal., 0 fat (0 sat. fat), 0 chol., 0 sod., 30g carb. (29g sugars, 0 fiber), 1g pro.

GRILLED SHRIMP WITH APRICOT SAUCE

Succulent bacon-wrapped shrimp get a flavor boost from the sweet-hot sauce. Served on skewers, they make a fabulous addition to a summer menu.
—Carole Resnick, Cleveland, OH

TAKES: 20 MIN.
MAKES: 2 SKEWERS (⅓ CUP SAUCE)

- ¼ cup apricot preserves
- 1 Tbsp. apricot nectar
- ⅛ tsp. ground chipotle powder
- 6 uncooked large shrimp, peeled and deveined
- 3 slices Canadian bacon, halved

1. In a small bowl, combine the preserves, apricot nectar and chipotle powder. Chill until serving.
2. Thread shrimp and bacon onto 2 metal or soaked wooden skewers. Grill, covered, over medium heat for 3-4 minutes on each side or until shrimp turn pink. Serve with sauce.
1 skewer: 208 cal., 4g fat (1g sat. fat), 80mg chol., 613mg sod., 28g carb. (16g sugars, 0 fiber), 17g pro.

PEANUT BUTTER, STRAWBERRY & HONEY SANDWICH

Who needs jam when you have fresh strawberries? Honey and mint make this sandwich stand out. If you prefer, use basil or thyme instead of mint.
—James Schend, Pleasant Prairie, WI

TAKES: 5 MIN. • **MAKES:** 1 SANDWICH

- 1 Tbsp. creamy peanut butter
- 1 slice crusty white bread
- ¼ cup sliced fresh strawberries
- 1 tsp. thinly sliced fresh mint
- 1 tsp. honey

Spread peanut butter over bread. Top with strawberries and mint; drizzle with honey.

1 open-faced sandwich: 208 cal., 9g fat (2g sat. fat), 0 chol., 211mg sod., 27g carb. (11g sugars, 2g fiber), 6g pro.

BACON QUESADILLA

This fuss-free quesadilla is so tasty, you'll feel like you're treating yourself. It's easy to just double or triple the ingredients as needed.
—Kathy Kittell, Lenexa, KS

TAKES: 10 MIN. • **MAKES:** 1 SERVING

- 1 Tbsp. butter, softened
- 2 flour tortillas (6 in.)
- ¼ cup shredded Colby-Monterey Jack cheese
- 2 bacon strips, cooked and crumbled
- 1 Tbsp. salsa
  Optional: Sour cream, guacamole and additional salsa

1. Butter 1 side of 1 tortilla; place in a small skillet, buttered side down. Top with cheese, bacon and salsa. Butter the remaining tortilla; place on top, buttered side up.
2. Cook over low heat 1-2 minutes on each side or until the cheese is melted. Cut into wedges. Serve with sour cream, guacamole and additional salsa if desired.

1 quesadilla: 388 cal., 23g fat (10g sat. fat), 46mg chol., 1,000mg sod., 28g carb. (1g sugars, 0 fiber), 18g pro.

CHOCOLATE PEANUT BUTTER SHAKES

These rich chocolate peanut butter shakes will make you feel as if you're sitting in a 1950s soda fountain! To make it modern, try an over-the-top garnish like skewered doughnut holes or chocolate-dipped cookies.
—*Taste of Home* Test Kitchen

TAKES: 10 MIN. • **MAKES:** 2 SERVINGS

- ¾ cup 2% milk
- 1½ cups chocolate ice cream
- ¼ cup creamy peanut butter
- 2 Tbsp. chocolate syrup
  Optional: Sweetened whipped cream; miniature peanut butter cups, quartered; additional chocolate syrup

In a blender, combine the milk, ice cream, peanut butter and syrup; cover and process until smooth. If desired, garnish with whipped cream, peanut butter cups and additional chocolate syrup.

1 cup: 501 cal., 29g fat (11g sat. fat), 41mg chol., 262mg sod., 51g carb. (43g sugars, 3g fiber), 14g pro.

ORANGE COCONUT COOKIES

The sunny taste of these crisp cookies always makes me smile—no matter what the weather.
—Evelyn Acheson, Nanaimo, BC

TAKES: 30 MIN. • **MAKES:** 15 COOKIES

- ½ cup butter, softened
- ½ cup confectioners' sugar
- ½ tsp. grated orange zest
- ½ cup all-purpose flour
- ¼ cup cornstarch
- 1 cup sweetened shredded coconut

1. Preheat oven to 350°. In a bowl, cream butter and sugar until light and fluffy. Stir in orange zest. Combine flour and cornstarch; add to the creamed mixture; stir until blended.
2. Shape dough into 1-in. balls, then roll each ball in coconut. Place 2 in. apart on ungreased baking sheets.
3. Bake for 14-16 minutes or until the coconut is lightly browned and the cookies are set. Remove to wire racks to cool.

1 cookie: 39 cal., 3g fat (2g sat. fat), 5mg chol., 20mg sod., 4g carb. (2g sugars, 0 fiber), 0 pro.

DILL SPIRAL BITES

It takes only six ingredients to roll out these savory pinwheels. They're great for lunch, as a snack or with soup.
—Valerie Belley, St. Louis, MO

PREP: 15 MIN. + CHILLING
MAKES: 2 SERVINGS

- 3 oz. cream cheese, softened
- 1 Tbsp. minced chives
- 1 Tbsp. snipped fresh dill
- 2 flour tortillas (8 in.)
- 6 thin slices tomato
- 6 large spinach leaves

1. In a small bowl, beat the cream cheese, chives and dill until blended. Spread about 1 Tbsp. over 1 side of each tortilla. Layer with tomato and spinach; spread with the remaining cream cheese mixture.
2. Roll up tortillas tightly; wrap securely. Refrigerate for at least 1 hour.
3. Unwrap rolls and cut each into 4 pieces.

4 spiral bites: 271 cal., 12g fat (6g sat. fat), 30mg chol., 458mg sod., 31g carb. (3g sugars, 2g fiber), 10g pro.

SIMPLE SWISS CHEESE FONDUE

When I was growing up, my friend's mother would make this fondue whenever I spent the night. Now, every time I make it, the rich flavor brings back fond memories. Happy dipping!
—Tracy Lawson, Plain City, UT

TAKES: 20 MIN. • **MAKES:** ¾ CUP

- 1 cup shredded Swiss cheese
- 1 Tbsp. all-purpose flour
- ⅛ tsp. ground mustard
  Dash ground nutmeg
- ¼ cup half-and-half cream
- ¼ cup beer or nonalcoholic beer
  French bread cubes

1. In a small bowl, combine the cheese, flour, mustard and nutmeg. In a small saucepan, heat cream and beer over medium heat until bubbles form around the sides of pan. Stir in cheese mixture. Bring just to a gentle boil; cook and stir until combined and smooth, 1-2 minutes.
2. Transfer to a small fondue pot or slow cooker and keep warm. Serve with bread cubes for dipping.

6 Tbsp.: 280 cal., 20g fat (12g sat. fat), 65mg chol., 117mg sod., 6g carb. (2g sugars, 0 fiber), 16g pro.

DID YOU KNOW?

Fondue started centuries ago as a way for villagers to make aged cheese and stale bread not just palatable, but delicious. It has been modernized since then, and now is the national dish of Switzerland.

EASY HOT SPICED CIDER

It's such a treat to come to come home to this warm, comforting cider after a day of playing in the snow.
—Trinda Heinrich, Lakemoor, IL

PREP: 5 MIN. • **COOK:** 2 HOURS
MAKES: 3 SERVINGS

- 2½ cups apple cider or unsweetened apple juice
- ⅔ cup orange juice
- ⅓ cup sugar
- 2 Tbsp. lemon juice
- ¼ tsp. ground nutmeg
- 1 cinnamon stick (3 in.)
- 12 whole cloves

1. In a 1½-qt. slow cooker, combine the first 5 ingredients. Place the cinnamon stick and cloves on a double thickness of cheesecloth; bring up the corners of the cloth and tie with string to form a bag. Place bag in slow cooker. Cook, covered, on low for 1 hour.
2. Discard spice bag; continue to cook for 1-2 hours or until heated through.

1 cup: 218 cal., 0 fat (0 sat. fat), 0 chol., 21mg sod., 54g carb. (49g sugars, 0 fiber), 0 pro.

CRAB & CREAM CHEESE DIP

Who says you have to wait for a big party to enjoy a great dip? This is the perfect accompaniment to any menu. It's delicious on crisp crackers.
—Nadine McGehee, Greenville, MS

PREP: 10 MIN. + CHILLING
MAKES: 2 SERVINGS

- 3 oz. cream cheese, softened
- 2 Tbsp. mayonnaise
- 1½ tsp. thinly sliced green onion
- 1½ tsp. diced pimiento, drained
- 1½ tsp. Worcestershire sauce
- ½ tsp. prepared horseradish
- ⅓ cup crabmeat, drained, flaked and cartilage removed
- 1 Tbsp. finely chopped pecans
  Assorted crackers

In a bowl, combine cream cheese and mayonnaise. Stir in the green onion, pimiento, Worcestershire sauce and horseradish; mix well. Stir in crab. Place in a 1-cup serving bowl; sprinkle with chopped pecans. Refrigerate for at least 2 hours. Serve with crackers.

⅓ cup: 292 cal., 28g fat (11g sat. fat), 72mg chol., 322mg sod., 3g carb. (1g sugars, 0 fiber), 8g pro.

TEST KITCHEN TIP

If you opt for canned crabmeat, soak it in ice water for 10 minutes, then drain it and pat it dry. The ice water will freshen the flavor of the crab.

HERBED TORTILLA CHIPS

I thought of these when I found several packages of tortillas while cleaning out my freezer. They're an inexpensive, low-calorie treat for my husband and me.
—Angela Case, Monticello, AR

TAKES: 20 MIN.
MAKES: 1 DOZEN CHIPS

- 2 tsp. grated Parmesan cheese
- ½ tsp. dried oregano
- ½ tsp. dried parsley flakes
- ½ tsp. dried rosemary, crushed
- ¼ tsp. garlic powder
- ⅛ tsp. kosher salt
  Dash pepper
- 2 flour tortillas (6 in.)
- 2 tsp. olive oil

1. Preheat oven to 425°. In a small bowl, combine the first 7 ingredients. Brush tortillas with oil; cut each tortilla into 6 wedges. Arrange wedges in a single layer on a baking sheet coated with cooking spray, then sprinkle them with the seasoning mixture.
2. Bake for 5-7 minutes or until golden brown. Cool for 5 minutes.
4 chips: 94 cal., 5g fat (1g sat. fat), 1mg chol., 245mg sod., 9g carb. (0 sugars, 0 fiber), 3g pro. **Diabetic exchanges:** 1 fat, ½ starch.

GUACAMOLE DIP

Since guacamole is a favorite in this area, I decided to create my own recipe. I serve it as a dip for chips, with baked chicken or to top off a bed of lettuce.
—Virginia Burwell, Dayton, TX

TAKES: 10 MIN. • **MAKES:** ¾ CUP

- 1 large ripe avocado, peeled
- ¼ cup plain yogurt
- 2 Tbsp. picante sauce or salsa
- 1 Tbsp. finely chopped onion
- ⅛ tsp. salt
- 2 to 3 drops hot pepper sauce, optional
  Tortilla chips

In a small bowl, mash the avocado until smooth. Stir in yogurt, picante sauce, onion, salt and hot pepper sauce if desired. Cover the dip and refrigerate it until serving. Serve with tortilla chips.
6 Tbsp: 307 cal., 29g fat (5g sat. fat), 4mg chol., 291mg sod., 14g carb. (4g sugars, 8g fiber), 4g pro.

Divide cider and ginger ale between 2 glasses. Top each with ½ cup ice cream; drizzle with 1 Tbsp. caramel syrup. Garnish with chopped apples if desired.

1 float: 220 cal., 4g fat (2g sat. fat), 15mg chol., 102mg sod., 46g carb. (41g sugars, 0 fiber), 2g pro.

PEANUT BUTTER DELIGHTS

Made with refrigerated cookie dough, these tasty treats could not be quicker or easier. Everyone loves them.
—Janice Rasmussen, Atlantic, IA

TAKES: 30 MIN. • **MAKES:** 1 DOZEN

- 1 **pkg. (16 oz.) refrigerated ready-to-bake peanut butter cookie dough with candy pieces**
- 2 **Tbsp. creamy peanut butter**
- 3 **oz. milk chocolate candy coating, melted**

1. Bake 12 cookies according to package directions. Cool on wire racks.
2. Spread center of each cookie with ½ tsp. peanut butter; spoon melted chocolate over peanut butter. Let stand for 5 minutes or until set. Save any remaining cookie dough for another use.

1 cookie: 218 cal., 11g fat (3g sat. fat), 4mg chol., 189mg sod., 25g carb. (17g sugars, 1g fiber), 3g pro.

TEST KITCHEN TIP

You can use either cider or apple juice for this recipe—your choice! Juice will create the light golden drink shown; cider will produce a rich, caramel-colored look.

CARAMEL APPLE FLOAT

Who doesn't love the flavors of caramel, apples and vanilla ice cream together? If I'm feeling fancy, I drizzle caramel syrup around the inside of the glass before adding the apple cider and ginger ale.
—Cindy Reams, Philipsburg, PA

TAKES: 10 MIN. • **MAKES:** 2 SERVINGS

- 1 **cup chilled apple cider or unsweetened apple juice**
- 1 **cup chilled ginger ale or lemon-lime soda**
- 1 **cup vanilla ice cream**
- 2 **Tbsp. caramel sundae syrup**
  Finely chopped apple, optional

FRUITY DESSERT TACOS

Here's a dessert you can feel good about eating! Fresh fruit and zippy jalapenos make a tasty filling for sweetened tortillas. Drizzle fruit-flavored yogurt or honey over the tortillas if desired.
—Diane Halferty, Corpus Christi, TX

TAKES: 15 MIN. • **MAKES:** 2 SERVINGS

- 3 tsp. sugar, divided
- ½ tsp. ground cinnamon
- ½ cup cubed fresh pineapple
- ½ cup sliced peeled kiwifruit
- ½ cup sliced fresh strawberries
- 1 tsp. chopped seeded jalapeno pepper, optional
- 2 whole wheat tortillas (8 in.), room temperature
  Butter-flavored cooking spray

1. Mix 2 tsp. sugar and cinnamon. In another bowl, toss fruit with the remaining 1 tsp. sugar and, if desired, jalapeno.
2. Coat both sides of tortillas with cooking spray. In a large skillet, cook tortillas until golden brown, 45-60 seconds per side.
3. Remove from the pan and dust both sides immediately with sugar mixture. Top with fruit mixture; fold to serve.

Note: Wear disposable gloves when cutting hot peppers; the oils can burn skin. Avoid touching your face.

1 taco: 227 cal., 4g fat (0 sat. fat), 0 chol., 172mg sod., 43g carb. (17g sugars, 5g fiber), 5g pro.

CHICKEN NACHOS

You will so look forward to "me time" when you have the makings for these nachos on hand. I've had them many ways, and they're always so good!
—Regina Morales, Orlando, FL

TAKES: 10 MIN. • **MAKES:** 1 SERVING

- ¾ cup coarsely chopped ready-to-use grilled chicken breast strips
- 2 Tbsp. water
- ¼ tsp. taco seasoning
- ¼ cup shredded Mexican cheese blend
- 2 cups tortilla chips
- ½ cup refried black beans, warmed
- 1 Tbsp. salsa

1. In a small skillet, combine the chicken, water and taco seasoning. Bring to a boil. Reduce the heat; simmer, uncovered, for 2 minutes, stirring occasionally. Remove from the heat. Sprinkle with cheese; cover and let stand for 1 minute or until melted.
2. Arrange chips on a serving plate; top with beans, chicken mixture and salsa. Serve immediately.

1 serving: 580 cal., 22g fat (8g sat. fat), 82mg chol., 1488mg sod., 56g carb. (3g sugars, 8g fiber), 41g pro.

CHOCOLATE PEANUT BUTTER MUG CAKE

This is a delectable little cake in a coffee mug! Try it with almond milk, too.
—Angela Lively, Conroe, TX

TAKES: 15 MIN. • **MAKES:** 1 SERVING

- 6 Tbsp. 2% milk
- 2 Tbsp. canola oil
- 6 Tbsp. all-purpose flour
- 3 Tbsp. sugar
- 3 Tbsp. quick-cooking oats
- ½ tsp. baking powder
- ¼ tsp. salt
- 2 Tbsp. semisweet chocolate chips
- 1 Tbsp. creamy peanut butter

1. Spray a 12-oz. coffee mug with cooking spray. Combine milk and oil in mug. Add flour, sugar, oats, baking powder and salt; stir to combine. Add chocolate chips; dollop center with peanut butter.
2. Microwave on high for about 2½ minutes, or until a toothpick inserted in the center comes out clean. Serve immediately.
1 mug cake: 862 cal., 46g fat (9g sat. fat), 7mg chol., 945mg sod., 105g carb. (56g sugars, 5g fiber), 14g pro.

SUNSHINE LIME RICKEY

This is my re-creation of the lime rickey sodas served at my favorite burger place. I even tried a version using my own homemade bitters.
—Shelly Bevington, Hermiston, OR

TAKES: 5 MIN. • **MAKES:** 2 SERVINGS

- 4 Tbsp. simple syrup
- 2 Tbsp. lime juice
- 2 Tbsp. orange juice
- 4 drops orange or lemon bitters
- 1 cup club soda, chilled
  Optional: Orange peel twists and fresh mint leaves

Fill 2 tall glasses three-fourths full with ice. Add half the simple syrup, lime juice, orange juice and bitters to each glass. Top each with ½ cup club soda; stir. Garnish as desired.
1 lime rickey: 130 cal., 0 fat (0 sat. fat), 0 chol., 25mg sod., 34g carb. (31g sugars, 0 fiber), 0 pro.

BROWNIE CUPCAKES

I grew up in my parents' bakery, which might explain why I don't like frosting! These cupcakes are just my style. They come out shiny on top and are great without frosting.
—Cindy Lang, Hays, KS

PREP: 15 MIN. • **BAKE:** 20 MIN. + COOLING
MAKES: 4 SERVINGS

- ¼ cup semisweet chocolate chips
- ¼ cup butter, cubed
- 1 large egg, room temperature
- ¼ cup sugar
- ¼ tsp. vanilla extract
- ¼ cup all-purpose flour
- ¼ cup chopped pecans

1. Preheat oven to 325°. In a microwave, melt the chocolate chips and butter; stir until smooth. Cool slightly. In a small bowl, beat egg and sugar. Stir in vanilla and the chocolate mixture. Gradually add flour; fold in pecans.
2. Fill paper-lined muffin cups two-thirds full. Bake until the tops begin to crack, 20-25 minutes. Cool in pans for 10 minutes before removing to a wire rack.
1 cupcake: 297 cal., 21g fat (10g sat. fat), 83mg chol., 99mg sod., 26g carb. (19g sugars, 2g fiber), 4g pro.

ZIPPY TORTILLA CHIPS

If store-bought tortilla chips are too salty for you, give these homemade southwestern chips a try. You'll be pleasantly surprised at how quick and easy they are to make, and you're sure to get a spicy kick out of them!
—Kim Sumrall, Aptos, CA

TAKES: 20 MIN. • **MAKES:** 2 SERVINGS

- ½ tsp. brown sugar
- ¼ tsp. paprika
- ¼ tsp. garlic powder
- ¼ tsp. onion powder
- ¼ tsp. ground cumin
- ⅛ tsp. cayenne pepper
- 4 corn tortillas (6 in.)
  Cooking spray

1. Preheat oven to 375°. In a small bowl, combine the first 6 ingredients. Stack the tortillas; cut into 6 wedges. Arrange wedges in a single layer on a baking sheet coated with cooking spray.
2. Spritz the wedges with cooking spray; sprinkle with seasoning mixture. Bake for 9-10 minutes or until lightly browned. Cool for 5 minutes.

12 chips: 138 cal., 3g fat (0 sat. fat), 0 chol., 85mg sod., 26g carb. (2g sugars, 3g fiber), 3g pro. **Diabetic exchanges:** 1½ starch, ½ fat.

CHOCOLATY CARAMEL APPLES

You'll love these easy-to-make caramel apples from our Test Kitchen. They're filled with classic flavor but capitalize on convenience products to keep things simple. Plus, they're a tasty way to sneak in an extra piece of fruit!
—*Taste of Home* Test Kitchen

PREP: 20 MIN. + COOLING
MAKES: 2 SERVINGS

- 2 medium apples
- 2 wooden pop sticks
- 18 Riesen's chewy chocolate-covered caramels
- 2 Tbsp. heavy whipping cream
- ¼ cup dry-roasted peanuts, chopped

1. Wash and dry apples; remove stems. Insert wooden pop sticks into apples. Place on a buttered baking sheet; set aside.
2. In a small saucepan, melt the caramels in cream over low heat until smooth, stirring occasionally. Place the peanuts in shallow dish; set aside.
3. Working quickly, dip each apple into the hot caramel mixture to completely coat, then dip the bottom and sides into peanuts. Place on prepared pan; let stand until set.

1 caramel apple: 590 cal., 27g fat (12g sat. fat), 20mg chol., 185mg sod., 83g carb. (47g sugars, 5g fiber), 7g pro.

PEANUT BUTTER S'MORES SANDWICH

Your favorite s'more flavors come together in this tasty peanut butter sandwich—no campfire required.
—James Schend, Pleasant Prairie, WI

TAKES: 10 MIN. • **MAKES:** 1 SANDWICH

- 1 Tbsp. creamy peanut butter
- 1 slice crusty white bread
- 1 Tbsp. milk chocolate chips
- 2 Tbsp. miniature marshmallows

Spread peanut butter over bread. Place on a baking sheet; top with chocolate chips and marshmallows. Broil 4-5 in. from heat until lightly browned, 30-60 seconds.

1 open-faced sandwich: 249 cal., 12g fat (4g sat. fat), 2mg chol., 224mg sod., 29g carb. (12g sugars, 2g fiber), 7g pro.

SANTA FE DEVILED EGGS

My deviled eggs have a zippy southwestern flair. The smoky, spicy flavor is a hit with my husband.
—Patricia Harmon, Baden, PA

TAKES: 15 MIN. • **MAKES:** 2 SERVINGS

- 2 hard-boiled large eggs
- 1 Tbsp. mayonnaise
- 1 Tbsp. canned chopped green chiles
- ½ tsp. chipotle pepper in adobo sauce
- ⅛ tsp. garlic salt
- 4 tsp. salsa
- 1 pitted ripe olive, sliced
- 1½ tsp. thinly sliced green onion

1. Cut eggs in half lengthwise. Remove yolks; set whites aside. In a small bowl, mash yolks. Stir in the mayonnaise, chiles, chipotle pepper and garlic salt. Stuff or pipe into egg whites.
2. Top each egg half with salsa, an olive slice and green onion slices. Refrigerate until serving.

2 filled egg halves: 136 cal., 11g fat (2g sat. fat), 215mg chol., 298mg sod., 2g carb. (1g sugars, 0 fiber), 6g pro.

DEEP-FRIED ONIONS WITH DIPPING SAUCE

Enjoy this steakhouse appetizer right in your own home. We covered onion wedges with a golden batter and fried them to perfection. The spicy dipping sauce really heats things up!
—*Taste of Home* Test Kitchen

TAKES: 25 MIN. • **MAKES:** 2 SERVINGS

- 1 sweet onion
- ½ cup all-purpose flour
- 1 tsp. paprika
- ½ tsp. garlic powder
- ⅛ tsp. cayenne pepper
- ⅛ tsp. pepper

BEER BATTER
- ⅓ cup all-purpose flour
- 1 Tbsp. cornstarch
- ½ tsp. garlic powder
- ½ tsp. paprika
- ¼ tsp. salt
- ¼ tsp. pepper
- 7 Tbsp. beer or nonalcoholic beer
  Oil for deep-fat frying

DIPPING SAUCE
- ¼ cup sour cream
- 2 Tbsp. chili sauce
- ¼ tsp. ground cumin
- ⅛ tsp. cayenne pepper

1. Cut onion into 1-in. wedges and separate into pieces. In a shallow bowl, combine the flour, paprika, garlic powder, cayenne and pepper.
2. For batter, in another shallow bowl, combine the flour, cornstarch, garlic powder, paprika, salt and pepper. Stir in beer. Dip onions into the flour mixture, then into batter and again into the flour mixture.
3. In an electric skillet or deep-fat fryer, heat oil to 375°. Fry onions, a few at a time, for 1-2 minutes on each side or until golden brown. Drain on paper towels.
4. In a small bowl, combine the sauce ingredients. Serve with the onions.

1 serving: 686 cal., 12g fat (7g sat. fat), 40mg chol., 1085mg sod., 119g carb. (20g sugars, 7g fiber), 16g pro.

HAM & PICKLE WRAPS

I decided to try this recipe with my card club, and they loved it. The recipe can be changed in so many different ways, and it always turns out. What an easy, great-tasting centerpiece over a hand of cards.
—Detra Little, Moultrie, GA

PREP: 10 MIN. + CHILLING
MAKES: 1 DOZEN

- 2 oz. cream cheese, softened
- 1½ tsp. spicy ranch salad dressing mix
- 2 slices deli ham
- 2 whole dill pickles

In a small bowl, combine cream cheese and dressing mix. Spread over ham slices. Place a pickle on each ham slice. Roll up tightly; wrap securely. Refrigerate for at least 1 hour or until firm. Cut each wrap into 6 slices.

6 pieces: 137 cal., 10g fat (6g sat. fat), 41mg chol., 1113mg sod., 5g carb. (1g sugars, 0 fiber), 6g pro.

GREEK PIZZA

Take your snacks to the next level. This flatbread pizza is packed with mouthwatering Mediterranean flavors.
—Cathi Schuett, Omaha, NE

TAKES: 20 MIN. • **MAKES:** 2 SERVINGS

- 1 Italian herb flatbread wrap
- 2½ tsp. Greek vinaigrette
- ¼ cup crumbled feta cheese
- 2 Tbsp. grated Parmesan cheese
- ¼ cup Greek olives, sliced
- ¼ cup water-packed artichoke hearts, rinsed, drained and chopped
- ¼ cup ready-to-use grilled chicken breast strips, chopped

Dash each dried oregano, dried basil and pepper
- ½ cup shredded part-skim mozzarella cheese
  Fresh basil, optional

Place wrap on an ungreased baking sheet; brush with vinaigrette. Layer with remaining ingredients. Bake at 400° for 8-10 minutes or until the cheese is melted. Garnish with fresh basil, if desired.

½ flatbread: 295 cal., 17g fat (6g sat. fat), 39mg chol., 1,062mg sod., 17g carb. (2g sugars, 2g fiber), 19g pro.

1. Spread half the graham cracker quarters with peanut butter; top with the remaining crackers.

2. In a microwave-safe bowl, melt chocolate chips and shortening; stir until smooth. Dip the cracker sandwiches into chocolate; place on a waxed paper-lined pan. Refrigerate until set.

1 cookie: 201 cal., 13g fat (5g sat. fat), 0 chol., 84mg sod., 22g carb. (15g sugars, 2g fiber), 3g pro.

ALMOND CHEESE SPREAD

I love this recipe! It's a great way to use up leftover or different kinds of cheeses I've already got on hand.
—Joan Cooper, Lake Orion, MI

PREP: 10 MIN. + CHILLING
MAKES: 2 SERVINGS

- ½ cup shredded sharp white cheddar cheese
- 2 Tbsp. mayonnaise
- ⅛ tsp. onion powder
  Dash pepper
  Dash Louisiana-style hot sauce
- 1 green onion, chopped
- 1 Tbsp. sliced almonds
  Celery ribs or assorted crackers

In a small bowl, combine the first 5 ingredients; stir in green onion and almonds. Cover and refrigerate for at least 4 hours. Serve with celery or crackers.

¼ cup: 185 cal., 16g fat (7g sat. fat), 35mg chol., 297mg sod., 3g carb. (1g sugars, 1g fiber), 8g pro.

CHOCOLATE PEANUT GRAHAMS

Cinnamon graham crackers are the base for this tasty no-bake chocolate treat.
—*Taste of Home* Test Kitchen

TAKES: 30 MINUTES
MAKES: 8 COOKIES

- 4 whole cinnamon graham crackers, broken into quarters
- ¼ cup creamy peanut butter
- 1 cup semisweet chocolate chips
- 3 tsp. shortening

CHOCOLATE WRAPS

I was inspired to create this rich dessert after seeing a similar recipe in our newspaper. I love that it frees up my oven for the main course. It is easy and wonderful!
—Sunny Goodyear, Camp Hill, PA

PREP: 15 MIN. + CHILLING
MAKES: 2 WRAPS

- 3 Tbsp. semisweet chocolate chips
- ¾ tsp. butter
- 3 oz. cream cheese, softened
- 3 Tbsp. peanut butter
- 1¼ tsp. confectioners' sugar
- 2 flour tortillas (6 in.)

GLAZE
- 1 Tbsp. semisweet chocolate chips
- ½ tsp. butter
- ½ tsp. corn syrup
- ½ tsp. hot water

1. In a microwave, melt chocolate chips and butter; stir until smooth. Cool slightly. Stir in cream cheese, peanut butter and confectioners' sugar until blended. Spread over tortillas. Roll up tightly; wrap securely. Refrigerate for at least 30 minutes.
2. For glaze, in a microwave-safe bowl, melt chocolate chips, butter and corn syrup; stir in hot water until smooth. Drizzle over wraps.
1 wrap: 459 cal., 32g fat (13g sat. fat), 33mg chol., 539mg sod., 35g carb. (17g sugars, 3g fiber), 14g pro.

BACON JALAPENO POPPERS

For a delicious appetizer for two, try this spicy recipe. The bacon adds a smoky flavor to the poppers.
—Bernice Knutson, Danbury, IA

TAKES: 30 MIN. • **MAKES:** 4 POPPERS

- 2 bacon strips, halved
- 4 tsp. cream cheese, softened
- 4 tsp. shredded Colby cheese
- 2 jalapeno peppers, halved lengthwise and seeded

1. Preheat oven to 350°. In a small skillet, cook bacon over medium heat until partially cooked but not crisp. Remove to paper towels to drain; keep warm.
2. Combine cheeses; spread into each pepper half. Wrap a piece of bacon around each pepper half. Place on a foil-lined baking sheet.
3. Bake, uncovered, 20-25 minutes or until the bacon is crisp and filling is heated through.
Note: Wear disposable gloves when cutting hot peppers; the oils can burn skin. Avoid touching your face.
1 popper: 80 cal., 8g fat (3g sat. fat), 16mg chol., 123mg sod., 1g carb. (1g sugars, 0 fiber), 3g pro.

SAUSAGE CHEESE BALLS

These bite-sized meatballs are a favorite of mine. Feel free to swap in different cheese for the cheddar or serve with Dijon mustard instead of barbecue and sweet-and-sour sauces.
—Anna Damon, Bozeman, MT

TAKES: 30 MIN. • **MAKES:** 1 DOZEN

- ½ cup shredded cheddar cheese
- 3 Tbsp. biscuit/baking mix
- 1 Tbsp. finely chopped onion
- 1 Tbsp. finely chopped celery
- ⅛ tsp. garlic powder
- ⅛ tsp. pepper
- ¼ lb. bulk pork sausage
  Optional: Sweet-and-sour and barbecue sauces

1. Preheat oven to 375°. In a small bowl, combine the first 6 ingredients. Crumble sausage over the mixture and mix well. Shape into 1-in. balls.
2. Place in a shallow baking pan coated with cooking spray. Bake, uncovered, for 12-15 minutes or until meat is no longer pink. Drain on paper towels. Serve with sauces if desired.

6 meatballs: 265 cal., 18g fat (8g sat. fat), 60mg chol., 685mg sod., 10g carb. (2g sugars, 0 fiber), 18g pro.

SUGAR COOKIE S'MORES

Change up traditional s'mores by using sugar cookies and candy bars in place of the expected ingredients. This fun twist on the campfire classic will delight everyone, and it couldn't be easier to scale up or down!
—Taste of Home Test Kitchen

TAKES: 15 MIN.
MAKES: 4 SANDWICH COOKIES

- 8 fun-size Milky Way candy bars
- 8 sugar cookies (3 in.)
- 4 large marshmallows

1. Place 2 candy bars on each of 4 cookies; place on grill rack. Grill, uncovered, over medium-hot heat for 1-1½ minutes or until bottoms of cookies are browned.
2. Meanwhile, using a long-handled fork, toast the marshmallows 6 in. from the heat until golden brown, turning occasionally. Remove marshmallows from fork and place over candy bars; top with remaining 4 cookies. Serve immediately.

1 sandwich cookie: 271 cal., 10g fat (5g sat. fat), 13mg chol., 123mg sod., 43g carb. (31g sugars, 1g fiber), 3g pro.

DID YOU KNOW?

Created in 1923, the Milky Way was the first mass-produced chocolate bar with a filling. It came in both chocolate and vanilla flavors.

BREAKFAST

Mornings are twice as nice when they start with any of these easy, delicious, sized-right dishes—from golden waffles to exceptional eggs. Rise and shine!

BLUEBERRY PANCAKE SMOOTHIE

A smoothie loaded with fruit, oatmeal, maple syrup and cinnamon is great in the morning or at any time of day. If your berries are fresh (not frozen), freeze the banana ahead of time.
—Kailey Thompson, Palm Bay, FL

TAKES: 5 MIN. • **MAKES:** 2 SERVINGS

- 1 cup unsweetened almond milk
- 1 medium banana
- ½ cup frozen unsweetened blueberries
- ¼ cup instant plain oatmeal
- 1 tsp. maple syrup
- ½ tsp. ground cinnamon
  Dash sea salt

Place the first 6 ingredients in a blender; cover and process until smooth. Pour mixture into 2 chilled glasses; sprinkle with the sea salt. Serve immediately.

1 cup: 153 cal., 3g fat (0 sat. fat), 0 chol., 191mg sod., 31g carb. (13g sugars, 5g fiber), 3g pro. **Diabetic exchanges:** 2 starch.

CHEESY EGG QUESADILLAS

Here's my fun spin on breakfast for dinner—or breakfast! These egg quesadillas are easy to make, full of protein and plain delicious any time of day.
—Barbara Blommer, Woodland Park, CO

TAKES: 25 MIN. • **MAKES:** 2 SERVINGS

- 3 large eggs
- 3 Tbsp. 2% milk
- ⅛ tsp. pepper
- 1 Tbsp. plus 2 tsp. butter, divided
- 4 flour tortillas (8 in.)
- ½ cup refried beans
- ¼ cup salsa
- ⅔ cup shredded cheddar cheese
  Optional: Sour cream and additional salsa

1. Preheat oven to 425°. Whisk together the first 3 ingredients. In a large nonstick skillet over medium heat, melt 1 Tbsp. butter. Add the egg mixture; cook and stir until eggs are thickened and no liquid egg remains. Remove from heat.
2. Place 2 tortillas on a baking sheet. Spread with beans; top with eggs, salsa, cheese and remaining tortillas. Melt the remaining 2 tsp. butter; brush over tops.
3. Bake until golden brown and cheese is melted, 10-12 minutes. If desired, serve with sour cream and additional salsa.

1 quesadilla: 738 cal., 38g fat (18g sat. fat), 344mg chol., 1248mg sod., 67g carb. (3g sugars, 5g fiber), 30g pro.

HEALTH TIP

Butter adds richness to these quesadillas, but it's not essential. Cook the eggs in a few spritzes of cooking spray and don't butter the tortillas—you'll decrease the fat by about one-third.

EASY SPICED MORNING MOCHA

This recipe is a delicious morning pick-me-up and still tastes great when made with low-fat milk.
—Vickie Wright, Omaha, NE

TAKES: 10 MIN. • **MAKES:** 1 SERVING

- 1 Tbsp. French vanilla powdered nondairy creamer
- 1½ tsp. sugar
- 1 tsp. instant coffee granules
- 1 tsp. baking cocoa
- ¼ tsp. ground ginger
- ¼ tsp. ground cinnamon
- 1 cup hot 2% milk or water
  Sweetened whipped cream and additional ground cinnamon

Place the first 6 ingredients in a mug. Stir in hot milk until blended. Top with whipped cream; sprinkle with additional cinnamon.

1 cup: 188 cal., 7g fat (5g sat. fat), 20mg chol., 115mg sod., 24g carb. (18g sugars, 1g fiber), 9g pro.

BACON & EGG GRAVY

My husband, Ron, created this wonderful breakfast gravy. It's home-style and old-fashioned. Sometimes we ladle the gravy over homemade biscuits. Served with fruit salad, it's a great breakfast.
—Terry Bray, Winter Haven, FL

TAKES: 20 MIN. • **MAKES:** 2 SERVINGS

- 6 bacon strips, diced
- 5 Tbsp. all-purpose flour
- 1½ cups water
- 1 can (12 oz.) evaporated milk
- 3 hard-boiled large eggs, sliced
  Salt and pepper to taste
- 4 slices bread, toasted

1. In a skillet, cook bacon over medium heat until crisp; remove to paper towels.
2. Stir flour into the drippings until blended; cook over medium heat until browned, stirring constantly. Gradually add water and milk. Bring to a boil; cook and stir for 2 minutes or until thickened.
3. Add bacon, eggs, salt and pepper. Serve over toast.

1 serving: 934 cal., 61g fat (26g sat. fat), 424mg chol., 1030mg sod., 58g carb. (21g sugars, 2g fiber), 33g pro.

BERRY SMOOTHIE BOWL

We turned one of our favorite smoothies into a breakfast bowl and topped it with even more fresh fruit and a few toasted almonds for a little crunch.
—*Taste of Home* Test Kitchen

TAKES: 5 MIN. • **MAKES:** 2 SERVINGS

- 1 cup fat-free milk
- 1 cup frozen unsweetened strawberries
- ½ cup frozen unsweetened raspberries
- 3 Tbsp. sugar
- 1 cup ice cubes
  Optional: Sliced fresh strawberries, fresh raspberries, chia seeds, fresh pumpkin seeds, unsweetened shredded coconut and sliced almonds

Place the milk, berries and sugar in a blender; cover and process until smooth. Add ice cubes; cover and process until smooth. Divide mixture between 2 serving bowls. Add optional toppings as desired.

1½ cups: 155 cal., 0 fat (0 sat. fat), 2mg chol., 54mg sod., 35g carb. (30g sugars, 2g fiber), 5g pro.

MANMOSA

Here's a guy-friendly adaptation of the sweet and fruity mimosa. This combo of OJ and beer makes a tasty kickoff to Father's Day celebrations or a Bowl day party.
—Mike Dietiker, Elburn, IL

TAKES: 5 MIN. • **MAKES:** 2 SERVINGS

 1 **bottle (12 oz.) beer, chilled**
 1 **cup orange juice**
 2 **oz. Triple Sec**

Divide beer between 2 tall glasses. Add ½ cup orange juice and 1 oz. Triple Sec to each glass.
1⅓ cups: 229 cal., 0 fat (0 sat. fat), 0 chol., 7mg sod., 31g carb. (28g sugars, 0 fiber), 1g pro.

BACON, EGG & AVOCADO SANDWICHES

My husband wanted bacon and eggs for a late breakfast; I wanted a BLT. We settled our standoff with an irresistible sandwich we've had many times since.
—Patti Darwin, Lubbock, TX

TAKES: 25 MIN. • **MAKES:** 2 SERVINGS

 2 **bacon strips, halved crosswise**
 2 **large eggs**
 ⅛ **tsp. garlic salt**
 ⅛ **tsp. pepper**
 2 **Tbsp. Miracle Whip or mayonnaise**
 4 **slices sourdough bread, toasted**
 4 **thin slices tomato**
 ½ **medium ripe avocado, peeled and sliced**
   Optional: 2 slices Gouda cheese, 1 slice red onion, separated into rings,
 2 **tsp. butter, softened**

1. In a large nonstick skillet, cook bacon over medium heat until crisp. Remove to paper towels to drain. Pour off drippings.
2. In same skillet, break eggs, 1 at a time, into the pan; immediately reduce heat to low. Cook until the whites are completely set and yolks begin to thicken. Remove from heat; sprinkle with garlic salt and pepper.
3. Spread the Miracle Whip over 2 toast slices. Top with bacon, eggs, tomato, avocado and, if desired, cheese and onion. Spread butter over the remaining 2 toast slices; place over top.
1 sandwich: 448 cal., 23g fat (7g sat. fat), 209mg chol., 864mg sod., 44g carb. (7g sugars, 4g fiber), 18g pro.

HEALTH TIP

Avocados are known for their healthy monounsaturated fat, but they are also a good source of vitamins C, K, E and most B vitamins.

1 cup pitted dates, chopped
1 cup 2% milk
½ cup ground almonds
⅓ cup old-fashioned oats
2 Tbsp. baking cocoa
1 tsp. butter
1 tsp. vanilla extract
  Optional: Fresh raspberries
  and sliced almonds

1. Place dates in a heatproof bowl; cover with boiling water. Let stand until softened, about 10 minutes. Drain, reserving ⅓ cup liquid. Place dates and reserved liquid in a food processor; process until smooth.
2. In a small saucepan, whisk milk, almonds, oats, cocoa and ¼ cup date puree until blended. (Save the remaining puree for another use.) Bring to a boil over medium heat, stirring occasionally.
3. Remove from heat; stir in butter and vanilla. If desired, garnish with raspberries and sliced almonds.
¾ cup: 338 cal., 18g fat (4g sat. fat), 15mg chol., 73mg sod., 37g carb. (19g sugars, 7g fiber), 12g pro.

DID YOU KNOW?

Dates are naturally dehydrated and, as they age, they dry further and the sugars migrate to the surface. So don't worry about white spots—they're not mold, they're sugar!

BROWNIE BATTER OATMEAL

We all grew up eating bowls of lumpy oatmeal for breakfast, and everyone has favorite toppings to make porridge more palatable. My recipe transforms a ho-hum morning staple into something that will make the kids jump out of bed!
—Kristen Moyer, Bethlehem, PA

TAKES: 30 MIN. • **MAKES:** 2 SERVINGS

EGGS LORRAINE

Super easy and elegant, this is one of my favorite special-occasion dishes, It's absolutely delicious!
—Sandra Woolard, DeLand, FL

PREP: 15 MIN. • **BAKE:** 25 MIN.
MAKES: 2 SERVINGS

- 4   slices Canadian bacon
- 2   slices Swiss cheese
- 4   large eggs
- 2   Tbsp. sour cream
- ⅛   tsp. salt
- ⅛   tsp. pepper
         Minced chives, optional

1. Preheat oven to 350°. Coat 2 shallow oval 1½-cup baking dishes with cooking spray. Line each with Canadian bacon; top with cheese. Carefully break 2 eggs into each dish.
2. In a small bowl, whisk the sour cream, salt and pepper together until smooth; drop the mixture by teaspoonfuls onto the eggs.
3. Bake, uncovered, until eggs are set, 25-30 minutes. If desired, sprinkle with chives.

Note: Closer to ham than bacon, Canadian bacon is usually derived from a loin cut and is leaner and meatier than conventional bacon. It is cured, smoked and fully cooked and needs only to be warmed.

1 serving: 286 cal., 17g fat (6g sat. fat), 462mg chol., 1018mg sod., 3g carb. (3g sugars, 0 fiber), 28g pro.

PUMPKIN GINGER CHAI LATTE

This pumpkin chai latte is so good that we enjoy it year-round. It features bold chai, spicy ginger and sweet almond milk for an easy, healthy latte option!
—Courtney Stultz, Weir, KS

PREP: 15 MIN.
COOK: 10 MIN. + STANDING
MAKES: 1 SERVING

- ½   cup water
- 1   chai-flavored tea bag
- ½   cup refrigerated almond milk or coconut milk
- 3   Tbsp. canned pumpkin
- 1   Tbsp. honey
- ¼   tsp. ground ginger
         Dash each ground cinnamon, ground cardamom and ground cloves

1. In a small saucepan, bring water to a boil; remove from heat. Add tea bag; steep, covered, 5-10 minutes according to taste.
2. Discard tea bag. Transfer tea to a blender; add remaining ingredients. Cover and pulse to combine.

1 cup: 102 cal., 2g fat (0 sat. fat), 0 chol., 94mg sod., 23g carb. (19g sugars, 2g fiber), 1g pro.

PEANUT BUTTER BANANA OVERNIGHT OATS

Talk about wholesome and quick! You'll be satisfied right up until lunchtime with these easy, creamy overnight oats.
—*Taste of Home* Test Kitchen

PREP: 10 MIN. + CHILLING
MAKES: 1 SERVING

- 1   Tbsp. creamy peanut butter, warmed
- 1   Tbsp. honey
- 3   Tbsp. fat-free milk
- ⅓   cup old-fashioned oats
- ¼   cup mashed ripe banana
         Optional: Sliced ripe banana and honey

In a small container or Mason jar, combine peanut butter, honey, milk, oats and banana. Seal; refrigerate overnight. If desired, top with sliced bananas and drizzle with honey.

1 serving: 325 cal., 10g fat (2g sat. fat), 1mg chol., 89mg sod., 54g carb. (29g sugars, 5g fiber), 9g pro.

BREAKFAST BANANA SPLITS

I can't brag enough about this recipe. It's elegant enough for a formal brunch, yet simple and nutritious. With different fruits and cereals, there are endless potential variations.
—Renee Lloyd, Pearl, MS

TAKES: 10 MIN. • **MAKES:** 2 SERVINGS

- 1 medium banana
- ⅓ cup each fresh blueberries, halved seedless grapes, sliced peeled kiwifruit and halved fresh strawberries
- 1 cup vanilla yogurt
- ½ cup granola with fruit and nuts
- 2 maraschino cherries with stems

Cut banana crosswise in half. For each serving, split each banana in half lengthwise and place in a serving dish; top with ½ of each of the remaining ingredients.

1 serving: 337 cal., 6g fat (1g sat. fat), 6mg chol., 96mg sod., 66g carb. (42g sugars, 8g fiber), 12g pro.

TOAD IN THE HOLE BACON SANDWICH

Switch up the cheese—pepper jack comes with a nice kick—or use sliced kielbasa, ham or sausage in place of the bacon in this versatile grilled cheese sandwich. This recipe couldn't be easier to double to serve two.
—Kallee Krong-McCreery, Escondido, CA

TAKES: 15 MIN. • **MAKES:** 1 SERVING

- 2 slices sourdough bread
- 1 Tbsp. mayonnaise
- 1 large egg
- 1 slice cheddar cheese
- 2 cooked bacon strips

1. Using a biscuit cutter or round cookie cutter, cut out the center from 1 slice of bread (discard the center or save for another use). Spread mayonnaise on 1 side of both bread slices. In a large skillet coated with cooking spray, lightly toast the cutout slice, mayonnaise side down, over medium-low heat. Flip slice; crack an egg into the center hole. Add the remaining bread slice, mayonnaise side down, to the skillet; layer with cheese and bacon.
2. Cook, covered, until egg white is set, yolk is soft-set and cheese begins to melt. If needed, flip the slice with egg to finish cooking.
3. To assemble sandwich, use the solid slice as the bottom and the cutout slice as the top.

1 sandwich: 610 cal., 34g fat (11g sat. fat), 240mg chol., 1220mg sod., 46g carb. (4g sugars, 2g fiber), 30g pro.

TEST KITCHEN TIP

Nothing perks up a grilled cheese sandwich like fresh tomato—especially in the summer, when tomatoes are at their ripest and most luscious. Add a slice of tomato just after the cheese melts but before you assemble the sandwich.

PUMPKIN PIE OATMEAL

I love pumpkin pie and wanted it for breakfast—so I created this oatmeal recipe! You can use reduced-fat or fat-free milk instead of soy milk, and it will be just as creamy.
—Amber Rife, Columbus, OH

TAKES: 15 MIN. • **MAKES:** 2 SERVINGS

- 1   cup water
- 1   cup vanilla soy milk
- 1   cup old-fashioned oats
- ½   cup canned pumpkin
- ¼   tsp. pumpkin pie spice
- 2   Tbsp. sugar
- ¼   tsp. vanilla extract
      Optional: Dried cranberries and salted pumpkin seeds or pepitas

1. In a small saucepan, combine the water, milk, oats, pumpkin and pie spice. Bring to a boil; cook and stir for 5 minutes.
2. Remove from heat; stir in sugar and vanilla. If desired, sprinkle with cranberries and pumpkin seeds; drizzle with additional milk.
1 cup: 268 cal., 5g fat (0 sat. fat), 0 chol., 51mg sod., 49g carb. (18g sugars, 6g fiber), 10g pro.

FLAXSEED OATMEAL PANCAKES

I came up with this recipe because my husband loves pancakes, but they're not the healthiest breakfast option! These are healthy and really tasty— they have a pleasing texture and a delightful touch of cinnamon.
—Sharon Hansen, Pontiac, IL

TAKES: 20 MIN. • **MAKES:** 4 PANCAKES

- ⅓   cup whole wheat flour
- 3   Tbsp. quick-cooking oats
- 1   Tbsp. flaxseed
- ½   tsp. baking powder
- ¼   tsp. ground cinnamon
- ⅛   tsp. baking soda
      Dash salt
- 1   large egg, separated, room temperature
- ½   cup buttermilk
- 1   Tbsp. brown sugar
- 1   Tbsp. canola oil
- ½   tsp. vanilla extract

1. In a large bowl, combine the first 7 ingredients. In a small bowl, whisk egg yolk, buttermilk, brown sugar, oil and vanilla; stir into dry ingredients just until moistened.
2. In a small bowl, beat egg white on medium speed until stiff peaks form. Fold into the batter.
3. Pour batter by ¼ cupfuls onto a hot griddle coated with cooking spray; turn when bubbles form on top. Cook until the second side is golden brown.
Note: For each cup of buttermilk, you can use 1 Tbsp. white vinegar or lemon juice plus enough milk to measure 1 cup. Stir, then let stand for 5 minutes.
2 pancakes: 273 cal., 13g fat (2g sat. fat), 108mg chol., 357mg sod., 31g carb. (10g sugars, 5g fiber), 10g pro.
Diabetic exchanges: 2 starch, 2 fat.

DID YOU KNOW?

Another good replacement for buttermilk, if you don't have it on hand, is to use an equivalent measure of plain yogurt—traditional or Greek-style.

PEAR QUINOA BREAKFAST BAKE

In an effort to eat healthier, I've been trying to incorporate more whole grains into our diet. My husband and I enjoy quinoa, so I created this breakfast bake for Sunday brunch. The quinoa is a nice change of pace from oatmeal.
—Sue Gronholz, Beaver Dam, WI

PREP: 15 MIN.
BAKE: 55 MIN. + STANDING
MAKES: 2 SERVINGS

- 1 cup water
- ¼ cup quinoa, rinsed
- ¼ cup mashed peeled ripe pear
- 1 Tbsp. honey
- ¼ tsp. ground cinnamon
- ¼ tsp. vanilla extract
  Dash ground ginger
  Dash ground nutmeg

TOPPING

- ¼ cup sliced almonds
- 1 Tbsp. brown sugar
- 1 Tbsp. butter, softened
  Plain Greek yogurt, optional

1. Preheat oven to 350°. In a small bowl, combine first 8 ingredients; transfer the mixture to a greased 3-cup baking dish. Cover and bake for 50 minutes.
2. In another small bowl, combine almonds, brown sugar, and butter; sprinkle over quinoa mixture.
3. Bake, uncovered, until lightly browned, 5-10 minutes longer. Let stand 10 minutes before serving. If desired, serve with yogurt.
1 serving: 267 cal., 13g fat (4g sat. fat), 15mg chol., 49mg sod., 35g carb. (18g sugars, 4g fiber), 6g pro. **Diabetic exchanges:** 2½ fat, 2 starch.

CHEESE DANISH DESSERT

This pretty Danish makes a delicious breakfast pastry, or a sweet dessert any time of day. If you prefer, you can omit the sugar-cinnamon mixture.
—Mary Margaret Merritt, Washington Court House, OH

TAKES: 30 MIN. • **MAKES:** 2 SERVINGS

- 1 tube (4 oz.) refrigerated crescent rolls
- 1 (3 oz.) cream cheese, softened
- ¼ cup sugar
- ¼ tsp. vanilla extract
- 1 tsp. butter, melted
- ¼ cup sugar
- 2 tsp. cinnamon

1. Preheat oven to 350°. Unroll crescent roll dough and separate into 2 rectangles; place on an ungreased baking sheet and press the perforations together on each rectangle. Beat the cream cheese, sugar and vanilla until smooth. Spread over half of each rectangle; fold dough over filling and pinch to seal. Brush with butter. Combine sugar and cinnamon; sprinkle over the Danishes.
2. Bake for 15-20 minutes or until golden brown.
1 Danish: 486 cal., 29g fat (14g sat. fat), 52mg chol., 591mg sod., 48g carb. (29g sugars, 0 fiber), 7g pro.

BLUEBERRY CHEESECAKE PARFAIT

Fresh blueberries make this breakfast treat seem a little less decadent, but this cheesecake-flavored parfait will make your mouth water.
—Blair Lonergan, Rochelle, VA

TAKES: 10 MIN. • **MAKES:** 1 SERVING

- ½ cup reduced-fat ricotta cheese
- 1 tsp. sugar
- ¼ tsp. vanilla extract
- 3 Tbsp. blueberry preserves
- ½ cup fresh or frozen blueberries, thawed
- ¼ cup graham cracker crumbs
- 1 Tbsp. slivered almonds

In a small bowl, combine cheese, sugar and vanilla. Spoon 1 Tbsp. preserves, 2 Tbsp. blueberries, half the cheese mixture and 2 Tbsp. cracker crumbs into a parfait glass. Repeat layers. Top with the rest of the preserves, blueberries and slivered almonds.
1 parfait: 458 cal., 11g fat (4g sat. fat), 30mg chol., 238mg sod., 77g carb. (60g sugars, 3g fiber), 13g pro.

BACON-BROCCOLI QUICHE CUPS

Rich with veggies and melted cheese, this comforting and colorful egg bake has become a holiday brunch classic in our home. For a tasty variation, try substituting asparagus for the broccoli and Swiss for the cheddar cheese.
—Irene Steinmeyer, Denver, CO

PREP: 10 MIN. • **BAKE:** 25 MIN.
MAKES: 2 SERVINGS

- 4 bacon strips, chopped
- ¼ cup small fresh broccoli florets
- ¼ cup chopped onion
- 1 garlic clove, minced
- 3 large eggs
- 1 Tbsp. dried parsley flakes
- ⅛ tsp. seasoned salt
  Dash pepper
- ¼ cup shredded cheddar cheese
- 2 Tbsp. chopped tomato

1. Preheat oven to 400°. In a skillet, cook bacon over medium heat until crisp, stirring occasionally. Remove bacon with a slotted spoon; drain on paper towels. Pour off drippings, reserving 2 tsp. in pan.
2. Add broccoli and onion to the drippings in pan; cook and stir for 2-3 minutes or until tender. Add garlic; cook 1 minute longer.
3. Whisk eggs, parsley, seasoned salt and pepper until blended. Stir in the cheese, tomato, bacon and the broccoli mixture.
4. Divide combined mixture evenly between 2 greased 10-oz. ramekins or custard cups. Bake until a knife inserted in the center comes out clean, 22-25 minutes.

Freeze option: Cover and freeze unbaked quiche cups. Remove from freezer 30 minutes before baking (do not thaw). Bake as directed, increasing time as necessary for a knife to test clean. Cover loosely with foil if tops brown too quickly.
1 serving: 302 cal., 23g fat (9g sat. fat), 314mg chol., 597mg sod., 5g carb. (2g sugars, 1g fiber), 19g pro.

2 tsp. butter, divided
4 large eggs, beaten
4 slices (¾ in. thick) hearty Italian bread
⅛ tsp. salt
⅛ tsp. pepper
4 oz. smoked Gouda or smoked cheddar cheese, cut in 4 slices
1 medium pear, thinly sliced
4 slices Canadian bacon, cooked
½ cup fresh baby spinach

1. Heat 1 tsp. butter in a small nonstick skillet over medium heat; add eggs and scramble until set.
2. Divide eggs between 2 slices of bread; sprinkle each with salt and pepper. Layer bread with cheese slices, pear slices, Canadian bacon and spinach. Top with the remaining bread slices.
3. If using a panini maker, spread the remaining 1 tsp. butter on to both sides of the sandwiches. Grill according to the manufacturer's directions until golden brown and grill marks show, 6-8 minutes.
4. If using an indoor grill, spread ½ tsp. of the remaining butter on 1 side of the sandwiches. Place buttered side down on grill; press down with a heavy skillet or other weight. Grill over medium-high heat until golden brown and grill-marked, 3-5 minutes. Remove weight; spread the remaining ½ tsp. butter on other side of sandwiches. Return to grill, buttered side down; replace weight. Grill until golden brown, another 3-5 minutes.

1 sandwich: 629 cal., 33g fat (17g sat. fat), 461mg chol., 1510mg sod., 44g carb. (11g sugars, 4g fiber), 38g pro.

GRILLED BISTRO BREAKFAST SANDWICHES

I used to make a classic breakfast sandwich when my kids were still at home. Now that it's just my husband and me, I've jazzed it up with pear, smoked Gouda and spinach.
—Wendy Ball, Battle Creek, MI

TAKES: 30 MIN. • **MAKES:** 2 SERVINGS

UPSIDE-DOWN PEAR PANCAKE

There's a pear tree in my yard that inspires me to bake with its fragrant fruit. This upside-down pancake works best with a firm pear, not one that is fully ripe.
—Helen Nelander, Boulder Creek, CA

TAKES: 30 MIN. • **MAKES:** 2 SERVINGS

- ½ cup all-purpose flour
- ½ tsp. baking powder
- 1 large egg, room temperature
- ¼ cup 2% milk
- 1 Tbsp. butter
- 1 tsp. sugar
- 1 medium pear, peeled and thinly sliced lengthwise
  Confectioners' sugar

1. Preheat oven to 375°. In a large bowl, whisk the flour and baking powder. In a separate bowl, whisk egg and milk until blended. Add to the dry ingredients, stirring just until combined.
2. Meanwhile, in a small ovenproof skillet, melt butter over medium-low heat. Sprinkle with sugar. Add pear slices in a single layer; cook 5 minutes. Spread prepared batter over the pears. Cook, covered, until the top is set, about 5 minutes.
3. Transfer pan to the oven; bake until the edges are lightly brown, 8-10 minutes. Invert onto a serving plate. Sprinkle with confectioners' sugar. Serve warm.

½ pancake: 274 cal., 9g fat (5g sat. fat), 111mg chol., 197mg sod., 41g carb. (12g sugars, 4g fiber), 8g pro. **Diabetic exchanges:** 2 starch, 1½ fat, 1 medium-fat meat, ½ fruit.

AIR-FRYER RASPBERRY FRENCH TOAST CUPS

A delightful twist on French toast, these individual treats make any morning special. I made this recipe for my mom last Mother's Day, and we both enjoyed it.
—Sandi Tuttle, Hayward, WI

PREP: 20 MIN. + CHILLING
COOK: 20 MIN. • **MAKES:** 2 SERVINGS

- 2 slices Italian bread, cut into ½-in. cubes
- ½ cup fresh or frozen raspberries
- 2 oz. cream cheese, cut into ½-in. cubes
- 2 large eggs
- ½ cup 2% milk
- 1 Tbsp. maple syrup

RASPBERRY SYRUP
- 2 tsp. cornstarch
- ⅓ cup water
- 2 cups fresh or frozen raspberries, divided
- 1 Tbsp. lemon juice
- 1 Tbsp. maple syrup
- ½ tsp. grated lemon zest
  Ground cinnamon, optional

1. Divide half the bread cubes between 2 greased 8-oz. custard cups. Sprinkle with raspberries and cream cheese. Top with the remaining bread cubes. In a small bowl, whisk eggs, milk and syrup; pour over the bread. Cover and refrigerate for at least 1 hour.
2. Preheat air fryer to 325°. Place custard cups on tray in air-fryer basket. Cook until golden brown and puffed, 12-15 minutes.
3. Meanwhile, in a small saucepan, combine cornstarch and water until smooth. Add 1½ cups raspberries, the lemon juice, syrup and lemon zest. Bring to a boil; reduce heat. Cook and stir until thickened, about 2 minutes. Strain and discard the seeds; cool slightly.
4. Gently stir the remaining ½ cup of berries into syrup. If desired, sprinkle French toast cups with cinnamon; serve with syrup.

1 serving: 406 cal., 18g fat (8g sat. fat), 221mg chol., 301mg sod., 50g carb. (24g sugars, 11g fiber), 14g pro.

FRUIT & CREAM CREPES

This fresh and creamy breakfast is just the start—you can fill the light crepes with anything you like!
—Ruth Kaercher, Hudsonville, MI

PREP: 20 MIN. + CHILLING
COOK: 15 MIN. • **MAKES:** 2 SERVINGS

- ⅓ cup 2% milk
- 2 Tbsp. beaten egg
- ¼ tsp. vanilla extract
- ¼ cup all-purpose flour
- 1½ tsp. confectioners' sugar
- ¼ tsp. baking powder
  Dash salt
- 2 tsp. butter, divided

FILLING
- 2 oz. cream cheese, softened
- 3 Tbsp. plus ½ tsp. confectioners' sugar, divided
- 4 tsp. 2% milk
- ⅛ tsp. vanilla extract
- ⅓ cup each fresh blueberries, strawberries and raspberries

1. In a small bowl, combine the first 7 ingredients. Cover and refrigerate for 1 hour.
2. In an 8-in. nonstick skillet, melt 1 tsp. butter. Stir batter; pour about 2 Tbsp. into the center of skillet. Lift and tilt pan to evenly coat bottom. Cook until top appears dry; turn and cook 15-20 seconds longer. Remove to a wire rack. Make 3 more crepes, adding the remaining 1 tsp. butter to the skillet as needed.
3. For filling, beat cream cheese, 3 Tbsp. confectioners' sugar, milk and vanilla until smooth. Spread 1 rounded Tbsp. of filling on each crepe; top with ¼ cup fruit. Roll up; sprinkle with the remaining ½ tsp. confectioners' sugar.

2 filled crepes: 329 cal., 17g fat (10g sat. fat), 110mg chol., 273mg sod., 38g carb. (0 sugars, 2g fiber), 8g pro.

AIR-FRYER HAM & EGG POCKETS

Refrigerated crescent roll dough makes these savory breakfast pockets a snap to prepare.
—*Taste of Home* Test Kitchen

TAKES: 25 MIN. • **MAKES:** 2 SERVINGS

- 1 large egg
- 2 tsp. 2% milk
- 2 tsp. butter
- 1 oz. thinly sliced deli ham, chopped
- 2 Tbsp. shredded cheddar cheese
- 1 tube (4 oz.) refrigerated crescent rolls

1. Preheat air fryer to 300°. In a small bowl, combine egg and milk. In a small skillet, heat butter until hot. Add the egg mixture; cook and stir over medium heat until eggs are completely set. Remove from the heat. Fold in ham and cheese.
2. Separate the crescent dough into 2 rectangles. Seal perforations; spoon half the filling down the center of each rectangle. Fold dough over filling; pinch to seal.
3. Place in a single layer on greased tray in air-fryer basket. Cook until golden brown, 8-10 minutes.

1 pocket: 326 cal., 20g fat (5g sat. fat), 118mg chol., 735mg sod., 25g carb. (6g sugars, 0 fiber), 12g pro.

TEST KITCHEN TIP

If you don't have an air fryer, you can make this recipe in a regular oven instead. Just place the pockets on a greased baking sheet and bake at 375° for 10-15 minutes or until golden brown.

MICHELADA

Like your drinks with a south-of-the-border vibe? Try a kicked-up beer cocktail that's a zesty mix of Mexican lager, lime juice and hot sauce. There are many variations, but this easy recipe is perfect for rookie mixologists.
—Ian Cliffe, Milwaukee, WI

TAKES: 5 MIN. • **MAKES:** 2 SERVINGS

    Coarse salt
    Lime wedges
    Ice cubes
6 dashes hot sauce, such as Valentina or Tabasco
3 dashes Maggi seasoning or soy sauce
1 to 3 dashes Worcestershire sauce
¼ to ⅓ cup lime juice
1 bottle (12 oz.) beer, such as Corona, Modelo or Tecate

1. Place coarse salt in a shallow dish; run a lime wedge around rims of 2 cocktail glasses. Dip rims of glasses into salt, shaking off excess. Fill each glass with ice.
2. In a small pitcher, combine hot sauce, Maggi seasoning, Worcestershire sauce and lime juice. Add beer.
3. Pour mixture into glasses. Garnish with lime wedges. Serve immediately.

1 serving: 165 cal., 0 fat (0 sat. fat), 0 chol., 137mg sod., 17g carb. (12g sugars, 0 fiber), 1g pro.

SALMON CROQUETTE BREAKFAST SANDWICH

I'm obsessed with smoked salmon on bagels with all the accouterments—I could seriously eat it every day for breakfast! But smoked salmon can get pricey, so I found a cheaper alternative without losing the flavor.
—Jessi Hampton, Richmond Hill, GA

PREP: 25 MIN. • **COOK:** 10 MIN.
MAKES: 2 SERVINGS

1 large egg, lightly beaten
¼ cup dry bread crumbs
1 tsp. garlic powder
1 tsp. smoked paprika
1 pouch (6 oz.) boneless skinless pink salmon
1 Tbsp. olive oil
2 everything bagels, split and toasted
4 Tbsp. cream cheese, softened
1 Tbsp. capers, drained
1 medium tomato, sliced
½ medium red onion, thinly sliced into rings
    Snipped fresh dill, optional

1. In a small bowl, combine egg, bread crumbs, garlic powder and smoked paprika. Add salmon and mix lightly but thoroughly. Shape into 2 patties.
2. In a large skillet, cook patties in oil over medium heat until browned, 5-6 minutes on each side.
3. Spread cut sides of bagels with the cream cheese; sprinkle with capers. Serve patties on bagels with tomato, red onion and, if desired, dill.

1 sandwich: 656 cal., 25g fat (10g sat. fat), 152mg chol., 1205mg sod., 75g carb. (14g sugars, 4g fiber), 34g pro.

⏱ QUICK FRUIT COMPOTE

My mother used to make this recipe when I was a kid. My four children always ate more fruit when I dressed it up this way.
—Maxine Otis, Hobson, MT

PREP: 20 MIN. + CHILLING
MAKES: 2 SERVINGS

- 1 cup apricot nectar, divided
  Dash to ⅛ tsp. ground cloves
  Dash to ⅛ tsp. ground cinnamon
- 1 Tbsp. cornstarch
- 2 Tbsp. lemon juice
- 1 firm banana, cut into ½-in. slices
- 4 fresh strawberries, sliced
- 1 kiwifruit, halved and thinly sliced

1. In a small saucepan, bring ¾ cup apricot nectar, the cloves and cinnamon to a boil.
2. Combine cornstarch and the remaining ¼ cup apricot nectar until smooth; gradually whisk into the nectar mixture. Return to a boil; cook and stir until thickened and bubbly, 1-2 minutes. Remove from the heat; stir in lemon juice. Cool.
3. Stir in banana, strawberries and kiwi. Refrigerate, covered, for at least 1 hour before serving.
1 cup: 174 cal., 1g fat (0 sat. fat), 0 chol., 7mg sod., 44g carb. (29g sugars, 4g fiber), 2g pro.

⏱ 🗑 PRESSURE-COOKER STEEL-CUT OATS & BERRIES

This is a great alternative to a slow-cooked breakfast when you're short on time. I woke up one morning realizing I had forgotten to make overnight oats the night before. I tried out an idea in the multicooker and it turned out great! Serve with fresh seasonal fruit; my favorite are spring and summer berries.
—Mary Anne Thygesen, Portland, OR

PREP: 15 MIN.
COOK: 10 MIN. + RELEASING
MAKES: 3 SERVINGS

- 3¼ cups water, divided
- ¾ cup steel-cut oats
- ¾ cup sweetened shredded coconut
- 6 Tbsp. dried cranberries
- ⅜ tsp. each ground cinnamon, allspice, cardamom, and nutmeg
- ⅜ tsp. salt
- 1½ tsp. butter
  Optional: Yogurt, maple syrup and fresh berries

1. Place ¾ cup water, ¼ cup oats, ¼ cup coconut, 2 Tbsp. cranberries, ⅛ tsp. of each cinnamon, allspice, cardamom and nutmeg, and ⅛ tsp. salt in each of three 1-pint canning jars. Top each with ½ tsp. butter.
2. Place a trivet insert and the remaining 1 cup water in a 6-qt. electric pressure cooker. Set jars on trivet. Lock lid; close pressure-release valve. Adjust to pressure-cook on high for 10 minutes.
3. Let pressure release naturally. Remove jars. Let stand 3 minutes before serving. Serve with yogurt, syrup, fresh fruit or toppings of your choice.
1 serving: 349 cal., 13g fat (9g sat. fat), 5mg chol., 372mg sod., 55g carb. (26g sugars, 7g fiber), 6g pro.

STRAWBERRY OVERNIGHT OATS

This easy gluten-free and dairy-free breakfast will be ready and waiting for you in the morning. Use more or less sugar depending on the sweetness of your strawberries.
—Jolene Martinelli, Fremont, NH

PREP: 1¼ HOURS + CHILLING
MAKES: 1 SERVING

- 1 cup sliced fresh strawberries
- ½ tsp. sugar
- ¾ cup old-fashioned oats
- 3 Tbsp. powdered peanut butter
- 1½ tsp. chia seeds
- 1 cup unsweetened almond milk

Combine strawberries and sugar. Let stand 1 hour; mash if desired. In a pint jar, layer ¼ cup oats, 1 Tbsp. powdered peanut butter, ½ tsp. chia seeds and ⅓ cup strawberry mixture. Repeat layers twice. Pour almond milk over top; seal and refrigerate overnight.
1 serving: 352 cal., 10g fat (1g sat. fat), 0 chol., 183mg sod., 60g carb. (12g sugars, 12g fiber), 10g pro.

MIGAS BREAKFAST TACOS

Unless you grew up in the Southwest or visit there often, you might be hearing of migas for the first time. Just think of them as the best scrambled eggs ever. The secret ingredient is corn tortillas. They really make my migas tacos special!
—Stephen Exel, Des Moines, IA

TAKES: 30 MIN. • **MAKES:** 3 SERVINGS

- ¼ cup finely chopped onion
- 1 jalapeno pepper, seeded and chopped
- 1 Tbsp. canola oil
- 2 corn tortillas (6 in.), cut into thin strips
- 4 large eggs

- ¼ tsp. salt
- ⅛ tsp. pepper
- ½ cup crumbled queso fresco or shredded Monterey Jack cheese
- ¼ cup chopped seeded tomato
- 6 flour tortillas (6 in.), warmed
  Optional: Refried beans, sliced avocado, sour cream and minced fresh cilantro

In a large skillet, saute onion and jalapeno in oil until tender. Add tortilla strips; cook 3 minutes longer. In a small bowl, whisk the eggs, salt and pepper. Add to the skillet; cook and stir until almost set. Stir in cheese and tomato. Serve in flour tortillas with the toppings of your choice.
2 tacos: 424 cal., 21g fat (5g sat. fat), 295mg chol., 821mg sod., 39g carb. (2g sugars, 1g fiber), 21g pro.

TEST KITCHEN TIP

If your tortillas aren't soft enough to fold without splitting, first wrap them in a damp paper towel and then heat them in the microwave for 20 seconds. That's enough to make them soft and pliable..

- 2 Tbsp. chopped onion
- ¾ tsp. plus 2 tsp. olive oil, divided
- ½ cup grated peeled tart apple
- 1 Tbsp. minced fresh sage or ¾ tsp. rubbed sage
- ¼ tsp. salt
- ⅛ tsp. pepper
  Dash ground cinnamon
- ¼ lb. ground chicken or turkey

1. In a nonstick skillet, saute onion in ¾ tsp. oil until crisp-tender. Add apple; cook until tender, about 5 minutes. Let stand until cool enough to handle. Stir in the seasonings. Crumble chicken over apple mixture and mix lightly but thoroughly. Shape into four ½-in.-thick patties.
2. Cook patties in the remaining 2 tsp. oil over medium heat or until juices run clear.

2 patties: 159 cal., 11g fat (2g sat. fat), 38mg chol., 329mg sod., 7g carb. (5g sugars, 1g fiber), 9g pro. **Diabetic exchanges:** 2 lean meat, ½ fruit.

CHICKEN SAUSAGE PATTIES

Enjoy the taste of homemade breakfast sausage without guilt. This hearty recipe uses ground chicken in place of regular pork sausage for a lighter spin on the favorite breakfast fare.
—Mary Webb, Longwood, FL

TAKES: 25 MIN. • **MAKES:** 2 SERVINGS

DID YOU KNOW?

Chicken sausage is leaner than pork—with as little as half the saturated fat. However, sodium content is usually an issue with all prepackaged sausage. This recipe lets you control your salt intake.

LIME COCONUT SMOOTHIE BOWL

This ultra refreshing bowl is the best way to start a summer morning!
—Madeline Butler, Denver, CO

TAKES: 15 MIN. • **MAKES:** 2 SERVINGS

- 1 medium banana, peeled and frozen
- 1 cup fresh baby spinach
- ½ cup ice cubes
- ½ cup cubed fresh pineapple
- ½ cup chopped peeled mango or frozen mango chunks
- ½ cup plain Greek yogurt
- ¼ cup sweetened shredded coconut
- 3 Tbsp. honey
- 2 tsp. grated lime zest
- 1 tsp. lime juice
- ½ tsp. vanilla extract
- 1 Tbsp. spreadable cream cheese, optional
- Optional: Lime wedges, sliced banana, sliced almonds, granola, dark chocolate chips and additional shredded coconut

Place the first 11 ingredients in a blender; if desired, add cream cheese. Cover and process until smooth. Pour into chilled bowls. Serve immediately, with optional toppings as desired.
1 cup: 325 cal., 10g fat (7g sat. fat), 15mg chol., 80mg sod., 60g carb. (51g sugars, 4g fiber), 4g pro.

BACON & MUSHROOM OMELETS

I had grown tired of the same breakfast meals and wanted to make something more interesting. This fresh, flavorful omelet comes with a versatile sauce that can also be used as a nacho dip or topping, over mashed potatoes or inside burritos.
—Susan Kieboam, Amherstburg, ON

TAKES: 25 MIN. • **MAKES:** 2 SERVINGS

- 3 bacon strips, chopped
- 4 medium fresh mushrooms, sliced
- 4 large eggs
- ¼ tsp. salt
- 2 tsp. butter, divided

SAUCE
- 1 Tbsp. butter
- 1 Tbsp. all-purpose flour
- ½ cup 2% milk
- 3 Tbsp. shredded cheddar cheese
- 1 tsp. shredded Parmesan cheese
- 1 tsp. taco seasoning
- Optional: Shredded lettuce, chopped tomatoes and thinly sliced green onions

1. In a nonstick skillet, cook bacon and mushrooms over medium heat until mushrooms are tender and bacon is crisp, stirring occasionally. Remove with a slotted spoon; drain on paper towels. Discard drippings.
2. In a small bowl, whisk eggs and salt. In the skillet, heat 1 tsp. butter over medium-high heat. Pour in half of the egg mixture; it should set immediately at edges.
3. As the eggs set, push the cooked portions toward the center, letting uncooked eggs flow underneath. When eggs are thickened and no liquid egg remains, spoon half the mushroom mixture onto 1 side. Fold omelet in half; slide out of pan onto a plate. Repeat to make the second omelet.
4. For sauce, in a small saucepan, melt 1 Tbsp. butter over medium heat. Stir in flour until smooth; gradually whisk in milk. Bring to a boil, stirring constantly; cook and stir 2-3 minutes or until thickened. Stir in cheeses and taco seasoning until cheese is melted. Serve with omelets and toppings as desired.
1 omelet with ¼ cup sauce: 393 cal., 29g fat (14g sat. fat), 426mg chol., 981mg sod., 10g carb. (3g sugars, 0 fiber), 23g pro.

CHEESY VEGETABLE FRITTATA

This cheesy, flavorful egg bake is packed with veggies. My husband and I enjoy it just as much for late-night suppers as we do for brunch. Swap in an egg substitute if you're cutting the fat in your diet. A simple side of fresh fruit makes a perfect refreshing complement for this dish.
—Pauline Howard, Lago Vista, TX

PREP: 15 MIN. • **BAKE:** 20 MIN.
MAKES: 2 SERVINGS

- 4   large eggs, beaten
- 1   cup sliced fresh mushrooms
- ½   cup chopped fresh broccoli
- ¼   cup shredded sharp cheddar cheese
- 2   Tbsp. finely chopped onion
- 2   Tbsp. finely chopped green pepper
- 2   Tbsp. grated Parmesan cheese
- ⅛   tsp. salt
     Dash pepper

Preheat oven to 350°. In a large bowl, combine all the ingredients. Pour into a greased shallow 2-cup baking dish. Bake, uncovered, until a knife inserted in the center comes out clean, 20-25 minutes.
1 serving: 143 cal., 5g fat (3g sat. fat), 14mg chol., 587mg sod., 7g carb. (4g sugars, 1g fiber), 19g pro.

BLUEBERRY OAT WAFFLES

I truly enjoy recipes that make just enough for the two of us, like this one for yummy waffles. Instead of blueberries, you can slice ripe strawberries on top—or use the batter to make pancakes.
—Ruth Andrewson, Leavenworth, WA

TAKES: 25 MIN. • **MAKES:** 4 WAFFLES

- ⅔   cup all-purpose flour
- ½   cup quick-cooking oats
- 1   Tbsp. brown sugar
- 1   tsp. baking powder
- ½   tsp. salt
- 1   large egg, room temperature
- ⅔   cup 2% milk
- ¼   cup canola oil
- ½   tsp. lemon juice
- ¼   cup ground pecans
- ½   cup fresh or frozen blueberries
     Optional: Additional blueberries and chopped pecans, maple syrup and butter

1. In a bowl, combine flour, oats, brown sugar, baking powder and salt. In another bowl, combine the egg, milk, oil and lemon juice; stir into the dry ingredients just until combined. Fold in ground pecans and blueberries. Let stand for 5 minutes.

2. Bake mixture in a preheated waffle iron according to the manufacturer's directions until golden brown. If desired, top with additional blueberries and chopped pecans, and serve with maple syrup and butter.
2 waffles: 691 cal., 44g fat (5g sat. fat), 100mg chol., 907mg sod., 64g carb. (15g sugars, 5g fiber), 14g pro.

PORTOBELLO MUSHROOMS FLORENTINE

A fun and surprisingly hearty breakfast dish packed with flavor and richness.
—Sara Morris, Laguna Beach, CA

TAKES: 25 MIN. • **MAKES:** 2 SERVINGS

- 2 **large portobello mushrooms, stems removed**
  Cooking spray
- ⅛ **tsp. garlic salt**
- ⅛ **tsp. pepper**
- ½ **tsp. olive oil**
- 1 **small onion, chopped**
- 1 **cup fresh baby spinach**
- 2 **large eggs**
- ⅛ **tsp. salt**
- ¼ **cup crumbled goat cheese or feta cheese**
  Minced fresh basil, optional

1. Preheat oven to 425°. Spritz mushrooms with cooking spray; place in a 15x10x1-in. pan, stem side up. Sprinkle with garlic salt and pepper. Bake, uncovered, until tender, about 10 minutes.
2. Meanwhile, in a nonstick skillet, heat oil over medium-high heat; saute onion until tender. Stir in spinach until wilted.
3. Whisk together eggs and salt; add to skillet. Cook and stir until the eggs are thickened and no liquid egg remains; spoon onto the mushrooms. Sprinkle with cheese and, if desired, basil.

1 stuffed mushroom: 126 cal., 5g fat (2g sat. fat), 18mg chol., 472mg sod., 10g carb. (4g sugars, 3g fiber), 11g pro. **Diabetic exchanges:** 2 vegetable, 1 lean meat, ½ fat.

YANKEE RANCHEROS

After my in-laws began affectionately referring to me as a Yankee, I decided I had to learn to make some Mexican dishes. These are super easy and make my Tex-Mex-loving family happy—even if they do come from a Northerner!
—Darla Andrews, Boerne, TX

TAKES: 25 MIN. • **MAKES:** 4 SERVINGS

- 5 **cups frozen shredded hash brown potatoes (about 15 oz.)**
- 1 **cup refried beans**
- ¼ **cup salsa**
- 2 **naan flatbreads, halved**
- 4 **large eggs**
- ½ **cup shredded cheddar cheese or Mexican cheese blend**
  Additional salsa, optional

1. Cook potatoes according to package directions for stovetop.
2. Meanwhile, in a microwave-safe bowl, mix the beans and salsa. Microwave, covered, on high until heated through, 1-2 minutes, stirring once.
3. In large skillet, heat naan over medium-high heat until lightly browned, 2-3 minutes per side; remove from pan. Keep warm.
4. Coat same skillet with cooking spray; place over medium-high heat. Break eggs, 1 at a time, into pan; reduce heat to low. Cook until whites are set and yolks begin to thicken, turning once if desired.
5. To serve, spread bean mixture over naan. Top with potatoes, eggs and cheese. If desired, serve with additional salsa.

1 serving: 430 cal., 23g fat (6g sat. fat), 202mg chol., 703mg sod., 40g carb. (4g sugars, 4g fiber), 16g pro.

PECAN FRENCH TOAST

Make-ahead convenience is a bonus with this yummy brunch dish. It couldn't be easier to make, but it tastes like you worked all morning!
—Cindy Fish, Summerfield, NC

PREP: 10 MIN. + STANDING
BAKE: 30 MIN. • **MAKES:** 2 SERVINGS

- 2 large eggs
- ⅔ cup 2% milk
- ½ tsp. vanilla extract
- ⅛ tsp. salt
- 4 slices French bread (1 in. thick)
- ¼ cup packed brown sugar
- 2 Tbsp. butter, cubed
- 1 Tbsp. corn syrup
- ¼ cup chopped pecans

1. Preheat oven to 350°. In a bowl, whisk the eggs, milk, vanilla and salt; pour over bread. Let stand for 10 minutes, turning once.
2. Meanwhile, in a small saucepan, combine brown sugar, butter and corn syrup; cook over medium heat until thickened, 1-2 minutes.
3. Pour into a greased 8-in. square baking dish; sprinkle with pecans. Top with bread. Bake, uncovered, until a thermometer reads 160°, 30-35 minutes. Invert onto a serving platter. Serve immediately.
2 pieces: 577 cal., 30g fat (11g sat. fat), 249mg chol., 666mg sod., 65g carb. (37g sugars, 3g fiber), 14g pro.

SAUSAGE GRAVY WITH BISCUITS

This is one of our favorite quick dishes. My husband and I used to winter in Florida and after a day of golf, it was always a cinch to prepare this satisfying meal with a tossed salad.
—Alyce Wyman, Pembina, ND

TAKES: 25 MIN. • **MAKES:** 2 SERVINGS

- 2 individually frozen biscuits
- ¼ lb. bulk pork sausage
- 3 Tbsp. all-purpose flour
- ¼ tsp. salt, optional
- ¼ tsp. Italian seasoning
- ¼ tsp. rubbed sage
- ⅛ tsp. garlic powder
- ⅛ tsp. pepper
- 1½ cups 2% milk

1. Bake biscuits according to package directions. Meanwhile, crumble sausage into a small skillet. Cook over medium heat until no longer pink; drain.
2. Stir in flour and seasonings until blended. Gradually add milk. Bring to a boil; cook and stir for 2 minutes or until thickened.
3. Split biscuits in half; serve with sausage gravy.
¾ cup: 444 cal., 22g fat (7g sat. fat), 44mg chol., 1105mg sod., 42g carb. (13g sugars, 1g fiber), 21g pro.

PUMPKIN CREAM OF WHEAT

This autumn-inspired breakfast tastes like pumpkin pie! Double the recipe if you feel like sharing.
—Amy Bashtovoi, Sidney, NE

TAKES: 10 MIN. • **MAKES:** 1 SERVING

- ½ cup 2% milk
- ¼ cup half-and-half cream
- 3 Tbsp. Cream of Wheat
- ¼ cup canned pumpkin
- 2 tsp. sugar
- ⅛ tsp. ground cinnamon
  Additional 2% milk

In a small microwave-safe bowl, combine the milk, cream and Cream of Wheat. Microwave, uncovered, on high for 1 minute; stir until blended. Cover and cook for 1-2 minutes or until thickened, stirring every 30 seconds. Stir in the pumpkin, sugar and cinnamon. Serve with additional milk.
1 cup: 314 cal., 9g fat (6g sat. fat), 39mg chol., 96mg sod., 46g carb. (18g sugars, 4g fiber), 10g pro.

POACHED EGG BUDDHA BOWLS

My husband and I celebrate the arrival of spring with this dish, enjoying it in the backyard. I often include fresh peas and other spring delights.
—Amy McDonough, Carlton, OR

PREP: 10 MIN. • **COOK:** 65 MIN.
MAKES: 2 SERVINGS

- ¾ cup wheat berries
- 2 Tbsp. olive oil
- 2 Tbsp. lemon juice
- 1 Tbsp. thinly sliced fresh mint leaves
- ¼ tsp. salt
- ⅛ tsp. freshly ground pepper
- ½ cup quartered cherry tomatoes
- ½ cup reduced-fat ricotta cheese
- 2 Tbsp. sliced Greek olives
- 2 large eggs
  Optional: Additional olive oil and pepper

1. Place wheat berries and 2½ cups water in a large saucepan; bring to a boil. Reduce heat; simmer, covered, until tender, about 1 hour. Drain; transfer berries to a bowl. Cool slightly.

2. Stir in oil, lemon juice, mint, salt and pepper; divide between 2 bowls. Top with tomatoes, ricotta cheese and olives.

3. To poach the eggs, place ½ cup water in a small microwave-safe bowl or glass measuring cup. Break an egg into the water. Microwave, covered, on high 1 minute. Cook in 10-second intervals until white is set and yolk begins to thicken; let stand 1 minute. Repeat to poach the remaining egg.

4. Using a slotted spoon, transfer an egg to each bowl. If desired, drizzle with additional oil and sprinkle with more pepper.

1 bowl: 526 cal., 24g fat (5g sat. fat), 201mg chol., 563mg sod., 58g carb. (5g sugars, 10g fiber), 21g pro.

TEST KITCHEN TIP

Wheat berries are whole kernels of wheat. They cook up to a chewy texture with a hint of buttery flavor. Try topping this dish with your favorite veggies—grilled asparagus, steamed green beans, sauteed mushrooms and more.

LUNCH

Your noontime meal just might become the most delicious dish of the day! Whether packing an on-the-go lunch or getting cozy at home, you'll love these easy ideas.

1 tsp. butter
½ lb. uncooked shrimp (31-40 per lb.), peeled and deveined
1 garlic clove, minced
3 cups fresh baby spinach
½ medium ripe avocado, peeled and cubed
1 medium tomato, chopped
2 Tbsp. Italian salad dressing
1 Tbsp. grated Parmesan cheese

1. In a large nonstick skillet, toss bread cubes with oil and garlic salt. Cook over medium heat until bread is toasted, 3-4 minutes, stirring frequently. Remove from pan.
2. In the same skillet, heat butter over medium heat. Add shrimp and garlic; cook and stir until the shrimp turn pink, 2-3 minutes. Remove from heat.
3. Combine the spinach, avocado, tomato, toasted bread and shrimp; drizzle with the dressing and toss gently to coat. Sprinkle with grated cheese; serve immediately.

1 serving: 306 cal., 16g fat (3g sat. fat), 145mg chol., 567mg sod., 19g carb. (4g sugars, 5g fiber), 23g pro. **Diabetic exchanges:** 3 lean meat, 2 vegetable, 1 fat, ½ starch.

SHRIMP PANZANELLA SALAD

These days I'm cooking for two. After working in the garden, I can dash indoors and have this shrimp and bread salad on the table pronto.
—Kallee Krong-McCreery, Escondido, CA

TAKES: 20 MIN. • **MAKES:** 2 SERVINGS

1 cup cubed (¾ in.) French bread
1 tsp. olive oil
⅛ tsp. garlic salt

HEALTH TIP

To increase the fiber in this salad, use whole wheat bread instead! If you can't find whole wheat French bread, you can use cubed bread from a crusty whole wheat dinner roll.

BAKED POTATO SOUP

I found our favorite soup in an unexpected place—a children's cookbook! This creamy comfort food is not only delicious but also scaled down to make an amount that's perfect for my husband and me.
—Linda Mumm, Davenport, IA

TAKES: 20 MIN. • **MAKES:** 2 SERVINGS

- 2 medium potatoes, baked and cooled
- 1 can (14½ oz.) chicken broth
- 2 Tbsp. sour cream
- ⅛ tsp. pepper
- ¼ cup shredded cheddar cheese
- 1 Tbsp. crumbled cooked bacon or bacon bits
- 1 green onion, sliced

Peel the potatoes and cut into ½-in. cubes; place half in a blender. Add broth; cover and process until smooth. Pour into a saucepan. Stir in sour cream, pepper and remaining potatoes. Cook over low heat until heated through (do not boil). Garnish with cheese, bacon and onion.

1 cup: 277 cal., 8g fat (5g sat. fat), 28mg chol., 1061mg sod., 41g carb. (5g sugars, 4g fiber), 11g pro.

INDIAN FRY BREAD TACOS

Our son-in-law is half Comanche and half Kiowa, and this recipe is adapted from one he uses. I downsized it to serve two.
—LaDonna Reed, Ponca City, OK

PREP: 20 MIN. + STANDING
COOK: 15 MIN.
MAKES: 2 SERVINGS

- ¾ cup all-purpose flour
- ½ tsp. baking powder
- ¼ tsp. salt
- ⅓ cup hot water
- ½ lb. lean ground beef (90% lean)
- 2 Tbsp. taco seasoning
- ⅓ cup water
  Oil for frying
- 2 Tbsp. chopped lettuce
- 2 Tbsp. chopped tomato
- 2 Tbsp. salsa
- 2 Tbsp. sour cream

1. In a small bowl, combine the flour, baking powder and salt; stir in hot water to form a soft dough. Cover and let stand for 1 hour.

2. In a small skillet, cook beef over medium heat until no longer pink; drain. Stir in taco seasoning and water; simmer, uncovered, for 10 minutes. Keep warm.

3. Divide dough in half. On a lightly floured surface, roll each portion into a 4-in. circle.

4. In an electric skillet, heat 1 in. of oil to 350°. Fry bread circles in hot oil for 3-4 minutes on each side or until golden; drain on paper towels. Top each with meat mixture, lettuce and tomato. Serve with salsa and sour cream.

1 taco: 407 cal., 11g fat (5g sat. fat), 66mg chol., 1361mg sod., 45g carb. (2g sugars, 1g fiber), 27g pro.

SPEEDY CREAM OF WILD RICE SOUP

Add homemade touches to a can of potato soup to get comfort food on the table quickly. The result is a thick and creamy treat textured with wild rice and flavored with smoky bacon.
—Joanne Eickhoff, Pequot Lakes, MN

TAKES: 20 MIN. • **MAKES:** 2 SERVINGS

- ½ cup water
- 4½ tsp. dried minced onion
- ⅔ cup condensed cream of potato soup, undiluted
- ½ cup shredded Swiss cheese
- ½ cup cooked wild rice
- ½ cup half-and-half cream
- 2 bacon strips, cooked and crumbled

In a small saucepan, bring water and onion to a boil. Reduce heat. Stir in the potato soup, cheese, rice and cream; heat through (do not boil). Garnish with bacon.
1 cup: 333 cal., 18g fat (11g sat. fat), 68mg chol., 835mg sod., 24g carb. (5g sugars, 2g fiber), 15g pro.

BEST EVER GRILLED CHEESE SANDWICHES

You can use your imagination to come up with other fillings, such as chives, a sprinkle of Parmesan or Italian seasoning—even a spoonful of salsa.
—Edie DeSpain, Logan, UT

TAKES: 20 MIN. • **MAKES:** 2 SERVINGS

- 2 Tbsp. mayonnaise
- 1 tsp. Dijon mustard
- 4 slices sourdough bread
- 2 slices Swiss cheese
- 2 slices cheddar cheese
- 2 slices sweet onion
- 1 medium tomato, sliced
- 6 cooked bacon strips
- 2 Tbsp. butter, softened

1. Combine mayonnaise and mustard; spread over 2 bread slices. Layer with cheeses, onion, tomato and bacon; top with the remaining bread slices. Spread outsides of sandwiches with butter.
2. In a small skillet over medium heat, toast sandwiches until cheese is melted, 2-3 minutes on each side.
1 sandwich: 714 cal., 48g fat (23g sat. fat), 111mg chol., 1291mg sod., 41g carb. (4g sugars, 3g fiber), 29g pro.

TEST KITCHEN TIP

Many cheeses work great for grilled cheese—. just be sure to use a quality cheese that melts well. Cheddar, Monterey Jack and Swiss cheese work well, but feel free to step up to Gruyere, or experiment with varieties such as Brie or Manchego. A sprinkling of crumbled goat cheese along with the other varieties will make the sandwich extra creamy.

SPICY BUFFALO CHICKEN WRAPS

This recipe has a real kick and is one of my husband's favorites. It's ready in a flash, is easily doubled and the closest thing to restaurant Buffalo wings I've ever tasted in a light version.
—Jennifer Beck, Meridian, ID

TAKES: 25 MIN. • **MAKES:** 2 SERVINGS

- ½ lb. boneless skinless chicken breast, cubed
- ½ tsp. canola oil
- 2 Tbsp. Louisiana-style hot sauce
- 1 cup shredded lettuce
- 2 flour tortillas (6 in.), warmed
- 2 tsp. reduced-fat ranch salad dressing
- 2 Tbsp. crumbled blue cheese

1. In a large nonstick skillet, cook chicken in oil over medium heat for 6 minutes; drain. Stir in hot sauce. Bring to a boil. Reduce the heat; simmer, uncovered, until sauce is thickened and chicken is no longer pink, 3-5 minutes.

2. Place lettuce on tortillas; drizzle with ranch dressing. Top with the chicken mixture and blue cheese; roll up.

1 wrap: 273 cal., 11g fat (3g sat. fat), 70mg chol., 453mg sod., 15g carb. (1g sugars, 1g fiber), 28g pro.
Diabetic exchanges: 3 lean meat, 1½ fat, 1 starch.

CAULIFLOWER BROCCOLI CHEESE SOUP

My husband, who's never been a big fan of broccoli, digs into this creamy soup with gusto. It's a perfect way to enjoy the produce from our garden.
—Betty Corliss, Stratton, CO

TAKES: 30 MIN. • **MAKES:** 2 SERVINGS

- ¾ cup small cauliflowerets
- ¾ cup small broccoli florets
- ¼ cup chopped onion
- ¼ cup halved thinly sliced carrot
- 1 to 2 Tbsp. butter
- 1½ cups 2% milk, divided
- ½ tsp. chicken bouillon granules
- ¼ tsp. salt
  Dash pepper
- 2 Tbsp. all-purpose flour
- ⅓ cup cubed Velveeta

1. In a large saucepan, cook the cauliflower, broccoli, onion and carrot in butter until vegetables are crisp-tender, about 5 minutes. Stir in 1¼ cups milk, bouillon, salt and pepper. Bring to a boil. Reduce heat; simmer, uncovered, until the vegetables are tender, about 5 minutes, stirring occasionally.

2. Combine the flour and remaining ¼ cup milk until smooth; add to the saucepan. Bring to a boil; cook and stir until thickened, 1-2 minutes. Reduce heat; add cheese and stir until melted. Serve immediately.

1 cup: 267 cal., 15g fat (9g sat. fat), 48mg chol., 909mg sod., 23g carb. (13g sugars, 2g fiber), 12g pro.

THE ELVIS SANDWICH

Like the King himself sang, you'll be all shook up when you taste this savory-sweet sandwich.
—James Schend, Pleasant Prairie, WI

TAKES: 5 MIN. • **MAKES:** 1 SERVING

- 1 Tbsp. creamy peanut butter
- 1 slice crusty white bread
- ½ medium banana, sliced
- 1 bacon strip, cooked and crumbled

Spread peanut butter over bread. Top with banana and bacon.

1 open-faced sandwich: 266 cal., 13g fat (3g sat. fat), 8mg chol., 356mg sod., 31g carb. (11g sugars, 3g fiber), 10g pro.

DIY RAMEN SOUP

This favorite, prepared and served in a canning jar, is a healthier alternative to most commercial varieties. Feel free to customize the veggies.
—Michelle Clair, Seattle, WA

TAKES: 25 MIN. • **MAKES:** 2 SERVINGS

- 1   pkg. (3 oz.) ramen noodles
- 1   Tbsp. reduced-sodium chicken base
- 1   to 2 tsp. Sriracha chili sauce
- 1   tsp. minced fresh gingerroot
- ½   cup shredded carrots
- ½   cup shredded cabbage
- 2   radishes, halved and sliced
- ½   cup sliced fresh shiitake mushrooms
- 1   cup shredded cooked chicken breast
- ¼   cup fresh cilantro leaves
- 2   lime wedges
- 1   hard-boiled large egg, halved
- 4   cups boiling water

1. Cook ramen noodles according to the package directions (do not use seasoning packet); cool.
2. In each of two 1-qt. wide-mouth canning jars, layer half of each ingredient in the following order: ramen noodles, chicken base, chili sauce, ginger, carrots, cabbage, radishes, mushrooms, chicken and cilantro. Place lime wedges and egg halves in 4-oz. glass jars or other airtight containers. Cover all 4 containers and refrigerate until ready to serve.
3. To serve, pour 2 cups boiling water into each 1-qt. glass jar; let stand until warmed through or until chicken base has dissolved. Stir to combine seasonings. Squeeze lime juice over soup; place egg halves on top.

1 serving: 380 cal., 6g fat (1g sat. fat), 147mg chol., 1386mg sod., 47g carb. (4g sugars, 3g fiber), 32g pro.

CHICKEN ALFREDO STROMBOLI

I combined my favorite fettuccine Alfredo recipe with the flavors of chicken Alfredo pizza to come up with this satisfying open-faced sandwich.
—Tracy Haven, Henryville, IN

TAKES: 25 MIN. • **MAKES:** 2 SERVINGS

- 1   mini French bread baguette (5 oz.), halved lengthwise
- 6   oz. boneless skinless chicken breast, cubed
- 1   tsp. olive oil
- 4   tsp. butter, softened, divided

- ⅓   cup canned mushroom stems and pieces, drained
- ¼   tsp. salt
- ¼   tsp. garlic powder
- ¼   tsp. pepper
- ¼   cup sour cream
- ¼   cup grated Parmesan cheese
- ½   cup shredded part-skim mozzarella cheese

1. Place bread, cut side up, on an ungreased baking sheet. Broil 4-6 in. from heat for 2-3 minutes or until lightly toasted; set aside.
2. In a small skillet, saute chicken in oil and 1 tsp. butter until no longer pink. Add mushrooms, salt, garlic powder and pepper; heat through.

3. In a small bowl, combine the sour cream, Parmesan cheese and remaining butter; spread over the bread halves. Top with the chicken mixture and sprinkle with mozzarella cheese. Broil for 1-2 minutes or until the cheese is melted.

1 serving: 613 cal., 26g fat (12g sat. fat), 95mg chol., 1249mg sod., 58g carb. (3g sugars, 5g fiber), 38g pro.

CHICKEN & ONION CAESAR SALAD

My Caesar with grilled chicken is a healthier alternative to gravy-laden meat-and-potatoes dishes. After grilling kabobs, we toss them with romaine and cheese.
—Melissa Adams, Tooele, UT

TAKES: 30 MIN. • **MAKES:** 2 SERVINGS

- ½ lb. boneless skinless chicken breasts, cut into 1-in. pieces
- 1 large sweet onion, cut into 2-in. pieces
- 6 Tbsp. creamy Caesar salad dressing, divided
- 4 small red potatoes, halved
- ½ tsp. lemon juice
- ⅛ tsp. coarsely ground pepper
- 1 small bunch romaine, torn
- 2 Tbsp. shredded Parmesan cheese

1. In a large bowl, combine the chicken, onion and 2 Tbsp. salad dressing; toss to coat. In a small bowl, combine the potatoes with 2 Tbsp. salad dressing.

2. Alternately thread chicken and onion pieces onto metal or soaked wooden skewers, leaving space between each piece. Thread the potatoes onto separate metal or soaked wooden skewers.

3. On a greased grill rack, grill potatoes, covered, over medium heat 5 minutes. Add the chicken kabobs; grill until the chicken is no longer pink and potatoes are tender, 10-15 minutes, turning skewers occasionally.

4. In a large bowl, whisk lemon juice, pepper and remaining salad dressing. Add romaine, chicken, potatoes, onion and cheese; toss to coat.

1 serving: 441 cal., 21g fat (5g sat. fat), 81mg chol., 601mg sod., 31g carb. (10g sugars, 5g fiber), 31g pro.

LEMONY CHICKEN NOODLE SOUP

This isn't Grandma's chicken soup, but it is comforting in a whole new way. The lemon juice gives this easy soup enough zip to make it interesting.
—Bill Hilbrich, St. Cloud, MN

TAKES: 30 MIN. • **MAKES:** 2 SERVINGS

- 1 small onion, chopped
- 2 Tbsp. olive oil
- 1 Tbsp. butter
- ¼ lb. boneless skinless chicken breast, cubed
- 1 garlic clove, minced
- 2 cans (14½ oz. each) chicken broth
- 1 medium carrot, cut into ¼-in. slices
- ¼ cup fresh or frozen peas
- ½ tsp. dried basil
- 2 cups uncooked medium egg noodles
- 1 to 2 Tbsp. lemon juice

1. In a small saucepan, saute onion in oil and butter until tender. Add chicken; cook and stir until the chicken is lightly browned and meat is no longer pink. Add garlic; cook 1 minute longer.
2. Stir in broth, carrot, peas and basil. Bring to a boil. Reduce heat; cover and simmer for 5 minutes. Add noodles. Cover and simmer until the noodles are tender, 8-10 minutes. Stir in lemon juice.
1 cup: 435 cal., 23g fat (6g sat. fat), 83mg chol., 949mg sod., 38g carb. (7g sugars, 4g fiber), 21g pro.

GRILLED JERK SHRIMP ORZO SALAD

It doesn't matter what the temperature outside is—you'll feel as if you're in the Caribbean when you take your first bite of this salad.
—Eileen Budnyk, Palm Beach Gardens, FL

PREP: 25 MIN. • **GRILL:** 10 MIN.
MAKES: 2 SERVINGS

- ⅓ cup uncooked whole wheat orzo pasta
- ½ lb. uncooked shrimp (31-40 per lb.), peeled and deveined
- 1 Tbsp. Caribbean jerk seasoning
- 1 medium ear sweet corn, husked
- 1 tsp. olive oil
- 6 fresh asparagus spears, trimmed
- 1 small sweet red pepper, chopped

DRESSING
- 3 Tbsp. lime juice
- 1 Tbsp. water
- 1 Tbsp. olive oil
- ⅛ tsp. salt
- ⅛ tsp. pepper

1. Cook orzo according to package directions. Rinse with cold water; drain well. Meanwhile, toss shrimp with jerk seasoning; thread onto metal or soaked wooden skewers. Brush corn with oil.
2. On a covered grill over medium heat, cook corn until tender and lightly browned, 10-12 minutes, turning ears occasionally; and cook asparagus until crisp-tender, 5-7 minutes, turning occasionally. Grill shrimp until they turn pink, 1-2 minutes per side.
3. Cut corn from cob; cut asparagus into 1-in. pieces. Remove shrimp from skewers. In a large bowl, combine orzo, grilled vegetables, shrimp and red pepper. Whisk together dressing ingredients; toss with salad.
2 cups: 340 cal., 12g fat (2g sat. fat), 138mg chol., 716mg sod., 35g carb. (6g sugars, 7g fiber), 25g pro.
Diabetic exchanges: 3 lean meat, 2 starch, 1 vegetable, 1 fat.

CHEESE-STUFFED BURGERS

Here's a sandwich that does traditional burgers one better—with a surprise pocket of cheddar! My family really enjoys the melted-cheese center.
—Janet Wood, Windham, NH

TAKES: 25 MIN. • **MAKES:** 2 SERVINGS

- 1 Tbsp. finely chopped onion
- 1 Tbsp. ketchup
- 1 tsp. prepared mustard
- ¼ tsp. salt
- ⅛ tsp. pepper
- ½ lb. lean ground beef (90% lean)
- ¼ cup finely shredded cheddar cheese
- 2 hamburger buns, split
  Optional: Lettuce leaves and tomato slices

1. In a small bowl, combine the first 5 ingredients. Crumble beef over mixture and mix lightly but thoroughly. Shape mixture into 4 thin patties. Sprinkle the cheese over 2 of the patties; top with the remaining 2 patties and press edges firmly to seal.
2. Grill burgers, covered, over medium heat 5-6 minutes on each side or until a thermometer reads 160°. Serve on buns, with lettuce and tomato if desired.

1 burger: 357 cal., 15g fat (7g sat. fat), 84mg chol., 787mg sod., 25g carb. (4g sugars, 1g fiber), 28g pro. **Diabetic exchanges:** 3 lean meat, 1½ starch, 1½ fat.

SMALL-BATCH CHILI

This thick and hearty chili gives you all the flavor of a chili cook-off winner in a quantity just right for two. I serve it with a refreshing salad of grapefruit and avocado slices.
—Norma Grogg, St. Louis, MO

TAKES: 25 MIN. • **MAKES:** 2 SERVINGS

- ¼ lb. ground beef
- ¼ cup chopped onion
- 1 garlic clove, minced
- 1 can (16 oz.) chili beans, undrained
- 1 can (14½ oz.) diced tomatoes, undrained
- 1½ tsp. chili powder
- ½ tsp. ground cumin
  Optional: Sour cream, shredded cheddar cheese and chopped cilantro

1. In a large saucepan, cook beef and onion over medium heat until the meat is no longer pink. Add garlic; cook 1 minute longer. Drain. Stir the in beans, tomatoes and spices; bring to a boil.
2. Reduce heat; cover and simmer until heated through, 10-15 minutes. If desired, top with sour cream, shredded cheddar cheese and chopped cilantro.

1 cup: 339 cal., 7g fat (3g sat. fat), 28mg chol., 948mg sod., 55g carb. (11g sugars, 17g fiber), 24g pro.

TEST KITCHEN TIP

Canned chili beans are either pinto or kidney beans in a chili sauce. You can use a can of plain beans to cut the sodium; add tomato paste, garlic powder and chili powder to boost the flavor.

1 large potato, peeled and cut into 1½-in. pieces
1 large carrot, cut into ½-in. slices
1½ cups water
1 cup reduced-sodium chicken broth
5 medium fresh mushrooms, halved
1 Tbsp. all-purpose flour
¼ cup reduced-fat evaporated milk
¼ cup shredded part-skim mozzarella cheese
½ lb. salmon fillet, cut into 1½-in. pieces
¼ tsp. pepper
⅛ tsp. salt
1 Tbsp. chopped fresh dill

1. Place the first 4 ingredients in a saucepan; bring to a boil. Reduce heat to medium; cook, uncovered, until the vegetables are tender, 10-15 minutes.
2. Add mushrooms. In a small bowl, mix flour and milk until smooth; stir into soup. Return to a boil; cook and stir until the mushrooms are tender. Reduce the heat to medium; stir in cheese until melted.
3. Reduce heat to medium-low. Add salmon; cook, uncovered, until the fish just begins to flake easily with a fork, 3-4 minutes. Stir in pepper and salt. Sprinkle with dill.
2½ cups: 398 cal., 14g fat (4g sat. fat), 71mg chol., 647mg sod., 37g carb. (7g sugars, 3g fiber), 30g pro. **Diabetic exchanges:** 3 lean meat, 2½ starch.

HEALTH TIP

Salmon is among the richest sources of healthy fats, making it an ideal source of omega-3 fatty acids. Salmon also contains calcium, vitamin D, and folate.

SALMON DILL SOUP

This is the best soup I have ever made, according to my husband, who loves salmon so much that he could eat it every day. When I get salmon, I try to make it a very special dish because it's a treat for both of us.
—Hidemi Walsh, Plainfield, IN

TAKES: 30 MIN. • **MAKES:** 2 SERVINGS

HONEY-DIJON CHICKEN SALAD

This delightful main-dish salad has an easy dressing that lends a sweet-tangy flavor to the mix. You can add or take away vegetables to suit your taste.
—Janelle Hensley, Harrisonburg, VA

PREP: 15 MIN. • **BAKE:** 20 MIN.
MAKES: 2 SERVINGS

- ½ lb. chicken tenderloins, cut into 1½-in. pieces
- 2 Tbsp. honey, divided
- 2 Tbsp. Dijon mustard, divided
- 3 cups torn leaf lettuce
- 2 hard-boiled large eggs, chopped
- 2 Tbsp. each chopped green, sweet orange and yellow pepper
- 1 Tbsp. chopped onion
- 2 tsp. sesame seeds

1. Preheat oven to 350°. Place chicken tenderloins in a greased 1½-qt. baking dish. Combine 1 Tbsp. each of honey and mustard; pour over chicken. Bake, covered, until the chicken is no longer pink, 20-25 minutes.

2. In a large bowl, combine the lettuce, eggs, peppers, onion and sesame seeds; divide between 2 plates. Top with chicken. Combine the remaining 1 Tbsp. each honey and mustard; drizzle over chicken.

2½ cups: 301 cal., 9g fat (2g sat. fat), 279mg chol., 498mg sod., 25g carb. (19g sugars, 2g fiber), 35g pro.
Diabetic exchanges: 4 lean meat, 2 vegetable, 1 starch.

QUICK CHICKEN LETTUCE WRAPS

Bundle up a tasty blend of garden flavors with these delightful wraps. Sweet and hot accents set these wraps apart.
—*Taste of Home* Test Kitchen

TAKES: 25 MIN. • **MAKES:** 2 SERVINGS

- 3 Tbsp. chicken broth
- 2 Tbsp. plus 2 tsp. reduced-sodium soy sauce, divided
- 1 Tbsp. sherry or additional chicken broth
- 1½ tsp. cornstarch
- ½ lb. ground chicken
- 1 tsp. canola oil
- ¼ cup shredded carrot
- 1 tsp. minced fresh gingerroot
- ⅓ cup plum or seedless raspberry preserves
- 2 tsp. hoisin sauce
- ⅛ tsp. hot pepper sauce
- 1 green onion, thinly sliced
- 4 Bibb or Boston lettuce leaves

1. In a small bowl, combine broth, 2 Tbsp. soy sauce, the sherry and cornstarch; set aside.

2. In a large skillet, cook chicken in oil over medium heat until the meat is no longer pink; drain. Add carrot and ginger; cook and stir for 2-3 minutes or until carrot is tender.

3. Meanwhile, for dipping sauce, combine the preserves, hoisin sauce, pepper sauce and remaining 2 tsp. soy sauce; set aside. Stir the cornstarch mixture; add to chicken. Cook and stir until thickened, about 2 minutes. Remove from the heat; stir in green onion.

4. Divide chicken mixture among lettuce leaves. Fold lettuce over filling. Serve with dipping sauce.

2 wraps: 354 cal., 12g fat (3g sat. fat), 75mg chol., 1025mg sod., 43g carb. (35g sugars, 1g fiber), 20g pro.

TUNA ARTICHOKE MELTS

After sampling a similar open-faced sandwich at a restaurant, I created my own version of lemon-seasoned tuna salad with artichoke hearts. Serve it on the patio for lunch with a friend.
—Evelyn Basinger, Linville, VA

TAKES: 15 MIN. • **MAKES:** 2 SERVINGS

- 1   can (6 oz.) light water-packed tuna, drained and flaked
- ⅓   cup coarsely chopped water-packed artichoke hearts, rinsed and drained
- 2   Tbsp. mayonnaise
- ½   cup shredded Mexican cheese blend, divided
- ¼   tsp. lemon-pepper seasoning
- ⅛   tsp. dried oregano
- 2   English muffins, split and toasted

1. Preheat broiler. In a small bowl, mix tuna, artichokes, mayonnaise, ¼ cup cheese, lemon pepper and oregano. Spread over English muffin halves.
2. Place on a baking sheet. Broil 4-6 in. from the heat until heated through, 3-5 minutes. Sprinkle with the remaining ¼ cup cheese; broil until the cheese is melted, 1-2 minutes longer.
2 topped muffin halves: 335 cal., 8g fat (4g sat. fat), 47mg chol., 989mg sod., 31g carb. (3g sugars, 2g fiber), 34g pro.

SAUSAGE & SPINACH TORTELLINI SOUP

My husband's grandmother used to make this soup with her own homemade sausage and tortellini. We don't make those ingredients from scratch, but this version is almost as good as hers. Plus, it's a great way to get the kids to eat spinach!
—Joyce Lulewicz, Brunswick, OH

PREP: 10 MIN. • **COOK:** 30 MIN.
MAKES: 2 SERVINGS

- ½   lb. bulk Italian sausage
- 1   small onion, thinly sliced
- 1   garlic clove, minced
- 1   can (14½ oz.) reduced-sodium chicken broth
- ½   cup water
- 1½   cups torn fresh spinach
- ¾   cup refrigerated cheese tortellini
- 2   Tbsp. shredded Parmesan cheese
  Crushed red pepper flakes, optional

1. In a small saucepan, cook the sausage over medium heat until no longer pink; drain. Add onion; cook and stir until tender. Add garlic; cook 1 minute longer. Stir in broth and water; bring to a boil. Reduce heat; simmer, uncovered, for 10 minutes.
2. Return to a boil. Reduce heat, add spinach and tortellini; cook until tortellini is tender, 7-9 minutes. Sprinkle with cheese. If desired, top with crushed red pepper flakes.
1¾ cups: 354 cal., 19g fat (8g sat. fat), 64mg chol., 1360mg sod., 23g carb. (4g sugars, 2g fiber), 23g pro.

HEALTH TIP

Italian sausage has a relatively high sodium content; if you want to cut the sodium, try using ground beef or turkey sausage mix instead. Try a different pasta, too—orzo is a winner here! . To add protein, throw in a can of drained cannelini or other white beans.

LEMONY MUSHROOM-ORZO SOUP

This versatile soup works as an appetizer or as a side for a sandwich lunch. It's loaded with mushrooms and orzo pasta—and lemon livens up its mild flavor.
—Edrie O'Brien, Denver, CO

TAKES: 30 MIN. • **MAKES:** 2 SERVINGS

- 2½ cups sliced fresh mushrooms
- 2 green onions, chopped
- 1 Tbsp. olive oil
- 1 garlic clove, minced
- 1½ cups reduced-sodium chicken broth
- 1½ tsp. minced fresh parsley
- ¼ tsp. dried thyme
- ⅛ tsp. pepper
- ¼ cup uncooked orzo pasta
- 1½ tsp. lemon juice
- ⅛ tsp. grated lemon zest

1. In a small saucepan, saute mushrooms and onions in oil until tender. Add garlic; cook 1 minute longer. Stir in the broth, parsley, thyme and pepper.
2. Bring to a boil. Stir in the orzo, lemon juice and zest. Cook until pasta is tender, 5-6 minutes.
1 cup: 191 cal., 8g fat (1g sat. fat), 0 chol., 437mg sod., 24g carb. (4g sugars, 2g fiber), 9g pro. **Diabetic exchanges:** 1½ fat, 1 starch, 1 vegetable.

SALMON & FETA WILTED SPINACH SALAD

A friend mentioned a Turkish salmon and couscous dish that sounded fantastic, so I started experimenting. I prefer this salad warm, but it's also tasty served cold.
—Jeni Pittard, Statham, GA

TAKES: 30 MIN. • **MAKES:** 2 SERVINGS

- 1 salmon fillet (8 oz.)
- 2 tsp. lemon juice
- ½ tsp. Greek seasoning
- ½ cup quinoa, rinsed
- 1 cup reduced-sodium chicken broth
- 1 tsp. olive oil
- 4 cups coarsely chopped fresh spinach
- 1 cup grape tomatoes, halved
- ¼ cup crumbled feta cheese
- 2 Tbsp. chopped fresh parsley
- 1 Tbsp. minced fresh oregano
- ⅛ tsp. pepper
  Lemon wedges

1. Preheat the oven to 375°. Place salmon on a foil-lined baking sheet, skin side down. Sprinkle with lemon juice and Greek seasoning. Bake until fish just begins to flake easily with a fork, 15-18 minutes.
2. Meanwhile, in a small saucepan, combine quinoa, broth and oil; bring to a boil. Reduce heat; simmer, covered, until liquid is absorbed and quinoa is tender, 12-15 minutes.
3. To serve, break salmon into 1-in. pieces using a fork. Place spinach, tomatoes, quinoa and salmon in a large bowl. Add cheese, herbs and pepper; toss gently to combine. Serve with lemon wedges.
2 cups: 427 cal., 18g fat (4g sat. fat), 64mg chol., 773mg sod., 34g carb. (3g sugars, 6g fiber), 32g pro. **Diabetic exchanges:** 3 lean meat, 2 vegetable, 1½ starch, 1 fat.

CHICKEN TZATZIKI CUCUMBER BOATS

I've tended a garden for decades, and these colorful boats made from cucumbers hold my homegrown tomatoes, peas and dill. It's absolute garden greatness.
—Ronna Farley, Rockville, MD

TAKES: 15 MIN. • **MAKES:** 2 SERVINGS

- 2 medium cucumbers
- ½ cup fat-free plain Greek yogurt
- 2 Tbsp. mayonnaise
- ½ tsp. garlic salt
- 3 tsp. snipped fresh dill, divided
- 1 cup chopped cooked chicken breast
- 1 cup chopped seeded tomato (about 1 large), divided
- ½ cup fresh or frozen peas, thawed

1. Cut each cucumber lengthwise in half; scoop out pulp, leaving a ¼-in. shell.
2. In a bowl, mix the Greek yogurt, mayonnaise, garlic salt and 1 tsp. dill; gently stir in chicken, ¾ cup tomato and the peas.
3. Spoon mixture into cucumber shells. Top with the remaining ¼ cup tomato and 2 tsp. dill.
2 filled cucumber halves: 312 cal., 12g fat (2g sat. fat), 55mg chol., 641mg sod., 18g carb. (10g sugars, 6g fiber), 34g pro. **Diabetic exchanges:** 4 lean meat, 2 vegetable, 2 fat, ½ starch.

COBB SALAD CLUB SANDWICH

Can't decide whether you want a salad or a sandwich? You'll never have to choose again. With the generous ingredients piled club-style high, this is a mouthwatering mashup. We affectionately call it the alpha Clobb sandwich!
—Carmell Childs, Orangeville, UT

TAKES: 25 MIN. • **MAKES:** 2 SERVINGS

- 3 Tbsp. butter, softened
- 3 slices rustic Italian bread
- 3 slices cheddar or provolone cheese
- 2 pieces leaf lettuce
- 3 slices tomato
- 7 thin slices deli smoked peppered turkey breast
- ½ medium ripe avocado, peeled and sliced
- 3 Tbsp. blue cheese spread
- 7 thin slices deli oven-roasted chicken
- 7 thin slices deli ham
- 5 crisp cooked bacon strips
- 1 hard-boiled large egg, sliced

1. Spread butter over 1 side of each bread slice. Place 1 slice cheese on each unbuttered side of bread. Toast bread slices, butter side down, in a large skillet or electric griddle over medium-low heat until golden brown, 4-5 minutes.
2. Layer 1 piece of toast with the lettuce, tomato, turkey and avocado. Top with another piece of toast and spread with blue cheese spread. Top with chicken, ham, bacon and egg. Top with the remaining piece of toast, cheese side down. Cut sandwich in half, secure with toothpicks and serve.
½ sandwich: 878 cal., 58g fat (26g sat. fat), 285mg chol., 2774mg sod., 32g carb. (5g sugars, 4g fiber), 58g pro.

GRILLED TUNA SALAD

I love cooking this tuna spinach salad! Tuna steaks are delicious and quick to cook, and always seem a little more elegant, even though they're pretty inexpensive. You can find them at most meat and seafood counters.
—De'Lawrence Reed, Durham, NC

TAKES: 30 MIN. • **MAKES:** 2 SERVINGS

- ½ lb. tuna steaks
- 1 tsp. olive oil
- ⅛ tsp. salt
- ⅛ tsp. pepper
- 3 cups fresh baby spinach
- ½ cup grape tomatoes
- ⅓ cup frozen shelled edamame, thawed
- ¼ cup frozen corn, thawed

CITRUS VINAIGRETTE
- 1 Tbsp. olive oil
- 1½ tsp. minced fresh basil
- 1½ tsp. white wine vinegar
- 1½ tsp. honey
- 1½ tsp. lime juice
- 1½ tsp. lemon juice
- 1½ tsp. orange juice
- ⅛ tsp. salt
- ⅛ tsp. pepper

1. Brush tuna with oil; sprinkle with salt and pepper. Grill, covered, over high heat on a greased grill rack or broil 3-4 in. from the heat for 3-4 minutes on each side or until slightly pink in the center (medium-rare.) Let stand for 5 minutes.
2. Meanwhile, in a large bowl, combine the spinach, tomatoes, edamame and corn. In a small bowl, whisk the vinaigrette ingredients; drizzle over salad and toss to coat.

3. Divide salad between 2 plates; slice tuna and arrange over the salads. Serve immediately.
2 cups salad with 3 oz. cooked tuna: 290 cal., 12g fat (2 g sat. fat), 51mg chol., 380mg sod., 16g carb., 3g fiber, 31g pro. **Diabetic exchanges:** 4 lean meat, 2 fat, 1 vegetable, ½ starch.

DID YOU KNOW?

Edamame are soybeans that are harvested early, before they become hard. The young beans are parboiled and frozen to retain their freshness and can be found in the freezer section.

FLAVORFUL TOMATO SOUP

A cookbook soup recipe called for ingredients I didn't have on hand, so I improvised and came up with this. I often make it for friends at church, and I've shared the recipe many times.
—Jean Sullivan, Denver, CO

TAKES: 15 MIN. • **MAKES:** 2 SERVINGS

- ¼ cup finely chopped onion
- 1 Tbsp. butter
- ¼ tsp. dried basil
- ¼ tsp. paprika
- ⅛ tsp. garlic powder
- 1 can (10¾ oz.) condensed tomato soup, undiluted
- 1 cup 2% milk
  Fresh basil leaves, optional

In a saucepan, saute onion in butter until tender. Add basil, paprika and garlic powder. Stir in soup and milk until well blended. Over medium heat, cook until heated through, 6-8 minutes. If desired, top with fresh basil leaves.

1 cup: 233 cal., 8g fat (5g sat. fat), 24mg chol., 989mg sod., 33g carb. (22g sugars, 2g fiber), 7g pro.

BLACKENED PORK CAESAR SALAD

This Caesar salad with pork has fantastic flavor even when the meat is chilled—so you can serve it either warm or cold.
—Penny Hedges, Dewdney, BC

TAKES: 30 MIN. • **MAKES:** 2 SERVINGS

- 2 Tbsp. mayonnaise
- 1 Tbsp. olive oil
- 1 Tbsp. lemon juice
- 1 garlic clove, minced
- ⅛ tsp. seasoned salt
- ⅛ tsp. pepper

SALAD

- ¾ lb. pork tenderloin, cut into 1-in. cubes
- 1 Tbsp. blackened seasoning
- 1 Tbsp. canola oil
- 6 cups torn romaine
  Optional: Shredded Parmesan cheese and salad croutons

1. For dressing, in a small bowl, mix the first 6 ingredients until blended; set aside.
2. Toss the cubed pork with blackened seasoning. In a large skillet, heat oil over medium-high heat. Add pork; cook and stir until tender, 5-7 minutes.
3. To serve, place romaine in a large bowl; add dressing and toss to coat. Top with pork and, if desired, croutons and cheese.

2½ cups: 458 cal., 31g fat (5g sat. fat), 100mg chol., 464mg sod., 8g carb. (2g sugars, 3g fiber), 36g pro.

GRILLED PEPPERONI PIZZA SANDWICHES

If pizza and grilled cheese are among your favorite foods, you're in for an ooey-gooey treat!
—Chris Anderson, Mounds View, MN

TAKES: 20 MIN. • **MAKES:** 2 SERVINGS

- 4 slices Italian bread
- 2 Tbsp. marinara sauce
- 16 slices pepperoni
- ½ cup shredded Italian cheese blend
- 2 Tbsp. butter, softened
- ⅛ tsp. garlic powder

1. Spread all 4 bread slices with marinara sauce; layer 2 slices with pepperoni and cheese. Top with the remaining bread slices. Combine the butter and garlic powder. Spread over the outsides of the sandwiches.
2. In a small skillet over medium heat, toast the sandwiches for 2-3 minutes on each side or until the cheese is melted.

1 sandwich: 439 cal., 27g fat (14g sat. fat), 63mg chol., 964mg sod., 33g carb. (2g sugars, 2g fiber), 15g pro.

 FLAVORFUL SLOPPY JOES

Do you like sloppy joes but not all the leftovers? This recipe makes just enough for two hearty sandwiches. The sauce level in the meat mixture is low, making it a little less messy to eat on a bun.
—Nancy Collins, Clearfield, PA

TAKES: 25 MIN. • **MAKES:** 2 SERVINGS

- ½ lb. lean ground beef (90% lean)
- 2 Tbsp. chopped onion
- 2 Tbsp. chopped green pepper
- ½ cup ketchup
- 1½ tsp. brown sugar
- 1½ tsp. prepared mustard
- 1½ tsp. Worcestershire sauce
- 2 hamburger buns, split

1. In a small skillet, cook the beef, onion and green pepper over medium heat until the meat is no longer pink; drain.
2. Stir in the ketchup, brown sugar, mustard and Worcestershire sauce. Bring to a boil. Reduce the heat; simmer, uncovered, for 5 minutes. Serve on buns.

1 serving: 379 cal., 11g fat (4g sat. fat), 56mg chol., 1112mg sod., 44g carb. (14g sugars, 2g fiber), 27g pro. **Diabetic exchanges:** 3 lean meat, 2 starch, 2 vegetable.

GRILLED SHRIMP COBB SALAD

This salad is both healthy and delicious. I often use a grill pan for the shrimp, but you can simply saute them, too. Use any greens you like—it's a very versatile salad.
—Nicholas Monfre, Hudson, FL

TAKES: 30 MIN. • **MAKES:** 2 SERVINGS

- ½ lb. uncooked shrimp (31-40 per lb.), peeled and deveined
- 2 Tbsp. olive oil
- 1 tsp. lemon juice
- ½ tsp. salt
- ¼ tsp. white pepper

DRESSING
- ¼ cup mayonnaise
- 2 Tbsp. crumbled Gorgonzola cheese
- 1 Tbsp. water
- ½ tsp. dried parsley flakes
- ¼ tsp. white wine vinegar

SALAD
- 4 cups spring mix salad greens
- 1 medium ripe avocado, peeled and cut into wedges
- 4 pieces bacon strips, cooked and chopped
- 2 hard-boiled large eggs, sliced
- 1 medium tomato, sliced
- ¼ cup slices red onion

1. Toss the shrimp with oil, lemon juice, salt and pepper; refrigerate, covered, for 15 minutes.
2. Mix the dressing ingredients, mashing the cheese with a fork. Place greens on a platter; arrange remaining ingredients over top.
3. Grill the shrimp, covered, over medium heat until pink, 2-3 minutes per side. Place over salad. Serve with dressing.

1 serving: 726 cal., 59g fat (12g sat. fat), 349mg chol., 1392mg sod., 16g carb. (3g sugars, 8g fiber), 36g pro.

2 tsp. olive oil
½ medium red onion, thinly sliced
6 oz. sliced deli turkey, coarsely chopped
6 cherry tomatoes, halved
2 tsp. balsamic vinegar
6 Bibb or Boston lettuce leaves
½ medium ripe avocado, peeled and cubed
¼ cup shredded Swiss cheese
¼ cup alfalfa sprouts, optional

1. In a large skillet, heat oil over medium-high heat. Add onion; cook and stir until tender, 3-4 minutes. Add turkey; heat through. Stir in tomatoes and vinegar just until combined.

2. Serve in lettuce leaves. Top with avocado, cheese and, if desired, sprouts.

3 wraps: 270 cal., 16g fat (4g sat. fat), 43mg chol., 799mg sod., 11g carb. (4g sugars, 4g fiber), 22g pro. **Diabetic exchanges:** 3 lean meat, 1½ fat, 1 vegetable.

HEALTH TIP

Deli meat, such as the turkey used in these low-carb wraps, is typically lean. But it's also high in sodium. Switch to leftover cooked turkey or chicken to cut back on sodium.

DELI TURKEY LETTUCE WRAPS

I used to make these during my training days when I worked at a restaurant in Hawaii. They're low-fat, low-carb, high-protein, quick and delicious—a great choice before or after a workout.
—Duncan Omarzu, Astoria, NY

TAKES: 25 MIN. • **MAKES:** 6 WRAPS

MUSHROOM BARLEY SOUP

This is part of my favorite meal, quick and easy to prepare and the perfect amount for two. The mushrooms, carrots and barley are a good combination for flavor and color.
—Aimee Lawrence, Wimberley, TX

PREP: 15 MIN. • **COOK:** 40 MIN.
MAKES: 3 CUPS

- 1   cup sliced fresh mushrooms
- 2   garlic cloves, minced
- 1   Tbsp. butter
- 2   cans (14½ oz. each) reduced-sodium chicken broth
- ⅓   cup medium pearl barley
- 1   Tbsp. reduced-sodium soy sauce
- 1   medium carrot, sliced
- ½   tsp. dill weed
      Salt and pepper to taste

1. In a small saucepan, saute mushrooms and garlic in butter for 3 minutes. Stir in the broth, barley and soy sauce. Bring to a boil. Reduce heat; simmer, covered, for 20 minutes.
2. Add the carrot, dill, salt and pepper. Simmer, covered, until barley and carrot are tender, about 15 minutes.
1½ cups: 230 cal., 6g fat (4g sat. fat), 15mg chol., 1543mg sod., 34g carb. (5g sugars, 7g fiber), 12g pro.

STEAK & NEW POTATO TOSS

I usually use leftover barbecued steak to make this fabulous main dish salad. It's pretty, too, with the red pepper, green broccoli and white potatoes. The salad can be served warm or cold.
—Deyanne Davies, Rossland, BC

TAKES: 30 MIN. • **MAKES:** 2 SERVINGS

- ½   lb. small red potatoes, scrubbed and cut into wedges
- 10   oz. beef top sirloin steak
- 1½   cups fresh broccoli florets
- ½   cup chopped sweet red pepper

VINAIGRETTE
- 2   Tbsp. olive oil
- 1   Tbsp. cider vinegar
- 1   green onion, thinly sliced
- 1   garlic clove, minced
- ¼   tsp. ground mustard
- ¼   tsp. paprika
- ⅛   tsp. pepper

1. Place potatoes in a large saucepan and cover with water. Bring to a boil. Reduce the heat; cook, covered, for 10-15 minutes or until tender.
2. Meanwhile, grill steak, covered, over medium heat for 8-11 minutes on each side or until meat reaches desired doneness (for medium-rare, a thermometer should read 135°; medium, 140°; medium-well, 145°). Let stand 10 minutes, then thinly slice across the grain.
3. Place the broccoli florets in a steamer basket. Place basket in a saucepan over 1 in. of water. Bring to a boil. Steam, covered, for 2-3 minutes or until broccoli is crisp-tender.
4. In a small bowl, combine the vinaigrette ingredients.

5. Drain the broccoli and potatoes; place in a large bowl. Add beef and red pepper; drizzle with vinaigrette and toss to coat.
1½ cups: 416 cal., 20g fat (4g sat. fat), 57mg chol., 88mg sod., 25g carb. (4g sugars, 5g fiber), 35g pro.

SAUSAGE SPINACH SALAD

Want a fast way to turn a salad into a hearty meal? Add sausage! The mustard dressing also goes with smoked salmon or chicken.
—Deborah Williams, Peoria, AZ

TAKES: 20 MIN. • **MAKES:** 2 SERVINGS

- 4 tsp. olive oil, divided
- 2 fully cooked Italian chicken sausage links (3 oz. each), cut into ¼-in. slices
- ½ medium onion, halved and sliced
- 4 cups fresh baby spinach
- 1½ tsp. balsamic vinegar
- 1 tsp. stone-ground mustard

1. In a large nonstick skillet, heat 1 tsp. oil over medium heat. Add sausage and onion; cook and stir until sausage is lightly browned and onion is crisp-tender.
2. Place spinach in a large bowl. In a small bowl, whisk vinegar, mustard and remaining 1 Tbsp. oil. Drizzle dressing over spinach; toss to coat. Add the sausage mixture; serve immediately.

2½ cups: 244 cal., 16g fat (3g sat. fat), 65mg chol., 581mg sod., 8g carb. (3g sugars, 2g fiber), 17g pro. **Diabetic exchanges:** 2 vegetable, 2 lean meat, 2 fat.

SPICY PEANUT BUTTER & PORK SANDWICH

A little spicy, a little sweet—and with just a hint of curry—this flavor combo is something you just have to try.
—James Schend, Pleasant Prairie, WI

TAKES: 10 MIN. • **MAKES:** 1 SERVING

- 1 Tbsp. creamy peanut butter
- 1 slice crusty white bread
- 2 Tbsp. shredded cooked pork
- 1 tsp. Sriracha chili sauce
  Curry powder
  Thinly sliced jalapeno pepper

Spread peanut butter over bread. Layer with pork and chili sauce. Sprinkle with curry powder; top with jalapeno.

1 open-faced sandwich: 215 cal., 11g fat (2g sat. fat), 16mg chol., 381mg sod., 20g carb. (5g sugars, 2g fiber), 11g pro.

GRILLED PEPPER JACK CHICKEN SANDWICHES

With zesty cheese, bacon and grilled chicken flavor, these sandwiches taste like specialties from a restaurant.
—Linda Foreman, Locust Grove, OK

TAKES: 25 MIN. • **MAKES:** 2 SERVINGS

- 2 boneless skinless chicken breast halves (4 oz. each)
- 1 tsp. poultry seasoning
- 2 slices (½ oz. each) pepper jack cheese
- 2 center-cut bacon strips, cooked and halved
- 2 hamburger buns, split
- 4 lettuce leaves
- 4 slices tomato
- 1 slice onion, separated into rings
  Dill pickle slices, optional

Sprinkle the chicken with poultry seasoning. Place on a greased grill rack. Grill, covered, or broil 4 in. from the heat until a thermometer reads 165°, 4-7 minutes on each side. Top with cheese and bacon; cook, covered, until the cheese is melted, 1-2 minutes longer. Serve on buns with lettuce, tomato, onion and, if desired, pickles.

1 sandwich: 335 cal., 11g fat (4g sat. fat), 85mg chol., 456mg sod., 25g carb. (4g sugars, 2g fiber), 33g pro. **Diabetic exchanges:** 4 lean meat, 1½ starch.

COOL COUSCOUS SALAD

Here's a refreshing lunch or dinner for hot summer days or any time you want to eat light. I combine hearty couscous and tangy feta cheese for Mediterranean flair, and then top it off with my favorite balsamic vinaigrette for a punch of flavor.
—Tiffany Blepp, Olathe, KS

PREP: 15 MIN. + CHILLING
MAKES: 2 SERVINGS

- ⅓ **cup water**
- ¼ **cup uncooked couscous**
- ⅓ **cup garbanzo beans or chickpeas, rinsed and drained**
- ¼ **cup seeded chopped cucumber**
- 1 **small plum tomato, seeded and chopped**
- ¼ **cup prepared balsamic vinaigrette**
- 2 **lettuce leaves**
- 2 **Tbsp. crumbled feta cheese**

1. In a small saucepan, bring water to a boil. Stir in couscous. Cover and remove from the heat; let stand for 5-10 minutes or until water is absorbed. Fluff with a fork; refrigerate, covered, at least 1 hour.
2. In a small bowl, combine the garbanzo beans, cucumber, tomato and couscous. Pour dressing over the mixture; toss to coat.
3. To serve, top lettuce leaves with the couscous mixture; sprinkle with crumbled cheese.

¾ cup: 212 cal., 7g fat (1g sat. fat), 4mg chol., 484mg sod., 29g carb. (5g sugars, 3g fiber), 7g pro. **Diabetic exchanges:** 2 starch, 1½ fat.

MEXICAN LEEK SOUP

This soup is so satisfying. You can substitute other beans, swap kale for the spinach or add corn. For brunch, I add a fried egg on top. And for dinner, my husband adds lots of hot sauce!
—Donna Ahnert, Scotia, NY

TAKES: 20 MIN. • **MAKES:** 2 SERVINGS

- 1 **can (15 oz.) pinto beans, rinsed and drained**
- 2 **medium leeks (white portion only), chopped**
- ½ **cup water**
- ¾ **cup coarsely chopped fresh spinach**
- 1 **cup shredded cheddar cheese**
- 2 **Tbsp. grated Parmesan cheese**
- 2 **Tbsp. grated Romano cheese**
- ½ **tsp. ground cumin**
- ½ **tsp. coarsely ground pepper**
- ¼ **tsp. cayenne pepper**
- ⅛ **tsp. salt**
- ¼ **cup heavy whipping cream**
- ¼ **cup french-fried onions**
- 2 **bacon strips, cooked and crumbled**
  Chopped fresh cilantro, optional

1. Place the beans, leeks and water in a 1-qt. microwave-safe bowl. Cover and microwave on high until tender, 4-5 minutes.
2. In a blender, process the bean mixture and spinach until smooth. Return to the bowl; add cheeses and seasonings. Whisk in cream.
3. Microwave, covered, on high until heated through, stirring once, 2-3 minutes. To serve, sprinkle with onions and bacon and, if desired, chopped cilantro.

1½ cups: 641 cal., 34g fat (19g sat. fat), 100mg chol., 1240mg sod., 54g carb. (9g sugars, 11g fiber), 34g pro.

CRABMEAT BOATS

I've been making this recipe for more than 40 years. You can also spread the filling on small rolls and serve them as an appetizer.
—June Strang, Grand Blanc, MI

PREP: 20 MIN. • **BAKE:** 15 MIN.
MAKES: 2 SERVINGS

- 2 kaiser rolls, split
- 2 tsp. butter, softened
- 1 can (6 oz.) lump crabmeat, drained
- 4 oz. Swiss cheese, cubed
- 1 celery rib, chopped
- ¼ cup mayonnaise
- 1 tsp. minced fresh parsley
- ¼ tsp. seafood seasoning, optional
- ¼ tsp. paprika

1. Preheat oven to 400°. Carefully hollow out each kaiser roll, leaving a ½-in. shell (save removed bread for another use). Spread inside of rolls with butter.
2. In a large bowl, combine the crab, cheese, celery, mayonnaise, parsley, seafood seasoning (if desired) and paprika; divide between rolls.
3. Wrap each roll in foil; place on a baking sheet. Bake until cheese is melted, 15-20 minutes.

1 serving: 661 cal., 44g fat (16g sat. fat), 148mg chol., 863mg sod., 25g carb. (3g sugars, 2g fiber), 38g pro.

GRILLED CAPRESE QUESADILLAS

Here's a quick and easy summer lunch that makes great use of garden-grown tomatoes. Feel free to make your quesadillas heartier by adding grilled chicken.
—Amy Mongiovi, Lititz, PA

TAKES: 20 MIN. • **MAKES:** 2 SERVINGS

- 4 whole wheat tortillas (8 in.)
- 6 oz. fresh mozzarella cheese, sliced
- 2 medium tomatoes, sliced and patted dry
- ⅓ cup julienned fresh basil
- ¼ cup pitted Greek olives, chopped
  Freshly ground pepper to taste

1. Layer half of each tortilla with cheese and tomatoes; sprinkle with basil, olives and pepper to taste. Fold tortillas to close.
2. Grill, covered, over medium-high heat until lightly browned and cheese is melted, 2-3 minutes per side.

1 quesadilla: 535 cal., 25g fat (13g sat. fat), 67mg chol., 665mg sod., 52g carb. (5g sugars, 8g fiber), 25g pro.

PEPPERONI BISCUIT BITES

I'm single and I love finding recipes that are both inexpensive and fast to fix. These little pizza-flavored pockets just call for on-hand ingredients and bake in 10 minutes in the toaster oven.
—Yvonne Roche, Lebanon, MO

TAKES: 20 MIN. • **MAKES:** 2 SERVINGS

- 3 Tbsp. tomato sauce
- ¾ tsp. olive oil
- ¼ tsp. onion powder
- ¼ tsp. dried oregano
- ⅛ tsp. garlic powder
- 1 tube (6 oz.) refrigerated flaky buttermilk biscuits
- 10 slices pepperoni
- 2 Tbsp. grated Parmesan cheese

1. In a small bowl, combine the tomato sauce, oil and seasonings. Cut each biscuit in half. Place 1 pepperoni slice on each half; fold dough over the pepperoni and pinch edges to seal. Dip in tomato mixture.
2. Place bites in a shallow baking pan coated with cooking spray. Sprinkle with the Parmesan cheese. Bake in a toaster oven at 450° for 10-12 minutes or until golden brown.

5 bites: 277 cal., 6g fat (2g sat. fat), 17mg chol., 1123mg sod., 43g carb. (1g sugars, 0 fiber), 12g pro.

ZIPPY EGG SALAD

Egg salad is a refreshing, tasty change from lunchmeat or peanut butter sandwiches. The touch of mustard and lemon juice gives it extra zip.
—Annemarie Pietila, Farmington Hills, MI

TAKES: 10 MIN. • **MAKES:** 2 SERVINGS

- 3 Tbsp. mayonnaise
- 1½ tsp. prepared mustard
- ⅛ tsp. salt
- ⅛ tsp. pepper
- ⅛ tsp. lemon juice
- 3 hard-boiled large eggs, coarsely chopped
- 1 Tbsp. minced green onion
- 2 slices bread
  Diced tomato, optional

Mix the first 5 ingredients. Stir in eggs and green onion. Serve on bread. If desired, top with tomato.
1 open-faced sandwich: 332 cal., 24g fat (5g sat. fat), 281mg chol., 530mg sod., 16g carb. (3g sugars, 1g fiber), 12g pro.

GROUND BEEF TACO SALAD

In spring, we look for something light and refreshing on the menu after the heavier comfort food of winter. Everyone at our house loves this salad.
—Muriel Bertrand, Shoreview, MN

TAKES: 25 MIN. • **MAKES:** 2 SERVINGS

- ½ lb. ground beef
- ⅓ cup bean dip
- 1 tsp. chili powder
- ¼ tsp. salt
- 1 cup canned diced tomatoes plus 2 Tbsp. liquid
- 2 cups chopped lettuce
- ½ cup shredded cheddar cheese
- 2 green onions, sliced
- 2 Tbsp. sliced ripe olives
- ½ cup corn chips

1. In a large skillet, cook beef over medium heat until no longer pink, crumbling meat; drain. Stir in the bean dip, chili powder, salt and tomato liquid. Remove from heat.
2. In a large bowl, combine the tomatoes, lettuce, cheese, onions and olives. Add beef mixture; toss to coat. Top with the chips. Serve salad immediately.
2 cups: 469 cal., 28g fat (12g sat. fat), 107mg chol., 1007mg sod., 25g carb. (5g sugars, 4g fiber), 32g pro.

TEST KITCHEN TIP

Refried beans, either canned or homemade, make a good substitute for the bean dip in this recipe. .

BEEF & CHICKEN DINNERS

For a duo, the perfect dinner doesn't have to mean going to a restaurant. These recipes feature beef, chicken (and some turkey!) in meals that rival any restaurant fare.

AIR-FRYER GARLIC-BUTTER STEAK

This quick and easy entree is definitely restaurant-quality and sure to become a staple at your house, too!
—Lily Julow, Lawrenceville, GA

TAKES: 20 MIN. • **MAKES:** 2 SERVINGS

- 1 beef flat iron steak or boneless top sirloin steak (¾ lb.)
- ⅛ tsp. salt
- ⅛ tsp. pepper
- 1 Tbsp. butter, softened
- 1 tsp. minced fresh parsley
- ½ tsp. minced garlic
- ¼ tsp. reduced-sodium soy sauce

1. Preheat air fryer to 400°. Sprinkle steak with salt and pepper. Place steak on tray in air-fryer basket. Cook until meat reaches desired doneness (for medium-rare, a thermometer should read 135°; medium, 140°; medium-well, 145°), 8-10 minutes, turning halfway through cooking.
2. Meanwhile, combine butter, parsley, garlic and soy sauce. Serve with steak.

4 oz. cooked beef with 2 tsp. garlic butter: 353 cal., 24g fat (11g sat. fat), 125mg chol., 322mg sod., 0 carb. (0 sugars, 0 fiber), 33g pro.

MUSHROOM STEAK SALAD WITH WALNUT VINAIGRETTE

When I want to prepare a romantic dinner for my husband and me, I fix this elegant yet easy salad. I just add crusty French bread and a glass of wine.
—Candace McMenamin, Lexington, SC

TAKES: 30 MIN. • **MAKES:** 2 SERVINGS

- 8 oz. boneless beef sirloin steak (¾ in. thick)
- 3 Tbsp. olive oil, divided
- 1 cup each sliced fresh baby portobello, shiitake and button mushrooms
- 2 Tbsp. balsamic vinegar
- 1 Tbsp. minced fresh thyme or 1 tsp. dried thyme
- 2 Tbsp. walnut oil
- 2 Tbsp. finely chopped walnuts
- 3 cups torn mixed salad greens
- 1 shallot, sliced
- 2 Tbsp. crumbled goat cheese

1. In a large skillet over medium heat, cook steak in 1 Tbsp. olive oil until meat reaches desired doneness (for medium-rare, a thermometer should read 135°; medium, 140°; medium-well, 145°), 4-6 minutes on each side. Remove from the skillet; let stand for 5 minutes before slicing.
2. Meanwhile, in the same skillet, saute mushrooms until tender. In a small bowl, combine vinegar and thyme. Whisk in walnut oil and remaining 2 Tbsp. olive oil. Stir in chopped walnuts.
3. Divide salad greens and shallot between 2 serving bowls. Cut steak into slices. Top salads with steak and mushrooms. Drizzle with dressing; sprinkle with cheese.

1 serving: 602 cal., 48g fat (9g sat. fat), 75mg chol., 151mg sod., 14g carb. (5g sugars, 4g fiber), 31g pro.

DID YOU KNOW?

Baby portobello mushrooms, a young version of portobellos, are also called crimini (or cremini) or Italian brown mushrooms. They can be used interchangeably with white button mushrooms, but do have a slightly richer flavor.

THAI CHICKEN PASTA

I try to buy fresh chicken when it's on sale. I cook a big batch in the slow cooker, then cut it up and package it in small amounts suitable for recipes like this. When I want it, I just need to pull a package out of the freezer to thaw.
—Jeni Pittard, Statham, GA

TAKES: 25 MIN. • **MAKES:** 2 SERVINGS

- 3 oz. uncooked whole wheat linguine
- ½ cup salsa
- 2 Tbsp. reduced-fat creamy peanut butter
- 1 Tbsp. orange juice
- 1½ tsp. honey
- 1 tsp. reduced-sodium soy sauce
- 1 cup cubed cooked chicken breast
- 1 Tbsp. chopped unsalted peanuts
- 1 Tbsp. minced fresh cilantro

1. Cook linguine according to package directions.
2. Meanwhile, in a microwave-safe dish, combine the salsa, peanut butter, orange juice, honey and soy sauce. Cover and microwave on high for 1 minute; stir. Add the chicken; heat through.
3. Drain linguine. Serve with chicken mixture. Garnish with peanuts and cilantro.
1 serving: 409 cal., 10g fat (2g sat. fat), 54mg chol., 474mg sod., 46g carb. (10g sugars, 6g fiber), 33g pro.

CAMPING HAYSTACKS

Try this layered dish for a satisfying meal after a busy day. We love the easy combo of canned chili, corn chips and taco toppings.
—Gaylene Anderson, Sandy, UT

TAKES: 15 MIN. • **MAKES:** 2 SERVINGS

- 1 can (15 oz.) chili with beans
- 2 pkg. (1 oz. each) corn chips
- ½ cup shredded cheddar cheese
- 1½ cups chopped lettuce
- 1 small tomato, chopped
- ½ cup salsa
- 2 Tbsp. sliced ripe olives
- 2 Tbsp. sour cream

In a small saucepan, heat chili. Divide corn chips between two plates; top with chili. Layer with cheese, lettuce, tomato, salsa, olives and sour cream. Serve immediately.

1 serving: 620 cal., 30g fat (11g sat. fat), 61mg chol., 1654mg sod., 61g carb. (8g sugars, 10g fiber), 25g pro.

BUFFALO SLOPPY JOES

Think you know sloppy joes? Think again! A hefty splash of hot sauce and optional blue cheese lend authentic Buffalo-style flavor to this take on the popular sandwich.
—Maria Regakis, Saugus, MA

TAKES: 30 MIN. • **MAKES:** 2 SERVINGS

- ½ lb. extra-lean ground turkey
- ¼ cup chopped celery
- 3 Tbsp. chopped onion
- 2 Tbsp. grated carrots
- 1 garlic clove, minced
- 3 Tbsp. tomato sauce
- 2 Tbsp. reduced-sodium chicken broth
- 1 Tbsp. Louisiana-style hot sauce
- 1½ tsp. brown sugar
- 1½ tsp. red wine vinegar
- ¾ tsp. Worcestershire sauce
  Dash pepper
- 2 hamburger buns, split
- ¼ cup crumbled blue cheese, optional

1. In a Dutch oven, cook the first 5 ingredients over medium heat until the turkey is no longer pink.
2. Stir in the tomato sauce, chicken broth, hot sauce, brown sugar, vinegar, Worcestershire sauce and pepper; heat through.
3. Serve on buns; sprinkle with cheese if desired.
1 sandwich: 276 cal., 3g fat (0 sat. fat), 45mg chol., 445mg sod., 30g carb. (8g sugars, 2g fiber), 33g pro.
Diabetic exchanges: 4 lean meat, 2 starch.

AIR-FRYER GROUND BEEF WELLINGTON

Trying new recipes—like this air-fryer Wellington—is one of my favorite hobbies. I replaced the filet mignon with ground beef to make it easier, while still keeping the beefy goodness.
—Julie Frankamp, Nicollet, MN

PREP: 30 MIN. • **COOK:** 20 MIN.
MAKES: 2 SERVINGS

- 1 Tbsp. butter
- ½ cup chopped fresh mushrooms
- 2 tsp. all-purpose flour
- ¼ tsp. pepper, divided
- ½ cup half-and-half cream
- 1 large egg yolk
- 2 Tbsp. finely chopped onion
- ¼ tsp. salt
- ½ lb. ground beef
- 1 tube (4 oz.) refrigerated crescent rolls
- 1 large egg, lightly beaten, optional
- 1 tsp. dried parsley flakes

1. Preheat air fryer to 300°. In a saucepan, heat butter over medium-high heat. Add chopped mushrooms; cook and stir until tender, 5-6 minutes. Stir in flour and ⅛ tsp. pepper until blended. Gradually add cream. Bring to a boil; cook and stir for 2 minutes or until thickened. Remove from heat and set aside.
2. In a bowl, combine egg yolk, onion, 2 Tbsp. mushroom sauce, salt and the remaining ⅛ tsp. pepper. Crumble beef over mixture and mix well. Shape into 2 loaves.
3. Unroll crescent dough and separate into 2 rectangles; press perforations to seal. Place a meat loaf on each rectangle. Bring edges together and pinch to seal. If desired, brush with beaten egg.
4. Place Wellingtons in a single layer on greased tray in air-fryer basket. Cook until golden brown and a thermometer inserted into loaf reads 160°, 18-22 minutes.
5. Meanwhile, warm remaining sauce over low heat; stir in parsley. Serve sauce with Wellingtons.
1 serving: 585 cal., 38g fat (14g sat. fat), 208mg chol., 865mg sod., 30g carb. (9g sugars, 1g fiber), 29g pro.

TEST KITCHEN TIP

To make this recipe in an oven, bake at 350° for 24-28 minutes.

- 1 boneless skinless chicken breast half, cut into 1½-in. pieces
- 2 tsp. canola oil
- 7 snow peas
- 1 cup fresh broccoli florets
- ⅓ cup julienned sweet red pepper
- 3 medium fresh mushrooms, sliced
- ¾ cup sliced onion
- 1 Tbsp. cornstarch
- 1 tsp. sugar
- ½ cup cold water
- 3 to 4 Tbsp. soy sauce Hot cooked rice
- 1 tsp. sesame seeds, toasted Thinly sliced green onions, optional

1. In a large skillet or wok, stir-fry chicken in oil for 6-8 minutes or until juices run clear. Remove chicken and set aside.
2. In the same skillet, stir-fry peas, broccoli and red pepper for 2-3 minutes. Add mushrooms and onion; stir-fry for 3-4 minutes.
3. Combine cornstarch and sugar; stir in water and soy sauce until smooth. Add to the pan. Bring to a boil; cook and stir for 1-2 minutes or until thickened.
4. Return chicken to the pan; cook until mixture is heated through and vegetables are tender. Serve over rice. Sprinkle with sesame seeds and, if desired, sliced green onions.
1 serving: 398 cal., 14g fat (2g sat. fat), 63mg chol., 2858mg sod., 33g carb. (16g sugars, 7g fiber), 36g pro.

SESAME CHICKEN STIR-FRY

When our children were little, my husband frequently worked late. This eye-catching stir-fry, easily adapted to serve more, was a satisfying alternative to a big dinner when it was just me and the kids.
—Michelle McWilliams, Fort Lupton, CO

TAKES: 30 MIN. • **MAKES:** 1 SERVING

CRISPY ASIAN CHICKEN SALAD

Asian flavor, crunchy almonds and crispy chicken make this salad special.
—Beth Dauenhauer, Pueblo, CO

TAKES: 30 MIN. • **MAKES:** 2 SERVINGS

- 2 boneless skinless chicken breast halves (4 oz. each)
- 2 tsp. hoisin sauce
- 1 tsp. sesame oil
- ½ cup panko bread crumbs
- 4 tsp. sesame seeds
- 2 tsp. canola oil
- 4 cups spring mix salad greens
- 1 small green pepper, julienned
- 1 small sweet red pepper, julienned
- 1 medium carrot, julienned
- ½ cup sliced fresh mushrooms
- 2 Tbsp. thinly sliced onion
- 2 Tbsp. sliced almonds, toasted
- ¼ cup reduced-fat sesame ginger salad dressing

1. Flatten chicken breasts to ½-in. thickness. Combine hoisin sauce and sesame oil; brush over the chicken. In a shallow bowl, combine panko and sesame seeds; dip chicken in panko mixture.
2. In a large nonstick, cook the chicken in oil until no longer pink, 5-6 minutes on each side.
3. Meanwhile, divide salad greens between 2 plates. Top with peppers, carrot, mushrooms and onion. Slice chicken; place on top. Sprinkle with almonds and drizzle with dressing.

1 salad: 386 cal., 17g fat (2g sat. fat), 63mg chol., 620mg sod., 29g carb. (11g sugars, 6g fiber), 30g pro.
Diabetic exchanges: 3 lean meat, 2 vegetable, 2 fat, 1 starch.

YELLOW SQUASH TURKEY SALAD

This is my favorite fast recipe. With a wonderful mix of flavors, colors and textures, this impressive salad can be made in minutes for a light and lovely dinner on a busy weeknight.
—Mildred Sherrer, Fort Worth, TX

TAKES: 10 MIN. • **MAKES:** 2 SERVINGS

- 4 cups spring mix salad greens
- ¼ lb. thinly sliced deli smoked turkey, cut into 1-in. strips
- 1 small yellow summer squash, halved lengthwise and sliced
- 1 small pear, chopped
- ½ cup dried cranberries
- ⅓ cup honey-roasted sliced almonds
- ¼ cup cubed cheddar cheese
- ⅓ cup red wine vinaigrette

In a large bowl, combine the first 7 ingredients. Drizzle with vinaigrette and toss to coat. Serve immediately.
1 serving: 490 cal., 17g fat (3g sat. fat), 37mg chol., 1170mg sod., 61g carb. (48g sugars, 7g fiber), 22g pro.

SPANISH NOODLES & GROUND BEEF

Bacon adds smoky flavor to this comforting stovetop supper that my mom often made when we were growing up. Now I prepare it for my family.
—Kelli Jones, Peris, CA

TAKES: 30 MIN. • **MAKES:** 2 SERVINGS

- ½ lb. lean ground beef (90% lean)
- ¼ cup chopped green pepper
- 2 Tbsp. chopped onion
- 1½ cups uncooked medium egg noodles
- ¾ cup canned diced tomatoes
- ½ cup water
- 2 Tbsp. chili sauce
- ¼ tsp. salt
  Dash pepper
- 2 bacon strips, cooked and crumbled

1. In a large skillet, cook and crumble beef with green pepper and onion over medium-high heat until no longer pink, 4-6 minutes.
2. Stir in all remaining ingredients except the bacon; bring to a boil. Reduce heat; simmer, covered, until noodles are tender, 15-20 minutes, stirring occasionally. Top with bacon.
1¼ cups: 371 cal., 14g fat (5g sat. fat), 103mg chol., 887mg sod., 31g carb. (7g sugars, 3g fiber), 30g pro.

AIR-FRYER ALMOND CHICKEN

My husband bought an air fryer after seeing it on television—now we use it at least twice a week! Chicken is especially good in the air fryer because of how moist it remains. This chicken with almonds is a favorite, and it's perfect for our low-carb diet.
—Pamela Shank, Parkersburg, WV

TAKES: 30 MIN. • **MAKES:** 2 SERVINGS

- 1 large egg
- ¼ cup buttermilk
- 1 tsp. garlic salt
- ½ tsp. pepper
- 1 cup slivered almonds, finely chopped
- 2 boneless skinless chicken breast halves (6 oz. each)
  Optional: Ranch salad dressing, barbecue sauce and honey mustard

1. Preheat air fryer to 350°. In a shallow bowl, whisk the egg, buttermilk, garlic salt and pepper. Place almonds in another shallow bowl. Dip chicken into egg mixture, then into almonds; pat to help the coating adhere.
2. Place chicken in a single layer on greased tray in the air-fryer basket; spritz with cooking spray. Cook until a thermometer inserted in the chicken reads at least 165°, 15-18 minutes. If desired, serve with ranch dressing, barbecue sauce or mustard.

1 chicken breast half: 353 cal., 18g fat (2g sat. fat), 123mg chol., 230mg sod., 6g carb. (2g sugars, 3g fiber), 41g pro.

TROPICAL BBQ CHICKEN

Here is my favorite slow-cooker recipe. The delicious, slightly spicy sauce will win you over, too!
—Yvonne McKim, Vancouver, WA

PREP: 15 MIN. • **COOK:** 3 HOURS
MAKES: 2 SERVINGS

- 2 chicken leg quarters (8 oz. each), skin removed
- 3 Tbsp. ketchup
- 2 Tbsp. orange juice
- 1 Tbsp. brown sugar
- 1 Tbsp. red wine vinegar
- 1 Tbsp. olive oil
- 1 tsp. minced fresh parsley
- ½ tsp. Worcestershire sauce
- ¼ tsp. garlic salt
- ⅛ tsp. pepper
- 2 tsp. cornstarch
- 1 Tbsp. cold water
  Additional fresh parsley, optional

1. With a sharp knife, cut leg quarters at the joints if desired; place in a 1½-qt. slow cooker. In a small bowl, combine the ketchup, orange juice, brown sugar, vinegar, oil, parsley, Worcestershire sauce, garlic salt and pepper; pour over the chicken.
2. Cook, covered, on low until the meat is tender, 3-4 hours.
3. Remove chicken to a serving platter; keep warm. Skim fat from cooking juices; transfer ½ cup to a small saucepan. Bring liquid to a boil.
4. Combine cornstarch and water until smooth. Gradually stir into the pan. Return to a boil; cook and stir until thickened, about 2 minutes. Serve with chicken. If desired, top with additional fresh parsley.

1 serving: 301 cal., 14g fat (3g sat. fat), 83mg chol., 601mg sod., 18g carb. (14g sugars, 0 fiber), 25g pro.

SWEET-SOUR MEATBALLS

For a great meal on busy days, I pop ready-made meatballs in the slow cooker and come home later to the heartwarming aroma of this Asian-style specialty! Nothing is more convenient than coming home to dinner that's ready to go.
—Lisa Stepanski, Munnsville, NY

PREP: 10 MIN. • **COOK:** 5 HOURS
MAKES: 2 SERVINGS

- 16 frozen fully cooked homestyle meatballs (½ oz. each), thawed
- ½ cup sugar
- 2 Tbsp. plus 2 tsp. cornstarch
- ⅓ cup white vinegar
- 1 Tbsp. reduced-sodium soy sauce
- ½ medium green pepper, cut into 1-in. pieces
- 1 can (8 oz.) pineapple chunks, undrained
  Hot cooked rice, optional

1. Place meatballs in a 1½-qt. slow cooker. In a small bowl, combine sugar, cornstarch, vinegar and soy sauce; pour over meatballs. Add green pepper. Cook, covered, on low for 4½ hours or until pepper is crisp-tender.
2. Stir in pineapple; cover and cook 30 minutes longer. Serve with rice if desired.

8 meatballs: 794 cal., 29g fat (10g sat. fat), 186mg chol., 582mg sod., 94g carb. (63g sugars, 2g fiber), 39g pro.

CHICKEN & GOAT CHEESE SKILLET

My husband was completely bowled over by this made-on-a-whim skillet meal. I can't wait to make it again soon!
—Ericka Barber, Eureka, CA

TAKES: 20 MIN. • **MAKES:** 2 SERVINGS

- ½ lb. boneless skinless chicken breasts, cut into 1-in. pieces
- ¼ tsp. salt
- ⅛ tsp. pepper
- 2 tsp. olive oil
- 1 cup cut fresh asparagus (1-in. pieces)
- 1 garlic clove, minced
- 3 plum tomatoes, chopped
- 3 Tbsp. 2% milk
- 2 Tbsp. herbed fresh goat cheese, crumbled
  Hot cooked rice or pasta
  Additional goat cheese, optional

1. Toss chicken with salt and pepper. In a large skillet, heat oil over medium-high heat; saute chicken until no longer pink, 4-6 minutes. Remove from pan; keep warm.
2. Add asparagus to skillet; cook and stir over medium-high heat for 1 minute. Add garlic; cook and stir 30 seconds. Stir in tomatoes, milk and 2 Tbsp. cheese; cook, covered, over medium heat until the cheese begins to melt, 2-3 minutes. Stir in chicken. Serve with rice. If desired, top with additional cheese.

1½ cups chicken mixture: 251 cal., 11g fat (3g sat. fat), 74mg chol., 447mg sod., 8g carb. (5g sugars, 3g fiber), 29g pro. **Diabetic exchanges:** 4 lean meat, 2 fat, 1 vegetable.

TEST KITCHEN TIP

An unopened package of goat cheese can last a couple of months in the refrigerator; once opened, it will last up to two weeks. To keep it as fresh as possible, wrap it twice—once in the original packaging, waxed paper or parchment paper and a second time in heavy-duty foil. If the cheese starts to get moldy, throw it away.

CHICKEN STRAWBERRY SPINACH SALAD

This pretty spinach salad topped with grilled chicken, strawberries and almonds features a delectably sweet poppy-seed dressing. Made in moments, it's a refreshing lunch or light supper for two.
—Ginger Ellsworth, Caldwell, ID

TAKES: 30 MIN. • **MAKES:** 2 SERVINGS

- ¾ lb. boneless skinless chicken breasts, cut into strips
- ¼ cup reduced-sodium chicken broth
- ¼ cup poppy seed salad dressing, divided
- 2 cups fresh baby spinach
- 1 cup torn romaine
- 1 cup sliced fresh strawberries
- ¼ cup sliced almonds, toasted

1. Place chicken on a double thickness of heavy-duty foil (about 18 in. x 15 in.). Combine broth and 1 Tbsp. poppy seed dressing; spoon over chicken. Fold edges of foil around chicken mixture, leaving center open. Grill, covered, over medium heat until chicken is no longer pink, 10-12 minutes.
2. In a large salad bowl, combine spinach, romaine and strawberries. Add chicken and the remaining 3 Tbsp. poppy seed dressing; toss to coat. Sprinkle with almonds.
1 serving: 438 cal., 22g fat (3g sat. fat), 104mg chol., 386mg sod., 18g carb. (11g sugars, 5g fiber), 39g pro.

CAST-IRON SKILLET STEAK

If you've never cooked steak at home before, it can be a little intimidating. That's why I came up with this simple steak recipe that's so easy, you could make it any day of the week.
—James Schend, Pleasant Prairie, WI

PREP: 5 MIN. + STANDING
COOK: 5 MIN. • **MAKES:** 2 SERVINGS

- 3 tsp. kosher salt, divided
- 1 beef New York strip or ribeye steak (1 lb.), 1 in. thick

1. Remove steak from refrigerator and sprinkle with 2 tsp. salt; let stand 45-60 minutes.
2. Preheat a cast-iron skillet over high heat until extremely hot, 4-5 minutes. Sprinkle remaining 1 tsp. salt in bottom of skillet; pat beef dry with paper towels. Place steak in skillet and cook until easily moved, 1-2 minutes; flip, placing steak in a different section of the skillet. Cook 30 seconds and then begin moving steak, occasionally pressing slightly to ensure even contact with skillet.
3. Continue turning and flipping until cooked to desired degree of doneness (for medium-rare, a thermometer should read 135°; medium, 140°; medium-well, 145°), 1-2 minutes.
6 oz. cooked beef: 494 cal., 36g fat (15g sat. fat), 134mg chol., 2983mg sod., 0 carb. (0 sugars, 0 fiber), 40g pro.

TEST KITCHEN TIP

You may have heard to never use dish soap on cast iron, but for some messes, it's necessary. Use a little soap, don't soak the pan, dry it well, and all is good. Watch for dull spots in the finish—that indicates that it's time to reseason the pan.

CHICKEN CURRY

I love to try new recipes for my husband and myself, and I have cookbooks and recipes from all over the world to help. When I find a recipe that's well-received, I make a copy and put it in a protective sleeve in a loose-leaf binder. I now have quite a few huge binders!
—Sharon Delaney-Chronis, South Milwaukee, WI

PREP: 20 MIN. • **COOK:** 3 HOURS
MAKES: 2 SERVINGS

- 1 small onion, sliced
- 1 Tbsp. plus ⅓ cup water, divided
- ½ lb. boneless skinless chicken breasts, cubed
- 1 small apple, peeled and chopped
- ¼ cup raisins
- 1 garlic clove, minced
- 1 tsp. curry powder
- ¼ tsp. ground ginger
- ⅛ tsp. salt
- 1½ tsp. all-purpose flour
- 1 tsp. chicken bouillon granules
- ½ cup sour cream
- ¾ tsp. cornstarch
- 1 Tbsp. thinly sliced green onion
  Hot cooked rice

1. Place onion and 1 Tbsp. water in a microwave-safe bowl. Microwave, covered, on high until crisp-tender, 1 to 1½ minutes.

2. In a 1½-qt. slow cooker, combine the chicken, apple, raisins, garlic, curry, ginger, salt and onion. Combine the flour, bouillon and remaining ⅓ cup water; pour over the chicken mixture. Cook, covered, on low until the chicken juices run clear, 3 to 3½ hours.

3. Bring sour cream to room temperature. Remove the chicken mixture to a bowl; keep warm. Transfer cooking juices to a small saucepan. Combine cornstarch and sour cream until smooth; add to juices. Cook and stir over medium heat until thickened. Pour over the chicken mixture; toss to coat. Sprinkle with green onion and serve with rice.

1 cup: 354 cal., 13g fat (8g sat. fat), 103mg chol., 647mg sod., 30g carb. (19g sugars, 3g fiber), 26g pro.

1½ cups fresh spinach, chopped
⅓ cup julienned soft sun-dried tomatoes (not packed in oil), chopped
¼ cup crumbled goat cheese
2 garlic cloves, minced
½ tsp. pepper, divided
¼ tsp. salt, divided
2 boneless skinless chicken breasts (6 oz. each)
1 Tbsp. olive oil, divided
½ lb. fresh asparagus, trimmed
Optional: Aged balsamic vinegar or balsamic glaze

1. Preheat oven to 400°. In a small bowl, combine spinach, sun-dried tomatoes, goat cheese, garlic, ¼ tsp. pepper and ⅛ tsp. salt.
2. Cut a pocket horizontally in the thickest part of each chicken breast. Fill with spinach mixture; secure with toothpicks.
3. In an 8-in. cast-iron or other ovenproof skillet, heat 1½ tsp. oil over medium heat. Brown chicken on each side. Place in oven; bake 10 minutes.
4. Toss the asparagus with the remaining 1½ tsp. oil, ¼ tsp. pepper, and ⅛ tsp. salt; add to skillet. Bake until a thermometer inserted in chicken reads 165° and asparagus is tender, 10-15 minutes longer. If desired, drizzle with vinegar. Discard toothpicks before serving.

1 stuffed chicken breast: 347 cal., 14g fat (4g sat. fat), 111mg chol., 532mg sod., 13g carb. (6g sugars, 5g fiber), 39g pro. **Diabetic exchanges:** 7 lean meat, 1 vegetable, 1 fat.

GOAT CHEESE & SPINACH STUFFED CHICKEN

This stuffed chicken breast recipe is special to me because it has so much flavor yet not too many calories. I love Italian food, but most of the time it is too heavy. This is a healthy twist on an Italian dish!
—Nicole Stevens, Charleston, SC

PREP: 30 MIN. • **BAKE:** 20 MIN.
MAKES: 2 SERVINGS

MERLOT FILET MIGNON

Although this filet is such a simple recipe, you can feel confident serving it to your guests. The rich sauce adds a touch of elegance. Just add a salad and rolls.
—Jauneen Hosking, Waterford, WI

TAKES: 20 MIN. • **MAKES:** 2 SERVINGS

- 2 **beef tenderloin steaks (8 oz. each)**
- 3 **Tbsp. butter, divided**
- 1 **Tbsp. olive oil**
- 1 **cup merlot**
- 2 **Tbsp. heavy whipping cream**
- ⅛ **tsp. salt**

1. In a small skillet, cook steaks in 1 Tbsp. butter and the olive oil over medium heat until meat reaches desired doneness (for medium-rare, a thermometer should read 135°; medium, 140°; medium-well, 145°), 4-6 minutes on each side. Remove and keep warm.
2. In the same skillet, add wine, stirring to loosen any browned bits from pan. Bring to a boil; cook until liquid is reduced to ¼ cup. Add cream, salt and the remaining 2 Tbsp. butter; bring to a boil. Cook and stir until slightly thickened and butter is melted, 1-2 minutes. Serve sauce with steaks.

1 steak with 2 Tbsp. sauce: 690 cal., 43g fat (20g sat. fat), 165mg chol., 279mg sod., 4g carb. (1g sugars, 0 fiber), 49g pro.

CHICKEN CREOLE

I ladle this vegetable-packed chicken dish over jasmine rice, a long-grain rice that's not as sticky as most. If you prefer another variety of rice, feel free to substitute.
—Virginia Crowell, Lyons, OR

PREP: 20 MIN. • **COOK:** 30 MIN.
MAKES: 2 SERVINGS

- ½ **lb. boneless skinless chicken breasts, cubed**
- 1 **tsp. canola oil, divided**
- ½ **cup chopped green pepper**
- ¼ **cup thinly sliced onion**
- ¼ **cup chopped celery**
- 1 **garlic clove, minced**
- ¾ **cup sliced fresh mushrooms**
- ¾ **cup undrained diced tomatoes**
- 2 **Tbsp. chicken broth**
- 1½ **tsp. minced fresh oregano or ½ tsp. dried oregano**
- 1½ **tsp. lemon juice**
- ¾ **tsp. minced fresh basil or ¼ tsp. dried basil**
- ⅛ **tsp. salt**
- ⅛ **tsp. pepper**
- ⅛ **tsp. crushed red pepper flakes**
  Hot cooked rice
  Minced fresh parsley, optional

1. In a Dutch oven, cook chicken in ½ teaspoon oil over medium-high heat until no longer pink, 6-8 minutes. Remove; set aside.
2. In the same pot, cook green peppers, onion, celery and garlic in the remaining ½ teaspoon oil until tender, 5-7 minutes. Add mushrooms; cook until liquid has evaporated.
3. Stir in tomatoes, broth, oregano, lemon juice, basil and seasonings. Bring to a boil. Reduce heat; cook, covered, until slightly thickened and flavors are blended, 5-10 minutes.
4. Add chicken; heat through. Serve over rice; garnish with parsley if desired.

1 cup: 189 cal., 5g fat (1g sat. fat), 63mg chol., 398mg sod., 10g carb. (5g sugars, 3g fiber), 25g pro. **Diabetic exchanges:** 3 lean meat, 2 vegetable, ½ fat.

APRICOT-ORANGE SALSA CHICKEN

Sweet oranges and apricots blend perfectly with zippy salsa in this five-ingredient entree. Keep the heat to your liking with mild, medium or hot salsa. Served over rice, it's a dinner we've enjoyed time and again.
—LaDonna Reed, Ponca City, OK

PREP: 10 MIN. • **COOK:** 2½ HOURS
MAKES: 2 SERVINGS

- ¾ cup salsa
- ⅓ cup apricot preserves
- ¼ cup orange juice
- 2 boneless skinless chicken breast halves (5 oz. each)
- 1 cup hot cooked rice

1. In a small bowl, combine the salsa, preserves and orange juice. In a 1½-qt. slow cooker coated with cooking spray, layer ⅓ cup of salsa mixture and a chicken breast. Repeat layers. Top with the remaining salsa mixture.
2. Cook, covered, on low until chicken is tender, 2½ to 3 hours. If desired, thicken pan juices. Serve with rice.

1 chicken breast half with ½ cup rice: 427 cal., 4g fat (1g sat. fat), 78mg chol., 450mg sod., 66g carb. (25g sugars, 0 fiber), 31g pro.

TERRIFIC TURKEY ENCHILADAS

Enchiladas are a favorite dish in our home. Our little girl, who calls them "laladas," especially loves them. This is a really tasty take on the classic southwestern dish.
—Jenn Tidwell, Fair Oaks, CA

PREP: 35 MIN. • **BAKE:** 35 MIN.
MAKES: 3 SERVINGS

- 1¼ cups frozen corn, thawed
- 1 can (4 oz.) chopped green chiles
- 1 cup fresh cilantro leaves
- ⅓ cup heavy whipping cream
- ¼ tsp. salt
- ¼ tsp. pepper

ENCHILADAS
- ¾ lb. ground turkey
- ⅓ cup chopped onion
- 1 garlic clove, minced
- 1 Tbsp. olive oil
- ¾ cup salsa

- 1 Tbsp. cornmeal
- 2 tsp. chili powder
- 1½ tsp. ground cumin
- 1 tsp. dried oregano
- ⅛ tsp. salt
- ⅛ tsp. pepper
- 6 flour tortillas (8 in.), warmed
- 1¼ cups shredded Mexican cheese blend, divided
- ¼ cup sliced ripe olives
  Additional chopped fresh cilantro, optional

1. Preheat oven to 350°. Place first 6 ingredients in a food processor; cover and pulse until blended.
2. In a large skillet, cook turkey, onion and garlic in oil over medium heat until meat is no longer pink. Remove from heat; stir in salsa, cornmeal and seasonings.
3. Spoon ⅓ cup turkey mixture down the center of each tortilla; top each with 2 Tbsp. cheese. Roll up and place seam side down in a greased 11x7-in. baking dish. Spoon corn mixture over top; sprinkle with olives and remaining ½ cup cheese.
4. Cover and bake 30 minutes. Uncover; bake for 5-10 minutes or until heated through. If desired, top with additional chopped cilantro.

Freeze option: Cover and freeze unbaked enchiladas. To use, partially thaw in refrigerator overnight. Remove from refrigerator 30 minutes before baking. Preheat oven to 350°. Cover casserole with foil; bake until casserole is heated through, sauce is bubbling and cheese is melted, 30-35 minutes. Serve as directed.

2 enchiladas: 968 cal., 55g fat (23g sat. fat), 155mg chol., 1766mg sod., 81g carb. (4g sugars, 5g fiber), 41g pro.

FRY BREAD

While taking a trip to the Grand Canyon, my family drove through the Navajo reservation and stopped at a little cafe for dinner. I complimented the young Navajo waiter on the delicious bread and he gave me the recipe. It is very easy to make.
—Mildred Stephenson, Hartselle, AL

PREP: 5 MIN. + STANDING
COOK: 5 MIN. • **MAKES:** 2 SERVINGS

- 1   cup all-purpose flour
- 1   tsp. baking powder
- ⅛   tsp. salt
- ⅓   cup hot water
     Oil for deep-fat frying
     Optional: Seasoned taco meat, shredded cheddar cheese, sour cream, chopped tomatoes, sliced jalapeno pepper, shredded lettuce

1. In a small bowl, combine the flour, baking powder and salt; stir in hot water to form a soft dough. Cover and let stand for 30 minutes.
2. Divide dough in half. On a lightly floured surface, roll each portion into a 6-in. circle.
3. In an electric skillet, heat 1 in. of oil to 375°. Fry bread in hot oil for 2-3 minutes on each side or until golden brown; drain on paper towels. Serve with your desired toppings.

1 piece bread (calculated without toppings): 285 cal., 7g fat (1g sat. fat), 0 chol., 349mg sod., 48g carb. (1g sugars, 2g fiber), 6g pro.

TURKEY LEG POT ROAST

Well-seasoned turkey legs and tender veggies make an ideal dinner for a crisp fall day. Tender and satisfying, the recipe couldn't be easier!
—Rick & Vegas Pearson, Cadillac, MI

PREP: 15 MIN. • **COOK:** 5 HOURS
MAKES: 3 SERVINGS

- 3   medium potatoes, quartered
- 2   cups fresh baby carrots
- 2   celery ribs, cut into 2½-in. pieces
- 1   medium onion, peeled and quartered
- 3   garlic cloves, peeled and quartered
- ½   cup chicken broth
- 3   turkey drumsticks (12 oz. each), skin removed
- 2   tsp. seasoned salt
- 1   tsp. dried thyme
- 1   tsp. dried parsley flakes
- ¼   tsp. pepper
     Chopped fresh parsley, optional

1. In a greased 5-qt. slow cooker, combine the first 6 ingredients. Place drumsticks over vegetables. Sprinkle with seasoned salt, thyme, parsley and pepper.
2. Cook, covered, on low for 5 to 5½ hours or until turkey is tender. If desired, top with chopped fresh parsley just before serving.

1 serving: 460 cal., 7g fat (2g sat. fat), 202mg chol., 1416mg sod., 44g carb. (10g sugars, 6g fiber), 54g pro.

DID YOU KNOW?

Baby carrots aren't actually small carrots; they're trimmed pieces from normal-size carrots that didn't meet retail beauty standards. If you don't have baby carrots, just use a normal carrot, cut into thick slices.

MOM'S MEAT LOAF

If you're looking for a small but mighty meal, here's a great fit. You'll love the old-fashioned flavor and scrumptious sauce. The recipe is easy to double for sandwiches the next day.
—Michelle Beran, Claflin, KS

PREP: 15 MIN. • **BAKE:** 40 MIN.
MAKES: 2 MINI MEAT LOAVES

- 1 **large egg**
- ¼ **cup 2% milk**
- ⅓ **cup crushed saltines**
- 3 **Tbsp. chopped onion**
- ¼ **tsp. salt**
- ⅛ **tsp. rubbed sage**
  Dash pepper
- ½ **lb. lean ground beef (90% lean)**
- ¼ **cup ketchup**
- 2 **Tbsp. brown sugar**
- ¼ **tsp. Worcestershire sauce**

1. Preheat oven to 350°. In a large bowl, beat egg. Add milk, cracker crumbs, onion, salt, sage and pepper. Crumble beef over mixture and mix well. Shape into 2 loaves; place in a shallow baking dish coated with cooking spray.
2. Combine ketchup, brown sugar and Worcestershire sauce; spoon over meat loaves. Bake until the meat is no longer pink and a thermometer inserted in each loaf reads 160°, 40-45 minutes.
1 meat loaf: 337 cal., 12g fat (4g sat. fat), 162mg chol., 898mg sod., 31g carb. (18g sugars, 1g fiber), 27g pro.
Diabetic exchanges: 3 lean meat, 2 starch.

BEEF IN ONION GRAVY

I double this recipe to feed our family of four and to ensure leftovers to send with my husband to work for lunch. His coworkers tell him he's lucky to have someone who fixes him such special meals. It's our secret that it's an easy slow-cooker dinner!
—Denise Albers, Freeburg, IL

PREP: 5 MIN. + STANDING
COOK: 6 HOURS • **MAKES:** 3 SERVINGS

- 1 **can (10¾ oz.) condensed cream of mushroom soup, undiluted**
- 2 **Tbsp. onion soup mix**
- 2 **Tbsp. beef broth**
- 1 **Tbsp. quick-cooking tapioca**
- 1 **lb. beef stew meat, cut into 1-in. cubes**
  Hot cooked noodles or mashed potatoes

1. In a 1½-qt. slow cooker, combine the soup, soup mix, broth and tapioca; let stand for 15 minutes.
2. Stir in the beef. Cook, covered, on low for 6-8 hours or until the meat is tender. Serve over noodles or mashed potatoes.
1 serving: 326 cal., 15g fat (6g sat. fat), 98mg chol., 1220mg sod., 14g carb. (1g sugars, 1g fiber), 31g pro.

TASTY TURKEY & MUSHROOMS

Fresh mushrooms star in this tender turkey entree that comes together in 15 minutes. Served with a side of brown rice, it makes a light but satisfying dinner.
—Nancy Zimmerman, Cape May Court House, NJ

TAKES: 15 MIN. • **MAKES:** 2 SERVINGS

- 1 **garlic clove, minced**
- 1 **Tbsp. butter**
- ½ **lb. boneless skinless turkey breast, cut into 2-in. strips**
- ¾ **cup reduced-sodium beef broth**
- 1 **Tbsp. tomato paste**
- 2 **cups sliced fresh mushrooms**
- ⅛ **tsp. salt**

1. In a large nonstick skillet, saute garlic in butter until tender. Add turkey; cook until juices run clear. Remove and keep warm.
2. To the same skillet, add broth, tomato paste, mushrooms and salt; cook for 3-5 minutes or until mushrooms are tender, stirring occasionally. Return turkey to the pan and heat through.
1 cup: 209 cal., 7g fat (4g sat. fat), 88mg chol., 435mg sod., 5g carb. (3g sugars, 1g fiber), 31g pro.

BACON-WRAPPED FILETS WITH SCOTCHED MUSHROOMS

I got the idea for this recipe when I came across bacon-wrapped filets on sale in the grocery store. The rest was inspired by my husband, because he once made a Scotch and ginger ale sauce. This recipe is for two, but it can easily be doubled.
—Mary Kay LaBrie, Clermont, FL

TAKES: 30 MIN. • **MAKES:** 2 SERVINGS

- 2 bacon strips
- 2 beef tenderloin steaks (5 oz. each)
- ¼ tsp. salt
- ¼ tsp. coarsely ground pepper
- 3 tsp. olive oil, divided
- 2 cups sliced baby portobello mushrooms
- ¼ tsp. dried thyme
- 2 Tbsp. butter, divided
- ¼ cup Scotch whiskey
- ½ cup diet ginger ale
- 1 Tbsp. brown sugar
- 1½ tsp. reduced-sodium soy sauce
- ¼ tsp. rubbed sage

1. Preheat oven to 375°. In a small skillet, cook bacon over medium heat until partially cooked but not crisp. Remove to paper towels to drain.
2. Sprinkle steaks with salt and pepper; wrap a strip of bacon around the side of each steak and secure with toothpicks.
3. In a small ovenproof skillet coated with cooking spray, cook steaks in 1½ tsp. oil over medium-high heat, 2 minutes on each side.
4. Bake, uncovered, until meat reaches desired doneness (for medium-rare, a thermometer should read 135°; medium, 140°; medium-well, 145°), 8-12 minutes.

5. In a large skillet, saute mushrooms and thyme in 1 Tbsp. butter and remaining 1½ tsp. oil until tender; remove from heat. Add whiskey, stirring to loosen browned bits. Stir in ginger ale, brown sugar, soy sauce and sage.
6. Bring to a boil. Reduce heat; simmer, uncovered, until reduced by half, 3-5 minutes. Stir in the remaining 1 Tbsp. butter. Serve with steaks.

1 filet with ⅓ cup mushroom mixture: 581 cal., 37g fat (15g sat. fat), 108 mg chol., 729 mg sod., 10 g carb. (8 g sugars, 1 g fiber), 35 g pro.

TEST KITCHEN TIP

Ginger ale adds a subtle ginger flavor to the sauce without being overpowering. You can use regular ginger ale instead of diet, and cut back slightly on the brown sugar, if you prefer.

PESTO
- ¼ **cup loosely packed basil leaves**
- ¼ **cup packed fresh parsley leaves**
- ¼ **tsp. salt**
- ¼ **cup canned coconut milk**

1. Preheat oven to 350°. Combine the first 5 ingredients; brush over the chicken. Place in a greased 8-in. square baking dish. Bake until a thermometer reads 165°, 20-25 minutes.

2. Meanwhile, place basil, parsley and salt in a small food processor; pulse until chopped. While processing, gradually add coconut milk in a steady stream until the mixture is pureed. Serve pesto with chicken.

1 chicken breast half with 2 Tbsp. pesto: 261 cal., 11g fat (6g sat. fat), 94mg chol., 684mg sod., 4g carb. (3g sugars, 1g fiber), 35g pro. **Diabetic exchanges:** 5 lean meat, 1½ fat.

CREAMY PESTO CHICKEN

Basil usually takes over our garden in the middle of June, but we don't mind because we love this pesto! It's a dairy-free version but tastes so good. We love this mixture over cauliflower rice or gluten-free pasta.
—Courtney Stultz, Weir, KS

PREP: 20 MIN. • **BAKE:** 20 MIN.
MAKES: 2 SERVINGS

- 1 **Tbsp. balsamic vinegar**
- 1 **tsp. olive oil**
- 1 **tsp. dried oregano**
- ½ **tsp. minced garlic**
- ¼ **tsp. salt**
- 2 **boneless skinless chicken breast halves (6 oz. each)**

TEST KITCHEN TIP

It's important to get the correct coconut milk. The ones in the refrigerated dairy case tend to curdle in this recipe, so be sure to grab the canned variety. Try this pesto mixed with pasta, spooned onto fresh sliced tomatoes or drizzled over sunny-side-up eggs.

EASY SLOW-COOKED SWISS STEAK

Let your slow cooker simmer up this fuss-free and flavorful Swiss steak. It's perfect for busy days—the longer it cooks, the better it tastes!
—Sarah Burks, Wathena, KS

PREP: 10 MIN. • **COOK:** 6 HOURS
MAKES: 2 SERVINGS

1	Tbsp. all-purpose flour
¼	tsp. salt
⅛	tsp. pepper
¾	lb. beef top round steak
½	medium onion, cut into ¼-in. slices
⅓	cup chopped celery
1	can (8 oz.) tomato sauce

1. In a large shallow dish, combine the flour, salt and pepper. Cut beef into 2 portions; add to the dish and turn to coat.
2. Place onion slices in a 3-qt. slow cooker coated with cooking spray. Layer with the beef, celery and tomato sauce. Cook, covered, on low until meat is tender, 6-8 hours.
1 serving: 272 cal., 5g fat (2g sat. fat), 96mg chol., 882mg sod., 13g carb. (4g sugars, 2g fiber), 41g pro.

SIMPLE CHICKEN STEW

This stew was an experiment of my husband's. It turned out to be our favorite Sunday dinner!
—Amy Dulling, Rockwood, TN

PREP: 20 MIN. • **COOK:** 6 HOURS
MAKES: 2 SERVINGS

1	can (10¾ oz.) condensed cream of chicken soup, undiluted
1	cup water
½	lb. boneless skinless chicken breast, cubed
1	large potato, peeled and cubed
2	medium carrots, sliced
½	cup sliced fresh mushrooms
¼	cup chopped onion
1	tsp. chicken bouillon granules
¼	tsp. poultry seasoning

In a 1½-qt. slow cooker, combine all ingredients. Cook, covered, on low for 6-7 hours or until the chicken and vegetables are tender.
1½ cups: 427 cal., 6g fat (2g sat. fat), 75mg chol., 834mg sod., 62g carb. (11g sugars, 6g fiber), 30g pro.

NUTTY CHICKEN FINGERS

Please both your adult palate and your inner kid with these homemade chicken strips. The crunchy pecan coating makes them stand out and doesn't require a lot of ingredients. Keep things easy by using prepared sauces for dipping—or have fun creating your own!
—Beba Cates, Pearland, TX

TAKES: 30 MIN. • **MAKES:** 2 SERVINGS

½	cup finely chopped pecans
⅓	cup crushed cornflakes
1	Tbsp. dried parsley flakes
⅛	tsp. garlic powder
⅛	tsp. salt
2	Tbsp. 2% milk
¾	lb. boneless skinless chicken breasts, cut into 1-in. strips

1. Preheat oven to 400°. In a shallow bowl, combine first 5 ingredients. Place milk in another shallow bowl. Dip chicken strips in milk, then roll them in the pecan mixture.
2. Place in a single layer in an ungreased 15x10x1-in. baking pan. Bake, uncovered, until juices run clear, 12-15 minutes.
5 oz. cooked chicken: 436 cal., 24g fat (3g sat. fat), 96mg chol., 346mg sod., 18g carb. (3g sugars, 3g fiber), 38g pro.

COWBOY CASSEROLE

This quick and creamy Tater Tot bake is a great homey dinner, especially on a cold night.
—Donna Donhauser, Remsen, NY

PREP: 15 MIN. • **BAKE:** 20 MIN.
MAKES: 2 SERVINGS

- ½ lb. lean ground beef (90% lean)
- 1 can (8¾ oz.) whole kernel corn, drained
- ⅔ cup condensed cream of chicken soup, undiluted
- ½ cup shredded cheddar cheese, divided
- ⅓ cup 2% milk
- 2 Tbsp. sour cream
- ¾ tsp. onion powder
- ¼ tsp. pepper
- 2 cups frozen Tater Tots

1. Preheat oven to 375°. In a large skillet, cook beef over medium heat until no longer pink. Stir in the corn, soup, ¼ cup cheese, the milk, sour cream, onion powder and pepper.
2. Place 1 cup Tater Tots in a greased 3-cup baking dish. Layer with the beef mixture and the remaining 1 cup Tater Tots; sprinkle with the remaining ¼ cup cheese. Bake, uncovered, until bubbly, 20-25 minutes.

1 serving: 714 cal., 38g fat (15g sat. fat), 120mg chol., 1675mg sod., 56g carb. (9g sugars, 6g fiber), 37g pro.

STEAK STRIPS WITH DUMPLINGS

Enjoy a day out and come home to this delicious slow-cooked specialty! Homemade dumplings make it unique.
—John Smalldridge, Princeton, ID

PREP: 25 MIN. • **COOK:** 5 HOURS
MAKES: 2 SERVINGS

- ¾ lb. beef top round steak, cut into ½-in. strips
- ¼ tsp. pepper
- 2 tsp. canola oil
- ⅔ cup condensed cream of chicken soup, undiluted
- ½ cup beef broth
- 4 large fresh mushrooms, sliced
- ¼ cup each chopped onion, green pepper and celery

DUMPLINGS
- ½ cup all-purpose flour
- ¾ tsp. baking powder
- ¼ tsp. salt
- 2 Tbsp. beaten egg
- 3 Tbsp. 2% milk
- ½ tsp. dried parsley flakes

1. Sprinkle steak with pepper. In a small skillet, brown steak in oil over medium-high heat. Transfer to a 1½-qt. slow cooker.
2. Combine the soup, broth and vegetables; pour over steak. Cover and cook on low for 4-5 hours.
3. For dumplings, in a small bowl, combine flour, baking powder and salt. Stir in egg and milk just until blended. Drop by tablespoonfuls onto the meat mixture. Sprinkle with parsley.
4. Cook, covered, on high until a toothpick inserted in a dumpling comes out clean (do not lift the cover while cooking), about 1 hour.

¾ cup beef mixture with 3 dumplings: 506 cal., 17g fat (4g sat. fat), 168mg chol., 1372mg sod., 36g carb. (5g sugars, 3g fiber), 49g pro.

CHICKEN PAELLA

Turmeric lends flavor and a pretty golden color to this Spanish-style entree. Haven't tried arborio rice? You'll love its creamy texture.
—Taste of Home Test Kitchen

PREP: 10 MIN. • **COOK:** 45 MIN.
MAKES: 2 SERVINGS

- 2 boneless skinless chicken thighs (about ½ lb.), cut into 2-in. pieces
- ½ cup cubed fully cooked ham
- ⅓ cup chopped onion
- ⅓ cup julienned sweet red pepper
- 1 Tbsp. olive oil, divided
- ½ cup uncooked arborio rice
- ½ tsp. ground turmeric
- ½ tsp. ground cumin
- ½ tsp. minced garlic
- ⅛ tsp. salt
- 1 cup plus 2 Tbsp. chicken broth
- ¾ cup frozen peas, thawed

1. In a large skillet, saute the chicken, ham, onion and red pepper in 2 tsp. oil until the chicken is browned on all sides. Remove with a slotted spoon.
2. In the same skillet, saute rice in the remaining 1 tsp. oil until lightly browned. Stir in turmeric, cumin, garlic and salt. Return the meat and vegetables to the pan; toss lightly. Add broth; bring to a boil. Reduce heat to medium; cover and simmer until rice is tender, 30-35 minutes. Stir in peas.

1½ cups: 516 cal., 17g fat (4g sat. fat), 99mg chol., 1242mg sod., 52g carb. (5g sugars, 4g fiber), 36g pro.

SPINACH & FETA STUFFED CHICKEN

My chicken bundles are simple, clean and comforting. Served with wild rice and green beans, they're one of our favorite meals.
—Jim Knepper, Mount Holly Springs, PA

TAKES: 30 MIN. • **MAKES:** 2 SERVINGS

- 8 oz. fresh spinach (about 10 cups)
- 1½ tsp. cider vinegar
- ½ tsp. sugar
- ⅛ tsp. pepper
- 2 boneless skinless chicken thighs
- ½ tsp. chicken seasoning
- 3 Tbsp. crumbled feta cheese
- 1 tsp. olive oil
- ¾ cup reduced-sodium chicken broth
- 1 tsp. butter

1. Preheat oven to 375°. In a large skillet, cook and stir spinach over medium-high heat until wilted. Stir in vinegar, sugar and pepper; cool slightly.
2. Pound chicken thighs with a meat mallet to flatten slightly; sprinkle with chicken seasoning. Top each piece of chicken with half the spinach mixture and half the cheese. Roll up chicken, starting from a long side; tie securely with kitchen string.
3. In an ovenproof skillet, heat oil over medium-high heat; add chicken and brown on all sides. Transfer to oven; roast until a thermometer inserted in chicken reads 170°, 13-15 minutes.
4. Remove chicken from skillet; keep warm. Add broth and butter to the same skillet; bring to a boil on the stovetop, stirring to loosen browned bits from pan. Cook until slightly thickened, 3-5 minutes. Serve with chicken.

1 chicken roll-up with 2 Tbsp. sauce: 253 cal., 14g fat (5g sat. fat), 86mg chol., 601mg sod., 5g carb. (2g sugars, 2g fiber), 26g pro. **Diabetic exchanges:** 3 lean meat, 2 vegetable, 1½ fat.

TENDER BEEF OVER NOODLES

I dress up thrifty stew meat with noodles and sweet red sauce for this satisfying main dish. It's terrific with a salad and garlic bread.
—Olivia Gust, Salem, OR

PREP: 15 MIN. • **COOK:** 5½ HOURS
MAKES: 2 SERVINGS

- ½ lb. beef stew meat
- ⅓ cup chopped onion
- 1 tsp. canola oil
- 1 cup water, divided
- ⅓ cup ketchup
- 1 Tbsp. brown sugar
- 1 Tbsp. Worcestershire sauce
- ½ tsp. paprika
- ¼ tsp. ground mustard
- 3 Tbsp. all-purpose flour
- 1 cup uncooked egg noodles
- Minced fresh parsley, optional

1. In a small skillet, brown beef and onion in oil; drain. Transfer to a 1½-qt. slow cooker.
2. In a small bowl, combine ½ cup water, the ketchup, brown sugar, Worcestershire sauce, paprika and mustard; pour over meat. Cook, covered, on low until meat is tender, about 5 hours.
3. Combine flour and remaining ½ cup water until smooth; stir into the meat mixture. Cook, covered, until thickened, about 30 minutes longer.
4. Meanwhile, cook noodles according to package directions; drain. Stir in parsley if desired. Serve with beef.
1 cup beef mixture with ½ cup cooked noodles: 385 cal., 11g fat (3g sat. fat), 89mg chol., 611mg sod., 44g carb. (13g sugars, 2g fiber), 27g pro.

SAUCY BEEF WITH BROCCOLI

When I'm looking for a fast entree, I turn to this classic stir-fry. It features a tantalizing sauce made with garlic and ginger.
—Rosa Evans, Odessa, MO

TAKES: 30 MIN. • **MAKES:** 2 SERVINGS

- 1 Tbsp. cornstarch
- ½ cup reduced-sodium beef broth
- ¼ cup sherry or additional beef broth
- 2 Tbsp. reduced-sodium soy sauce
- 1 Tbsp. brown sugar
- 1 garlic clove, minced
- 1 tsp. minced fresh gingerroot
- 2 tsp. canola oil, divided
- ½ lb. beef top sirloin steak, cut into ¼-in.-thick strips
- 2 cups fresh small broccoli florets
- 8 green onions, cut into 1-in. pieces

1. Mix the first 7 ingredients. In a large nonstick skillet, heat 1 tsp. oil over medium-high heat; stir-fry beef until browned, 1-3 minutes. Remove from pan.
2. Stir-fry broccoli in remaining 1 tsp. oil until crisp-tender, 3-5 minutes. Add green onions; cook just until tender, 1-2 minutes.
3. Stir cornstarch mixture and add to pan. Bring to a boil; cook and stir until sauce is thickened, 2-3 minutes. Add beef and heat through.
1¼ cups: 313 cal., 11g fat (3g sat. fat), 68mg chol., 816mg sod., 20g carb. (11g sugars, 4g fiber), 29g pro.
Diabetic exchanges: 3 lean meat, 1 starch, 1 vegetable, 1 fat.

TEST KITCHEN TIP

If you like, you can adjust this recipe by loading it up with extra veggies like julienned red peppers or carrots, sesame seed topping, or fresh mushrooms. If you like things spicy, sprinkle in some red pepper flakes.

MOROCCAN CHICKEN THIGHS

My husband and I love Mediterranean and Middle Eastern food. This recipe has lots of tasty flavor, so it's quickly become one of our favorites.
—Susan Mills, Three Rivers, CA

PREP: 25 MIN. • **COOK:** 40 MIN.
MAKES: 2 SERVINGS

- ½ tsp. brown sugar
- ½ tsp. ground coriander
- ½ tsp. ground cumin
- ½ tsp. paprika
- ¼ tsp. ground cinnamon
- ⅛ tsp. garlic powder
- ⅛ tsp. salt
- ⅛ tsp. pepper
- 2 tsp. all-purpose flour
- 4 bone-in chicken thighs (about 1½ lbs.), skin removed
- 1 Tbsp. olive oil

SAUCE
- 3 shallots, chopped
- ½ cup plus 2 Tbsp. reduced-sodium chicken broth, divided
- 4 pitted dates, chopped
- 1 tsp. all-purpose flour
- 1½ tsp. minced fresh cilantro

COUSCOUS
- ¼ cup water
- 3 Tbsp. reduced-sodium chicken broth
- ⅛ tsp. salt
  Dash ground cumin
- ⅓ cup uncooked couscous
- 1½ tsp. slivered almonds, toasted

1. In a small bowl, combine the first 8 ingredients. Set aside 1 tsp. spice mixture; add flour to the remaining mixture and sprinkle over chicken.
2. In a large nonstick skillet, brown chicken in oil on both sides. Remove and keep warm.
3. Add shallots to the pan; cook and stir over medium heat for 3 minutes. Stir in ½ cup broth and the dates. Bring to a boil. Reduce heat; return chicken to the pan. Simmer, covered, until chicken juices run clear, 20-25 minutes.
4. Remove chicken; keep warm. Combine flour with remaining 1 tsp. spice mixture and 2 Tbsp. broth until smooth; gradually stir into the pan. Bring to a boil; cook and stir until thickened, about 2 minutes. Stir in cilantro.
5. For couscous, in a small saucepan, bring the water, broth, salt and cumin to a boil. Stir in couscous. Cover and remove from heat; let stand until the water is absorbed, 5-10 minutes. Fluff with a fork, then stir in almonds. Serve with chicken and sauce.

1 serving: 644 cal., 24g fat (6g sat. fat), 174mg chol., 685mg sod., 51g carb. (15g sugars, 4g fiber), 57g pro.

2 oz. thick rice noodles
½ lb. lean ground turkey
1 small onion, chopped
½ cup shredded red cabbage
½ cup chopped fresh kale
¼ cup packed fresh parsley sprigs, chopped
1 tsp. coconut or olive oil
½ tsp. pepper
¼ tsp. salt
3 green onions, thinly sliced
1 jalapeno pepper, sliced
2 tsp. Sriracha chili sauce
Thai peanut sauce, optional

1. Cook noodles according to package directions. Meanwhile, in a large skillet, cook turkey, onion, cabbage and kale over medium-high heat until turkey is no longer pink and vegetables are tender, 8-10 minutes, breaking up turkey into crumbles.
2. Drain the noodles; add to skillet. Stir in parsley, coconut oil, pepper and salt. Serve with green onions, jalapeno, chili sauce and if desired, peanut sauce.
Note: Wear disposable gloves when cutting hot peppers; the oils can burn skin. Avoid touching your face.
2 cups: 332 cal., 11g fat (4g sat. fat), 78mg chol., 588mg sod., 32g carb. (4g sugars, 3g fiber), 25g pro.
Diabetic exchanges: 3 lean meat, 2 starch, ½ fat.

SPICY TURKEY STIR-FRY WITH NOODLES

I created this ground turkey stir-fry recipe when I began my journey to get fit. Healthy eating always sounds so bland and boring, so I wanted to bring life to the world of healthy eating. I think I did it with this spicy dish.
—Jermell Clark, Desert Hot Springs, CA

TAKES: 30 MIN. • **MAKES:** 2 SERVINGS

DID YOU KNOW?

Sriracha is made of a mix of red jalapeno and serrano peppers, garlic, sugar, salt and vinegar. If you don't have it, you can use another hot sauce.

SLOW-COOKED BEEF & VEGGIES

My husband and I came up with this soothing slow-cooker recipe. It's simple and filling with lots of flavor.
—LaDonna Reed, Ponca City, OK

PREP: 15 MIN. + MARINATING
COOK: 8 HOURS • **MAKES:** 2 SERVINGS

- 1 boneless beef top round steak (½ lb.), cut into 2 pieces
  Dash seasoned salt, optional
  Dash pepper
  Dash garlic powder
- 1 cup Italian salad dressing
- ½ cup water
- 1 Tbsp. browning sauce, optional
- 2 medium carrots, cut into 2-in. pieces
- 2 medium red potatoes, cubed
- 1 small onion, sliced
- ½ small green pepper, cut into small chunks

1. Sprinkle 1 side of each piece of steak with seasoned salt if desired and pepper; sprinkle other side with garlic powder. Refrigerate, covered, for 2-3 hours or overnight.
2. In a 3-qt. slow cooker, combine the salad dressing, water and, if desired, browning sauce. Add carrots and potatoes; toss to coat. Add steak and coat with sauce. Top with onion and green pepper.
3. Cook, covered, on low until the meat is tender, 8-9 hours.

1 serving: 505 cal., 22g fat (3g sat. fat), 63mg chol., 1283mg sod., 36g carb. (14g sugars, 5g fiber), 29g pro.

CHICKEN QUINOA BOWLS WITH BALSAMIC DRESSING

This recipe is wonderful for two. But even when scaled up to feed more people, its simplicity still allows me to spend time with my family without sacrificing nutrition or taste.
—Allyson Meyler, Greensboro, NC

PREP: 30 MIN. + COOLING
BROIL: 10 MIN. • **MAKES:** 2 SERVINGS

- ¼ cup balsamic vinegar
- ⅔ cup water
- ⅓ cup quinoa, rinsed
- 2 boneless skinless chicken breast halves (6 oz. each)
- 3 tsp. olive or coconut oil, divided
- ¼ tsp. garlic powder
- ½ tsp. salt, divided
- ¼ tsp. pepper, divided
- ½ lb. fresh asparagus, trimmed
- ¼ cup plain Greek yogurt
- ½ tsp. spicy brown mustard
- ½ medium ripe avocado, peeled and sliced
- 6 cherry tomatoes, halved

1. Place vinegar in a small saucepan; bring to a boil. Cook until slightly thickened, 2-3 minutes. Transfer to a bowl; cool completely.
2. In a small saucepan, bring water to a boil. Add the quinoa. Reduce heat; simmer, covered, until the liquid is absorbed, 10-12 minutes. Keep warm.
3. Preheat broiler. Toss chicken with 2 tsp. oil, garlic powder, ¼ tsp. salt and ⅛ tsp. pepper. Place on 1 half of a 15x10x1-in. pan coated with cooking spray. Broil 4 in. from heat for 5 minutes.
4. Meanwhile, toss asparagus with remaining 1 tsp. oil, ¼ tsp. salt and ⅛ tsp. pepper.
5. Remove pan from oven; turn chicken over. Add asparagus. Broil until a thermometer inserted in chicken reads 165° and asparagus is tender, 3-5 minutes. Let chicken stand 5 minutes before slicing.
6. For dressing, stir yogurt and mustard into balsamic reduction. To serve, spoon quinoa into bowls; top with the chicken, asparagus, avocado and tomatoes. Serve with dressing.

1 serving: 491 cal., 21g fat (5g sat. fat), 101mg chol., 715mg sod., 35g carb. (12g sugars, 6g fiber), 42g pro.

PORK, SAUSAGE & OTHER ENTREES

Whether it's a savory pork tenderloin, elegant lamb chops, or a homemade pasta sauce that puts jarred sauce to shame, these dishes will make any small dinner special.

COUSCOUS & SAUSAGE-STUFFED ACORN SQUASH

With a tiny apartment, zero counter space and only two people to feed, hefty meals are out. This acorn squash with couscous is just the right size.
—Jessica Levinson, Nyack, NY

TAKES: 25 MIN. • **MAKES:** 2 SERVINGS

- 1 medium acorn squash (about 1½ lbs.)
- ¼ tsp. salt
- ¼ tsp. pepper
- 1 Tbsp. olive oil
- 1 medium onion, chopped
- 2 fully cooked spinach and feta chicken sausage links (3 oz. each), sliced
- ½ cup chicken stock
- ½ cup uncooked couscous
  Crumbled feta cheese, optional

1. Cut squash lengthwise in half; remove and discard seeds. Sprinkle squash with salt and pepper; place in a microwave-safe dish, cut side down. Microwave, covered, on high for 10-12 minutes or until tender.
2. Meanwhile, in a large skillet, heat oil over medium heat. Add onion; cook and stir 5-7 minutes or until tender and lightly browned. Add sausage; cook and stir 2-3 minutes or until lightly browned.
3. Add stock; bring to a boil. Stir in couscous. Remove from heat; let stand, covered, 5 minutes or until the stock is absorbed. Spoon over the squash. If desired, top with crumbled feta cheese.

1 stuffed squash half: 521 cal., 15g fat (4g sat. fat), 65mg chol., 979mg sod., 77g carb. (11g sugars, 8g fiber), 25g pro.

PRESSURE-COOKER PORK RIBS

When I was younger, my mom made these delicious ribs for special Saturday dinners. Now I can prepare them any weeknight with the help of an electric pressure cooker.
—Paula Zsiray, Logan, UT

PREP: 25 MIN.
COOK: 20 MIN. + RELEASING
MAKES: 2 SERVINGS

- 1 lb. boneless country-style pork ribs, cut into 2-in. chunks
- ½ tsp. onion salt
- ½ tsp. pepper
- ½ tsp. paprika
- 2 tsp. canola oil
- 1 cup water
- 2 Tbsp. ketchup
- 2 tsp. white vinegar
- ½ tsp. Worcestershire sauce
- ½ tsp. prepared mustard
- ⅛ tsp. celery seed

1. Sprinkle ribs with onion salt, pepper and paprika. Select saute setting on a 3- or 6-qt. electric pressure cooker. Adjust for medium heat; add oil. When oil is hot, brown meat on all sides; remove from pressure cooker.
2. Add water to pressure cooker. Cook 30 seconds, stirring to loosen browned bits from bottom of pressure cooker. Press cancel. Whisk in the remaining ingredients. Return ribs to pressure cooker.
3. Lock lid; close pressure-release valve. Adjust to pressure-cook on high for 20 minutes. Let pressure release naturally. If desired, skim fat and thicken cooking juices.

6 oz. cooked pork: 417 cal., 26g fat (8g sat. fat), 131mg chol., 764mg sod., 5g carb. (4g sugars, 0 fiber), 40g pro.

CREAMY HAM & POTATOES

If you love scalloped potatoes but have a small household, this downsized version with tender chunks of ham is just for you.
—Wendy Rowley, Green River, WY

PREP: 20 MIN. • **COOK:** 5 HOURS
MAKES: 2 SERVINGS

- 2 large red potatoes, cubed
- ⅓ cup cubed Velveeta
- ¾ cup cubed fully cooked ham
- 1 Tbsp. dried minced onion
- ⅔ cup condensed cream of celery soup, undiluted
- ⅔ cup 2% milk
- 1 Tbsp. all-purpose flour
- ¼ tsp. pepper

1. In a greased 1½-qt. slow cooker, layer the potatoes, cheese, ham and onion.
2. In a small bowl, combine soup and milk; whisk in flour and pepper. Pour over potatoes. Cook, covered, on low until the potatoes are tender, 5-6 hours. Stir before serving.

1½ cups: 398 cal., 15g fat (6g sat. fat), 52mg chol., 1534mg sod., 45g carb. (8g sugars, 4g fiber), 20g pro.

PRESSURE-COOKER MUSHROOM PORK RAGOUT

Savory, quickly made pork is luscious served in a delightful tomato gravy over noodles. It's a nice change from regular pork roast. I serve it with broccoli or green beans on the side.
—Connie McDowell, Greenwood, DE

PREP: 20 MIN. • **COOK:** 10 MIN.
MAKES: 2 SERVINGS

- 1 pork tenderloin (¾ lb.)
- ⅛ tsp. salt
- ⅛ tsp. pepper
- 1½ cups sliced fresh mushrooms
- ¾ cup canned crushed tomatoes
- ¾ cup reduced-sodium chicken broth, divided
- ⅓ cup sliced onion
- 1 Tbsp. chopped sun-dried tomatoes (not packed in oil)
- 1¼ tsp. dried savory
- 1 Tbsp. cornstarch
- 1½ cups hot cooked egg noodles

1. Rub tenderloin with salt and pepper; cut in half. Place in a 6-qt. electric pressure cooker. Top with sliced mushrooms, tomatoes, ½ cup broth, the onion, sun-dried tomatoes and savory.
2. Lock lid and close pressure-release valve. Adjust to pressure-cook on high for 6 minutes. Quick-release the pressure. (A thermometer inserted in the pork should read at least 145°.) Remove pork; keep warm.
3. In a small bowl, mix cornstarch and remaining ¼ cup broth until smooth; stir into pressure cooker. Select the saute setting and adjust for low heat. Simmer, stirring constantly, until thickened, 1-2 minutes. Serve over noodles.

1 serving: 387 cal., 8g fat (2g sat. fat), 119mg chol., 613mg sod., 37g carb. (8g sugars, 4g fiber), 43g pro. **Diabetic exchanges:** 5 lean meat, 2 vegetable, 1 starch.

DID YOU KNOW?

Although they sound similar, a ragu and a ragout are not the same. A *ragout* is a French-style, slow-cooked stew; a *ragú* is an Italian-style sauce for pasta.

SWEET ONION & CHERRY PORK CHOPS

When I want to jump-start supper, I opt for these tender pork chops. The sweet and savory cherry sauce makes the recipe a keeper. Try serving it with wild rice pilaf.
—Stephanie Ray, Naples, FL

PREP: 15 MIN. • **COOK:** 3 HOURS
MAKES: 2 SERVINGS

- ½ cup fresh or frozen pitted tart cherries, thawed
- 2 Tbsp. chopped sweet onion
- 1 Tbsp. honey
- ½ tsp. seasoned salt
- ¼ tsp. pepper
- 2 boneless pork loin chops (5 oz. each)
- 1 tsp. cornstarch
- 1 tsp. cold water

1. In a 1½-qt. slow cooker, combine the first 5 ingredients; top with pork chops. Cook, covered, on low until the meat is tender, 3-4 hours.
2. Remove meat to a serving platter; keep warm. Skim fat from the cooking juices; transfer to a small saucepan. Bring liquid to a boil. Combine cornstarch and water until smooth. Gradually stir into the pan. Bring to a boil; cook and stir until thickened, about 2 minutes. Serve with meat.

1 pork chop with ¼ cup cherry mixture: 278 cal., 8g fat (3g sat. fat), 68mg chol., 425mg sod., 23g carb. (9g sugars, 1g fiber), 28g pro.
Diabetic exchanges: 4 lean meat, 1 starch, ½ fat.

MAPLE PORK RIBS

A luscious maple-mustard sauce will take your next plate of ribs to a whole new level.
—Phyllis Schmalz, Kansas City, KS

PREP: 10 MIN. • **COOK:** 5 HOURS
MAKES: 2 SERVINGS

- 1 lb. boneless country-style pork ribs, trimmed and cut into 3-in. pieces
- 2 tsp. canola oil
- 1 medium onion, sliced and separated into rings
- 3 Tbsp. maple syrup
- 2 Tbsp. spicy brown or Dijon mustard

In a large skillet, brown ribs in oil on all sides; drain. Place ribs and onion in a 1½-qt. slow cooker. Combine syrup and mustard; pour over ribs. Cook, covered, on low until meat is tender, 5-6 hours.
4 oz. cooked pork: 428 cal., 20g fat (6g sat. fat), 98mg chol., 272mg sod., 27g carb. (24g sugars, 2g fiber), 31g pro.

DID YOU KNOW?

Despite the name, country-style ribs aren't ribs—they come from the pork shoulder and come either boneless or bone-in. This thick, meaty cut is ideal for slow cooking.

SPINACH- & GOUDA-STUFFED PORK CUTLETS

This started as a restaurant copycat dish made at home and evolved. Cheese just oozes out of the center, and mustard lends a lot of flavor.
—Joan Oakland, Troy, MT

TAKES: 30 MIN. • **MAKES:** 2 SERVINGS

- 3 Tbsp. dry bread crumbs
- 2 Tbsp. grated Parmesan cheese
- 2 pork sirloin cutlets (3 oz. each)
- ¼ tsp. salt
- ⅛ tsp. pepper
- 2 slices smoked Gouda cheese (about 2 oz.)
- 2 cups fresh baby spinach
- 2 Tbsp. horseradish mustard

1. Preheat oven to 400°. In a shallow bowl, mix the bread crumbs and Parmesan cheese.
2. Sprinkle tops of cutlets with salt and pepper. Layer the end of each cutlet with Gouda cheese and spinach. Fold the cutlets in half, enclosing the filling; secure with toothpicks. Brush mustard over outsides of pork; dip in bread crumb mixture, patting to help coating adhere.
3. Place on a greased foil-lined baking sheet. Bake until breading is golden brown and pork is tender, 12-15 minutes. Discard toothpicks before serving.

1 stuffed cutlet: 299 cal., 16g fat (7g sat. fat), 91mg chol., 898mg sod., 10g carb. (2g sugars, 2g fiber), 30g pro.

AIR-FRYER SWEET & SOUR PORK

Whether you're serving a party of two—or making a bigger batch for company—you'll find this pork tenderloin a succulent choice.
—Leigh Rys, Herndon, VA

PREP: 25 MIN. • **COOK:** 20 MIN.
MAKES: 2 SERVINGS

- ½ cup unsweetened crushed pineapple, undrained
- ½ cup cider vinegar
- ¼ cup sugar
- ¼ cup packed dark brown sugar
- ¼ cup ketchup
- 1 Tbsp. reduced-sodium soy sauce
- 1½ tsp. Dijon mustard
- ½ tsp. garlic powder
- 1 pork tenderloin (¾ lb.), halved
  Cooking spray
- ⅛ tsp. salt
- ⅛ tsp. pepper
  Sliced green onions, optional

1. In a small saucepan, combine first 8 ingredients. Bring to a boil; reduce heat. Simmer, uncovered, until thickened, 6-8 minutes, stirring occasionally.
2. Preheat air fryer to 350°. Sprinkle pork with salt and pepper. Place pork on greased tray in air-fryer basket; spritz with cooking spray. Cook until pork begins to brown around edges, 7-8 minutes. Turn; pour 2 Tbsp. sauce over pork. Cook until a thermometer inserted into the pork reads at least 145°, 10-12 minutes longer.
3. Let pork stand 5 minutes before slicing. Serve with remaining sauce. If desired, top with sliced green onions.

5 oz. cooked pork with ½ cup sauce: 502 cal., 7g fat (2g sat. fat), 95mg chol., 985mg sod., 72g carb. (69g sugars, 1g fiber), 35g pro.

HERBED LEMON PORK CHOPS

You'll receive plenty of compliments on these tender and juicy pork chops. Mixed herbs and a final squeeze of lemon pack on the flavor in just 20 minutes!
—Billi Jo Sylvester, New Smyrna Beach, FL

TAKES: 20 MIN. • **MAKES:** 2 SERVINGS

- 1 tsp. salt-free garlic seasoning blend
- ½ tsp. dried basil
- ½ tsp. dried oregano
- ½ tsp. dried parsley flakes
- ¼ tsp. salt
- ¼ tsp. garlic powder
- ¼ tsp. dried rosemary, crushed
- 2 bone-in pork loin chops (6 oz. each)
- 1 tsp. olive oil
- 1 Tbsp. lemon juice

1. Mix first 7 ingredients; rub over both sides of chops. In a large nonstick skillet, heat oil over medium-high heat. Add pork; cook until a thermometer reads 145°, 5-8 minutes per side.
2. Remove from heat; drizzle with lemon juice. Let stand, covered, 5 minutes before serving.

1 pork chop: 200 cal., 10g fat (3g sat. fat), 74mg chol., 350mg sod., 1g carb. (0 sugars, 0 fiber), 26g pro. **Diabetic exchanges:** 4 lean meat, ½ fat.

PORK CHOPS WITH MUSHROOM BOURBON SAUCE

These golden-crusted pork chops are accompanied with a rich mushroom sauce. This scrumptious entree is loved by my family and scales up well to makes a terrific company dish; it's wonderful with mashed potatoes!
—Nadine Mesch, Mount Healthy, OH

PREP: 20 MIN. • **COOK:** 30 MIN.
MAKES: 2 SERVINGS

- ½ lb. sliced fresh mushrooms
- 2 Tbsp. chopped onion
- 2 Tbsp. olive oil, divided
- 1 Tbsp. butter
- 1 garlic clove, minced
- ¼ cup white wine or reduced-sodium chicken broth
- 2 Tbsp. bourbon
- ½ cup reduced-sodium chicken broth
- ¼ cup heavy whipping cream
- 2 boneless pork loin chops (6 oz. each)
- ¼ tsp. salt
- ¼ tsp. paprika
- ⅛ tsp. pepper
- 1 large egg
- 2 Tbsp. water
- 3 Tbsp. all-purpose flour
- ½ cup panko bread crumbs
- 4 tsp. minced fresh basil

1. In a large skillet, saute the mushrooms and onion in 1 Tbsp. each of oil and butter until tender. Add garlic; cook 1 minute longer. Remove from the heat. Add wine and bourbon; cook over medium heat until liquid is evaporated. Add chicken broth and cream; bring to a boil. Reduce heat and simmer until sauce is thickened, stirring occasionally; keep warm.
2. Sprinkle chops with salt, paprika and pepper. In a shallow bowl, whisk egg and water. Place flour and bread crumbs in separate shallow bowls. Dip pork in the flour, the egg mixture, then the bread crumbs.
3. In a large skillet, cook chops over medium heat in remaining 1 Tbsp. oil until breading is crisp and the juices run clear, 4-5 minutes on each side. Stir basil into mushroom sauce; serve over pork.

1 pork chop with ⅓ cup sauce: 646 cal., 42g fat (16g sat. fat), 202mg chol., 601mg sod., 20g carb. (3g sugars, 2g fiber), 42g pro.

PORK CHOP SUPPER

My pork chop dinner is a perfect fall meal for two, featuring some of the season's best flavors.
—Pamela Shank, Parkersburg, WV

PREP: 20 MIN. • **COOK:** 3 HOURS
MAKES: 2 SERVINGS

- 2 boneless pork loin chops (5 oz. each)
- 2 tsp. canola oil
- 1 medium sweet potato, peeled and thinly sliced
- 1 small onion, sliced
- 1 small tart apple, peeled and sliced
- 1 Tbsp. brown sugar
- ½ tsp. ground cinnamon
- ¼ tsp. salt
- ¼ tsp. ground nutmeg
- ¼ tsp. pepper
- 1 can (8 oz.) sauerkraut, undrained

1. In a small nonstick skillet, brown chops in oil. Meanwhile, place the sweet potato, onion and apple in a 1½-qt. slow cooker.
2. Combine the brown sugar, cinnamon, salt, nutmeg and pepper; sprinkle over the top of the sweet potato mixture. Layer with pork chops and sauerkraut.
3. Cook, covered, on low 3-4 hours or until the meat is tender.

1 serving: 377 cal., 13g fat (3g sat. fat), 68mg chol., 1094mg sod., 35g carb. (21g sugars, 6g fiber), 30g pro.

CHORIZO SAUSAGE CORN CHOWDER

The spiciness of the sausage in this chowder is a wonderful counterpart to the corn's sweetness.
—Robin Haas, Cranston, RI

PREP: 25 MIN. • **COOK:** 20 MIN.
MAKES: 6 SERVINGS (2½ QT.)

- 3 cups frozen corn, thawed
- 1 large onion, chopped
- 1 celery rib, chopped
- 1 tsp. olive oil
- 2 garlic cloves, minced
- 3 cans (14½ oz. each) reduced-sodium chicken broth
- 1 Tbsp. sherry or additional reduced-sodium chicken broth
- 2 bay leaves
- 1 tsp. dried thyme
- ½ tsp. pepper
- 1 pkg. (12 oz.) fully cooked chorizo chicken sausage links or flavor of your choice, chopped
- 1 cup half-and-half cream
- 1 cup shredded smoked Gouda cheese
- 1 medium sweet red pepper, chopped
- 2 green onions, chopped

1. In a nonstick Dutch oven, saute the corn, onion and celery in oil until tender. Add garlic; cook 1 minute longer. Stir in the broth, sherry, bay leaves, thyme and pepper. Bring to a boil. Reduce heat; simmer, uncovered, for 8-10 minutes. Discard the bay leaves.
2. Cool slightly. In a food processor, process soup in batches until blended. Return all to pan.
3. Stir in sausage and cream; heat through. Sprinkle with cheese, red pepper and green onions.

1½ cups: 331 cal., 15g fat (8g sat. fat), 85mg chol., 1144mg sod., 28g carb. (8g sugars, 3g fiber), 22g pro.

FAMILY FAVORITE PASTA SAUCE

Sure, it's temptingly easy to just open a jar, but jarred sauces have nothing on this homemade classic!
—Jody Bober, St Clairsville, OH

PREP: 30 MIN. • **COOK:** 1¾ HOURS
MAKES: 2 SERVINGS

- ¼ lb. bulk Italian sausage
- ½ cup chopped onion
- 1 small garlic clove, minced
- ¾ tsp. olive oil
- 1 cup diced tomatoes
- 3 Tbsp. Italian tomato paste
- 2 Tbsp. water
- 1½ tsp. minced fresh parsley
- ¾ tsp. packed brown sugar
- ¾ tsp. balsamic vinegar
- ½ tsp. dried basil
- ¼ tsp. salt
- ⅛ tsp. Italian seasoning
  Dash coarsely ground pepper
  Hot cooked pasta of your choice

1. In a large saucepan, cook the sausage, onion and garlic in oil over medium heat until meat is no longer pink; drain.
2. Stir in the tomatoes, tomato paste, water, parsley, brown sugar, vinegar and seasonings. Bring to a boil. Reduce heat; simmer, uncovered, for 45 minutes or until flavors are blended. Serve with pasta.

¾ cup: 187 cal., 10g fat (3g sat. fat), 23mg chol., 950mg sod., 17g carb. (9g sugars, 3g fiber), 8g pro.

AIR-FRYER JAMAICAN JERK PORK CHOPS

These sweet, spicy chops can be thrown together in minutes, but they definitely don't taste like it. Serve them with a side of jasmine rice and you'll feel as if you're on a tropical vacation.
—Allison Ulrich, Frisco, TX

TAKES: 25 MIN. • **MAKES:** 4 SERVINGS

- 1 Tbsp. butter, softened
- ¼ cup peach preserves
- 4 boneless thin-cut pork loin chops (2 to 3 oz. each)
- 3 tsp. Caribbean jerk seasoning
- ½ tsp. salt
- ¼ tsp. pepper
- ½ medium sweet orange pepper
- ½ medium sweet yellow pepper
- ½ medium sweet red pepper
  Hot cooked rice, optional

1. Preheat air fryer to 350°. In a small bowl, mix the butter and peach preserves until combined.
2. Sprinkle chops with jerk seasoning, salt and pepper. Place on greased tray in air-fryer basket. Cook until meat is no longer pink, 2-3 minutes on each side. Remove and keep warm.
3. Cut peppers into thin strips. Place on greased tray in air-fryer basket. Cook until crisp-tender and lightly browned, 5-6 minutes, stirring occasionally.
4. Return chops to air fryer with peppers; top with butter mixture. Cook until the butter is melted, 1-2 minutes. If desired, serve with rice.

1 serving: 368 cal., 14g fat (7g sat. fat), 84mg chol., 1099mg sod., 32g carb. (28g sugars, 2g fiber), 28g pro.

TEST KITCHEN TIP

Jerk seasoning comes in either a dry rub or a marinade; this recipe calls for dry.

SPICE-RUBBED LAMB CHOPS

One of my absolute favorite meals to eat anytime is lamb chops! This recipe serves two but can easily be scaled up to feed more.
—Nareman Dietz, Beverly Hills, MI

PREP: 15 MIN. + CHILLING • **BAKE:** 5 MIN.
MAKES: 2 SERVINGS

- 2 tsp. lemon juice
- 2 tsp. Worcestershire sauce
- 1½ tsp. pepper
- 1¼ tsp. ground cumin
- 1¼ tsp. curry powder
- 1 garlic clove, minced
- ½ tsp. sea salt
- ½ tsp. onion powder
- ½ tsp. crushed red pepper flakes
- 4 lamb rib chops
- 1 Tbsp. olive oil

1. Mix the first 9 ingredients; spread over the lamb chops. Refrigerate, covered, overnight.
2. Preheat oven to 450°. In an ovenproof skillet, heat oil over medium-high heat; brown chops, about 2 minutes per side.
3. Transfer skillet to oven; roast until desired doneness (for medium-rare, a thermometer should read 135°; medium, 140°), 3-4 minutes.

2 lamb chops: 290 cal., 17g fat (4g sat. fat), 90mg chol., 620mg sod., 5g carb. (1g sugars, 2g fiber), 29g pro. **Diabetic exchanges:** 4 lean meat, 1½ fat.

SLOW-COOKED PEACH PORK CHOPS

I played around with many variations of this recipe until I came up with one that was just right. Warm peaches make an excellent side dish for pork.
—Bonnie Morrow, Spencerport, NY

PREP: 15 MIN. • **COOK:** 5 HOURS
MAKES: 2 SERVINGS

- 2 bone-in center-cut pork loin chops (7 oz. each)
- 2 tsp. canola oil
- 1 can (8¼ oz.) sliced peaches in extra-light syrup
- 1 can (8 oz.) tomato sauce
- ½ cup water
- 1 tsp. reduced-sodium soy sauce
- ⅛ tsp. dried rosemary, crushed
- ⅛ tsp. dried thyme
- ⅛ tsp. dried basil
  Dash to ⅛ tsp. cayenne pepper

1. In a small skillet, brown the pork chops in oil; drain. Transfer to a 1½-qt. slow cooker.
2. Drain peaches, reserving juice. In a bowl, combine the tomato sauce, water, soy sauce, rosemary, thyme, basil, cayenne and reserved peach juice; pour over pork. Top with peaches.
3. Cook, covered, on low until the pork is tender, about 5 hours.

1 pork chop: 389 cal., 22g fat (6g sat. fat), 97mg chol., 690mg sod., 15g carb. (11g sugars, 3g fiber), 34g pro.

TEST KITCHEN TIP

You can use boneless pork chops for this recipe or even substitute a pork tenderloin. If using a tenderloin, cut it in half before putting it in the slow cooker.

TENDER & TANGY RIBS

These ribs are so simple to prepare! Just brown them in the skillet and then combine them with the sauce ingredients in your slow cooker. Serve them for lunch or let them cook all day for fall-off-the-bone tenderness.
—Denise Hathaway Valasek, Perrysburg, OH

PREP: 15 MIN. • **COOK:** 4 HOURS
MAKES: 3 SERVINGS

- ¾ to 1 cup white vinegar
- ½ cup ketchup
- 2 Tbsp. sugar
- 2 Tbsp. Worcestershire sauce
- 1 garlic clove, minced
- 1 tsp. ground mustard
- 1 tsp. paprika
- ½ to 1 tsp. salt
- ⅛ tsp. pepper
- 2 lbs. pork spareribs
- 1 Tbsp. canola oil

Combine the first 9 ingredients in a 3-qt. slow cooker. Cut ribs into serving-sized pieces; brown in a skillet in oil. Transfer to the slow cooker. Stir to coat ribs in sauce. Cook, covered, on low 4-6 hours or until tender.

1 cup: 689 cal., 48g fat (16g sat. fat), 170mg chol., 1110mg sod., 22g carb. (13g sugars, 1g fiber), 42g pro.

PARMESAN PORK TENDERLOIN

I am of Danish descent and love all things pork, both old recipes and new. Here's a dish I came up with myself.
—John Hansen, Marstons Mills, MA

PREP: 25 MIN. • **COOK:** 25 MIN.
MAKES: 2 SERVINGS

- 1 pork tenderloin (¾ lb.)
- 6 Tbsp. grated Parmesan cheese
- 1 small sweet onion, sliced and separated into rings
- 1½ cups sliced fresh mushrooms
- 1 garlic clove, minced
- 2 tsp. butter, divided
- 2 tsp. olive oil, divided
- ¼ cup reduced-sodium beef broth
- 2 Tbsp. port wine or additional beef broth
- ⅛ tsp. salt, optional
- ⅛ tsp. each dried basil, thyme and rosemary, crushed
   Dash pepper
- ½ tsp. cornstarch
- 3 Tbsp. water

1. Cut pork into ½-in. slices; flatten to ⅛-in. thickness. Coat slices with Parmesan cheese.
2. In a large skillet, saute the onion, mushrooms and garlic in 1 tsp. butter and 1 tsp. oil until tender; remove and keep warm.
3. In the same skillet, cook pork in the remaining 1 tsp. butter and 1 tsp. oil in batches over medium heat until juices run clear, about 2 minutes on each side. Remove and keep warm.
4. Add broth to the pan, scraping to loosen browned bits. Stir in wine or additional broth; add seasonings. Bring to a boil. Reduce heat; simmer, uncovered, for 5 minutes.
5. Combine cornstarch and water until smooth; stir into pan juices. Bring to a boil; cook and stir until thickened, about 2 minutes. Serve the sauce with the pork and the onion mixture.

1 serving: 388 cal., 19g fat (8g sat. fat), 118mg chol., 472mg sod., 11g carb. (6g sugars, 2g fiber), 43g pro.

FISH & MEATLESS MAINS

Whether you enjoy seafood greats and meatless Mondays, or maybe you live a vegetarian lifestyle, this chapter offers dishes you'll turn to time and again.

LAZY LASAGNA

Lasagna may seem as if it's a lot of work on a busy evening, but one day when I had a craving for it, I devised this simple recipe. It worked out beautifully!
—Carol Mead, Los Alamos, NM

TAKES: 30 MIN. • **MAKES:** 2 SERVINGS

- 1 cup meatless spaghetti sauce
- ¾ cup shredded part-skim mozzarella cheese
- ½ cup 4% cottage cheese
- 1½ cups cooked wide egg noodles
- 2 Tbsp. grated Parmesan cheese
  Chopped fresh parsley, optional

1. Warm the spaghetti sauce; stir in mozzarella and cottage cheeses. Fold in noodles. Pour into 2 greased 2-cup baking dishes. Sprinkle with Parmesan cheese.
2. Bake, uncovered, at 375° until bubbly, about 20 minutes. If desired, top with parsley.
1 lasagna: 399 cal., 16g fat (8g sat. fat), 68mg chol., 1120mg sod., 37g carb. (12g sugars, 3g fiber), 25g pro.

FLAVORFUL SALMON FILLETS

Compliments are a sure thing when I fix these fabulous salmon fillets. A tasty marinade pumps up the flavor and keeps them moist and tender.
—Krista Frank, Rhododendron, OR

TAKES: 30 MIN. • **MAKES:** 2 SERVINGS

- ¼ cup packed brown sugar
- ¼ cup reduced-sodium soy sauce
- 3 Tbsp. unsweetened pineapple juice
- 3 Tbsp. red wine vinegar
- 1 Tbsp. lemon juice
- 3 garlic cloves, minced
- 1 tsp. ground ginger
- 1 tsp. pepper
- ¼ tsp. hot pepper sauce
- 2 salmon fillets (1 in. thick and 6 oz. each)

1. In a shallow dish, combine the first 9 ingredients. Add salmon and turn to coat; cover and refrigerate for 15 minutes, turning once.
2. Drain fillets, discarding the marinade. Place salmon on oiled grill rack, skin side down. Grill, covered, over medium heat or broil 4 in. from the heat until fish just begins to flake easily with a fork, 13-15 minutes.
6 oz.-weight: 330 cal., 18g fat (4g sat. fat), 100mg chol., 204mg sod., 4g carb. (3g sugars, 0 fiber), 34g pro.
Diabetic exchanges: 5 lean meat.

TEST KITCHEN TIP

Get creative when making the easy marinade for this salmon. Add fresh herbs, a dash of teriyaki sauce, red pepper flakes or even a little brown mustard.

1-2-3 GRILLED SALMON

I love salmon, but my husband doesn't. So I combined flavors I knew he liked to create this recipe, and now it's the only salmon recipe he will eat. It's so easy and only requires just a handful of ingredients.
—Nicole Clayton, Prescott, AZ

PREP: 10 MIN. + MARINATING
GRILL: 5 MIN. • **MAKES:** 2 SERVINGS

- 2 Tbsp. olive oil
- 1 Tbsp. reduced-sodium soy sauce
- 2 tsp. Dijon mustard
- ¼ tsp. dried minced garlic
- 2 salmon fillets (5 oz. each)
  Sliced green onions, optional

1. In a small bowl, combine oil, soy sauce, mustard and garlic. Pour half of marinade into a shallow dish. Add salmon; turn to coat. Cover; refrigerate 30 minutes. Cover and refrigerate remaining marinade.

2. Drain fish and discard marinade. On a greased grill rack, grill the salmon, covered, over high heat until fish flakes easily with a fork, 5-10 minutes. Drizzle with reserved marinade. If desired, sprinkle with green onions.

1 fillet: 322 cal., 23g fat (4g sat. fat), 71mg chol., 452mg sod., 2g carb. (0 sugars, 0 fiber), 24g pro. **Diabetic exchanges:** 4 lean meat, 2 fat.

ZESTY BAKED CATFISH

This catfish combines common pantry seasonings for a taste that's anything but basic.
—Karen Conklin, Supply, NC

TAKES: 20 MIN. • **MAKES:** 2 SERVINGS

- 1 tsp. canola oil
- 1 tsp. lemon juice
- 2 catfish fillets (6 oz. each)
- 1½ tsp. paprika
- ½ tsp. dried tarragon
- ½ tsp. dried basil
- ½ tsp. pepper
- ¼ tsp. salt
- ⅛ tsp. cayenne pepper

1. Combine oil and lemon juice; brush over both sides of fillets. Combine remaining ingredients; rub over both sides of fillets. Place fish in an ungreased 15x10x1-in. baking pan.

2. Bake, uncovered, at 350° for 10-15 minutes or until fish flakes easily with a fork.

1 serving: 259 cal., 16g fat (3g sat. fat), 80mg chol., 386mg sod., 2g carb. (0 sugars, 1g fiber), 27g pro.

SPEEDY SHRIMP FLATBREADS

My husband and I are hooked on flatbread pizzas. I make at least one a week just to have something tasty around as a snack. This one came together easily because I had all the ingredients on hand.
—Cheryl Woodson, Liberty, MO

TAKES: 15 MIN. • **MAKES:** 2 SERVINGS

- 2 naan flatbreads or whole pita breads
- 1 pkg. (5.2 oz.) garlic-herb spreadable cheese
- ½ lb. peeled and deveined cooked shrimp (31-40 per lb.)
- ½ cup chopped oil-packed sun-dried tomatoes
- ¼ cup fresh basil leaves
  Lemon wedges, optional

Preheat oven to 400°. Place flatbreads on a baking sheet. Spread with the cheese; top with shrimp and tomatoes. Bake until heated through, 4-6 minutes. Sprinkle with basil. If desired, serve with lemon wedges.

1 flatbread: 634 cal., 41g fat (24g sat. fat), 263mg chol., 1163mg sod., 38g carb. (3g sugars, 3g fiber), 33g pro.

1. Pat cod dry with paper towels; sprinkle with salt and pepper. In a large nonstick skillet, heat 2 Tbsp. oil over medium-high heat. Brown fillets lightly on both sides; remove from pan.

2. In same skillet, heat remaining 1 Tbsp. oil over medium heat. Add onion; cook and stir 4-5 minutes or until softened. Stir in wine; cook until onion is lightly browned, stirring occasionally, 3-4 minutes longer. Return cod to pan. Reduce heat to low; cook, covered, until fish just begins to flake easily with a fork, 2-3 minutes.

3. Remove cod from pan. Stir the cilantro and pine nuts into onion; serve with fish.

1 fillet with ¼ cup onion mixture: 378 cal., 24g fat (3g sat. fat), 65mg chol., 691mg sod., 8g carb. (5g sugars, 1g fiber), 28g pro.

TEST KITCHEN TIP

You'll know when cod is done when the fish starts to look solid white, reaches an internal temp of about 145° F and flakes easily with a fork.

PAN-SEARED COD

Cod has a soft, buttery appeal that goes great with cilantro, onions and crunchy pine nuts. This is the easiest, tastiest cod preparation I've found.
—Lucy Lu Wang, Seattle, WA

TAKES: 25 MIN. • **MAKES:** 2 SERVINGS

- 2 cod fillets (6 oz. each)
- ½ tsp. salt
- ¼ tsp. pepper
- 3 Tbsp. olive oil, divided
- ½ large sweet onion, thinly sliced
- ½ cup dry white wine
- ¼ cup coarsely chopped fresh cilantro
- 1 Tbsp. pine nuts or sliced almonds

SHRIMP & SCALLOPS TROPICAL SALAD

A fruity dressing makes this seafood salad shine. Served on a bed of greens, the scrumptious combination of grilled seafood, veggies and macadamia nuts is the perfect way to celebrate a special summer occasion.

—Jackie Pressinger, Stuart, WI

PREP: 35 MIN. • **COOK:** 5 MIN.
MAKES: 2 SERVINGS

- 2 Tbsp. diced peeled mango
- 1 Tbsp. diced fresh pineapple
- 1½ tsp. mango chutney
- 1½ tsp. olive oil
- 1 tsp. rice vinegar
- ¾ tsp. lime juice
   Dash salt
   Dash crushed red pepper flakes
- 3 cups torn Bibb or Boston lettuce
- 1 cup chopped peeled cucumber
- ½ medium ripe avocado, peeled and sliced
- 2 Tbsp. coarsely chopped macadamia nuts, toasted
- 1 Tbsp. finely chopped red onion
- 1 Tbsp. minced fresh cilantro
- 2 Tbsp. canola oil
- 1½ tsp. Caribbean jerk seasoning
- 6 uncooked large shrimp, peeled and deveined
- 6 sea scallops, halved

1. Place the first 8 ingredients in a blender. Cover and process until blended; set aside. Divide lettuce, cucumber, avocado, nuts, onion and cilantro between 2 serving plates.
2. In a small bowl, combine the oil and jerk seasoning. Thread shrimp and scallops onto 2 metal or soaked wooden skewers; brush with the oil mixture.
3. Grill the skewers, covered, over medium heat until shrimp turn pink and scallops are firm and opaque, 2-3 minutes on each side. Place on salads; drizzle with dressing.
1 salad: 413 cal., 32g fat (4g sat. fat), 96mg chol., 523mg sod., 16g carb. (6g sugars, 5g fiber), 19g pro.

SWISS MACARONI & CHEESE

Whenever we visited my husband's good friend, his wife made this dish. I was too shy to ask for the recipe, so I came up with this one. It is very creamy and rich, with a mild Swiss cheese flavor.

—Kateri Scott, Amsterdam, NY

TAKES: 20 MIN. • **MAKES:** 2 SERVINGS

- ¾ cup uncooked elbow macaroni
- 2 Tbsp. chopped onion
- 2 Tbsp. butter
- 1 Tbsp. all-purpose flour
- 1 cup fat-free milk
- 1 cup shredded Swiss cheese
- ¼ tsp. salt
- ⅛ tsp. pepper

1. Cook macaroni according to package directions. Meanwhile, in a small saucepan, saute onion in butter until tender. Stir in flour until smooth; gradually add milk. Bring to a boil; cook and stir for 2 minutes or until thickened.
2. Add cheese, salt and pepper. Drain macaroni. Add to cheese mixture; toss gently to coat.
1 cup: 464 cal., 27g fat (17g sat. fat), 82mg chol., 569mg sod., 32g carb. (9g sugars, 1g fiber), 24g pro.

AIR-FRYER PORTOBELLO MELTS

We're always looking for satisfying vegetarian meals, and this one tops the list. These melts are especially delicious in the summer when we have tons of homegrown tomatoes.
—Amy Smalley, Morehead, KY

TAKES: 25 MIN. • **MAKES:** 2 SERVINGS

- 2   large portobello mushrooms (4 oz. each), stems removed
- ¼   cup olive oil
- 2   Tbsp. balsamic vinegar
- ½   tsp. salt
- ½   tsp. dried basil
- 4   tomato slices
- 2   slices mozzarella cheese
- 2   slices Italian bread (1 in. thick)
     Chopped fresh basil

1. Place mushrooms in a shallow bowl. Mix oil, vinegar, salt and dried basil; brush onto both sides of the mushrooms. Let stand 5 minutes. Reserve the remaining marinade. Preheat air fryer to 400°.

2. Place mushrooms on greased tray in air-fryer basket, stem side down. Cook 3-4 minutes per side or until tender. Remove from basket. Top stem sides with tomato and cheese; secure with toothpicks. Cook until cheese is melted, about 1 minute. Remove and keep warm; discard toothpicks.

3. Place bread on tray in air-fryer basket; brush with the reserved marinade. Cook until lightly toasted, 2-3 minutes. Top with mushrooms. Sprinkle with chopped basil.

1 open-faced sandwich: 427 cal., 30g fat (4g sat. fat), 4mg chol., 864mg sod., 33g carb. (8g sugars, 4g fiber), 8g pro.

SHRIMP PASTA PRIMAVERA

They say the way to a man's heart is through his stomach. So when I invite that special guy to dinner, I like to prepare something equally wonderful. This well-seasoned pasta dish has tons of flavor.
—Shari Neff, Takoma Park, MD

TAKES: 15 MIN. • **MAKES:** 2 SERVINGS

- 4   oz. uncooked angel hair pasta
- 8   jumbo shrimp, peeled and deveined
- 6   fresh asparagus spears, trimmed and cut into 2-in. pieces
- ¼   cup olive oil
- 2   garlic cloves, minced
- ½   cup sliced fresh mushrooms
- ½   cup chicken broth
- 1   small plum tomato, peeled, seeded and diced
- ¼   tsp. salt
- ⅛   tsp. crushed red pepper flakes
- 1   Tbsp. each minced fresh basil, oregano, thyme and parsley
- ¼   cup grated Parmesan cheese

1. Cook pasta according to package directions. Meanwhile, in a large skillet, saute shrimp and asparagus in oil 3-4 minutes or until shrimp turn pink. Add garlic; cook 1 minute longer. Add the mushrooms, broth, tomato, salt and pepper flakes; simmer, uncovered, for 2 minutes.

2. Drain pasta. Add the pasta and seasonings to skillet; toss to coat. Sprinkle with cheese.

1 serving: 581 cal., 32g fat (6g sat. fat), 89mg chol., 783mg sod., 49g carb. (4g sugars, 3g fiber), 24g pro.

AIR-FRYER COD

This air-fryer cod recipe will convert even the biggest fish skeptic. It's healthy and delicious, and there's no need for breading!
—Kim Russell, North Wales, PA

TAKES: 30 MIN. • **MAKES:** 2 SERVINGS

- ¼ cup fat-free Italian salad dressing
- ½ tsp. sugar
- ⅛ tsp. salt
- ⅛ tsp. garlic powder
- ⅛ tsp. curry powder
- ⅛ tsp. paprika
- ⅛ tsp. pepper
- 2 cod fillets (6 oz. each)
- 2 tsp. butter

1. Preheat air fryer to 370°. In a shallow bowl, mix the first 7 ingredients; add cod, turning to coat. Let stand 10-15 minutes.
2. Place fillets in a single layer on greased tray in air-fryer basket; discard remaining marinade. Cook until the fish just begins to flake easily with a fork, 8-10 minutes. Top with butter.

1 fillet: 168 cal., 5g fat (3g sat. fat), 75mg chol., 366mg sod., 2g carb. (2g sugars, 0 fiber), 27g pro.
Diabetic exchanges: 4 lean meat, 1 fat.

CLASSIC CRAB BOIL

Dig in to Dungeness crab boiled in a special mix of spices.
—Matthew Hass, Ellison Bay, WI

PREP: 10 MIN. • **COOK:** 30 MIN.
MAKES: 2 SERVINGS

- 2 Tbsp. mustard seed
- 2 Tbsp. celery seed
- 1 Tbsp. dill seed
- 1 Tbsp. coriander seeds
- 1 Tbsp. whole allspice
- ½ tsp. whole cloves
- 4 bay leaves
- 8 qt. water
- ¼ cup salt
- ¼ cup lemon juice
- 1 tsp. cayenne pepper
- 2 whole live Dungeness crabs (2 lbs. each)
  Melted butter and lemon wedges

1. Place first 7 ingredients on a double thickness of cheesecloth. Gather corners of cloth to enclose seasonings; tie securely with string.
2. In a large stockpot, bring water, salt, lemon juice, cayenne and spice bag to a boil. Using tongs, add crab to stockpot; return to a boil. Reduce heat; simmer, covered, until shells turn bright red, about 15 minutes.
3. Using tongs, remove crab from pot. Run under cold water or plunge into ice water. Serve with melted butter and lemon wedges.

1 crab: 245 cal., 3g fat (0 sat. fat), 169mg chol., 956mg sod., 2g carb. (0 sugars, 0 fiber), 50g pro.

TEST KITCHEN TIP

If you enjoy whole crab, you may want to invest in a wooden seafood mallet, to crack the large shell, as well as a set of crab crackers and picks for the crab legs.

HOMEMADE FISH STICKS

I am a nutritionist and needed a healthy fish fix. Moist inside and crunchy outside, these are fantastic with oven fries or roasted veggies and homemade low-fat tartar sauce.
—Jennifer Rowland, Elizabethtown, KY

TAKES: 25 MIN. • **MAKES:** 2 SERVINGS

½ cup dry bread crumbs
½ tsp. salt
½ tsp. paprika
½ tsp. lemon-pepper seasoning
½ cup all-purpose flour
1 large egg, beaten
¾ lb. cod fillets, cut into 1-in. strips
     Butter-flavored cooking spray

1. Preheat oven to 400°. In a shallow bowl, mix the bread crumbs and seasonings. Place flour and egg in separate shallow bowls. Dip fish in flour to coat both sides; shake off excess. Dip in the egg, then in the crumb mixture, patting to help coating adhere.
2. Place on a baking sheet coated with cooking spray; spritz with butter-flavored cooking spray. Bake 10-12 minutes or until fish just begins to flake easily with a fork, turning once.
1 serving: 278 cal., 4g fat (1g sat. fat), 129mg chol., 718mg sod., 25g carb. (2g sugars, 1g fiber), 33g pro. **Diabetic exchanges:** 4 lean meat, 1½ starch.

SMOKED SALMON QUESADILLAS WITH CREAMY CHIPOTLE SAUCE

These quesadillas taste extra-special, but they take just minutes to make. A fresh burst of chopped fresh cilantro is the perfect finishing touch.
—Daniel Shemtob, Irvine, CA

TAKES: 25 MIN.
MAKES: 3 SERVINGS (⅔ CUP SAUCE)

½ cup creme fraiche or sour cream
2 Tbsp. minced chipotle peppers in adobo sauce
2 Tbsp. lime juice
⅛ tsp. salt
⅛ tsp. pepper
QUESADILLAS
¼ cup cream cheese, softened
2 oz. fresh goat cheese
3 flour tortillas (8 in.)

3 oz. smoked salmon or lox, chopped
¼ cup finely chopped shallots
¼ cup finely chopped roasted sweet red pepper
     Coarsely chopped fresh cilantro

1. In a small bowl, mix the first 5 ingredients. In another bowl, mix cream cheese and goat cheese until blended; spread over tortillas. Top half side of each with the salmon, shallots and red pepper; fold over.
2. Place quesadillas on a greased griddle. Cook over medium heat until lightly browned and cheeses are melted, 1-2 minutes on each side. Serve with the sauce and top with cilantro.
1 quesadilla with 3 Tbsp. sauce: 453 cal., 28g fat (16g sat. fat), 74mg chol., 1118mg sod., 33g carb. (2g sugars, 0 fiber), 15g pro.

DID YOU KNOW?

Smoked salmon is salmon that has undergone either a hot- or cold-smoking process. Cold-smoking, producing a product called lox, is brined or cured in salt and/or sugar before smoking at 70-90°F temperatures. Hot-smoking is a process in which salmon is smoked for hours in temperatures of 120-180°, producing a firm, flaky texture and a stronger smoky flavor.

FOUR-CHEESE STUFFED SHELLS

More cheese, please! You'll get your fill from these saucy jumbo pasta shells loaded with four kinds—ricotta, Asiago, mozzarella and cottage cheese. Do the prep work, and then freeze according to the recipe directions to have a ready-to-bake meal.
—*Taste of Home* Test Kitchen

PREP: 20 MIN. • **BAKE:** 25 MIN.
MAKES: 2 SERVINGS

- 6 uncooked jumbo pasta shells
- ½ cup shredded part-skim mozzarella cheese, divided
- ¼ cup shredded Asiago cheese
- ¼ cup ricotta cheese
- ¼ cup 4% cottage cheese
- 1 Tbsp. minced chives
- 1 pkg. (10 oz.) frozen chopped spinach, thawed and squeezed dry
- 1 cup meatless spaghetti sauce

1. Preheat oven to 350°. Cook pasta according to package directions. Meanwhile, in a bowl, combine ¼ cup mozzarella cheese, Asiago cheese, ricotta cheese, cottage cheese, chives and ½ cup spinach (save the remaining spinach for another use).
2. Spread ½ cup spaghetti sauce into a shallow 1½-qt. baking dish coated with cooking spray. Drain pasta; stuff with cheese mixture. Arrange in prepared dish. Top with the remaining spaghetti sauce and mozzarella.
3. Baked, covered, until heated through, 25-30 minutes.

Freeze option: Cover and freeze the unbaked casserole. To use, partially thaw in the refrigerator overnight. Remove from refrigerator 30 minutes before baking. Bake at 350° as directed, increasing the time as necessary to heat through and for a thermometer inserted in the center of 2 or 3 shells to read 165°.
3 stuffed shells: 376 cal., 14g fat (9g sat. fat), 49mg chol., 959mg sod., 39g carb. (13g sugars, 4g fiber), 25g pro.

TEST KITCHEN TIP

Serving a meat lover? Tuck cooked meatballs inside a few of the shells along with the cheese mixture. Proceed with the recipe as directed.

PENNE WITH VEGGIES & BLACK BEANS

Brimming with zucchini, tomato, sweet pepper and carrot, this pasta dish puts your garden harvest to good use.
—Vickie Spoerle, Carmel, IN

TAKES: 25 MIN. • **MAKES:** 2 SERVINGS

- ¾ cup uncooked penne pasta
- ⅓ cup sliced zucchini
- ⅓ cup sliced fresh carrot
- 4 medium fresh mushrooms, sliced
- ½ small green pepper, thinly sliced
- ½ small onion, thinly sliced
- 1 small garlic clove, minced
- ¼ tsp. each dried basil, oregano and thyme
- ¼ tsp. salt
- ⅛ tsp. pepper
- 2 tsp. olive oil, divided
- 1 cup canned black beans, rinsed and drained
- ¼ cup chopped seeded tomato
- 2 Tbsp. shredded Parmesan cheese
- 2 tsp. minced fresh parsley

1. Cook pasta according to package directions. Meanwhile, in a large nonstick skillet, saute the zucchini, carrot, mushrooms, green pepper, onion, garlic and seasonings in 1 tsp. oil until crisp-tender. Stir in the beans.
2. Drain pasta; add to the vegetable mixture. Add tomato and remaining olive oil; toss gently. Sprinkle with Parmesan cheese and parsley.

1⅓ cups: 300 cal., 7g fat (2g sat. fat), 4mg chol., 643mg sod., 47g carb. (6g sugars, 8g fiber), 14g pro.

SHEET-PAN TILAPIA & VEGETABLE MEDLEY

Unlike some one-pan dinners that require precooking in a skillet or pot, this one, with fish and spring veggies, uses just the sheet pan—period.
—Judy Batson, Tampa, FL

PREP: 15 MIN. • **BAKE:** 25 MIN.
MAKES: 2 SERVINGS

- 2 medium Yukon Gold potatoes, cut into wedges
- 3 large fresh Brussels sprouts, thinly sliced
- 3 large radishes, thinly sliced
- 1 cup fresh sugar snap peas, cut into ½-in. pieces
- 1 small carrot, thinly sliced
- 2 Tbsp. butter, melted
- ½ tsp. garlic salt
- ½ tsp. pepper
- 2 tilapia fillets (6 oz. each)
- 2 tsp. minced fresh tarragon or ½ tsp. dried tarragon
- ⅛ tsp. salt
- 1 Tbsp. butter, softened
  Optional: Lemon wedges and tartar sauce

1. Preheat oven to 450°. Line a 15x10x1-in. baking pan with foil; grease foil.
2. In a large bowl, combine the first 5 ingredients. Add melted butter, garlic salt and pepper; toss to coat. Place vegetables in a single layer in prepared pan; bake until potatoes are tender, about 20 minutes.
3. Remove from oven; preheat broiler. Arrange vegetables on 1 side of sheet pan. Add fish to other side. Sprinkle fillets with tarragon and salt; dot with softened butter. Broil 4-5 in. from heat until fish flakes easily with a fork, about 5 minutes. If desired, serve with lemon wedges and tartar sauce.

1 serving: 555 cal., 20g fat (12g sat. fat), 129mg chol., 892mg sod., 56g carb. (8g sugars, 8g fiber), 41g pro.

NAKED FISH TACOS

This is one of my husband's all-time favorite meals. I've even converted some friends to fish after eating this. I serve it with fresh melon when it's in season to balance the subtle heat of the cabbage mixture.
—Elizabeth Bramkamp, Gig Harbor, WA

TAKES: 25 MIN. • **MAKES:** 2 SERVINGS

- 1 cup coleslaw mix
- ¼ cup chopped fresh cilantro
- 1 green onion, sliced
- 1 tsp. chopped seeded jalapeno pepper
- 4 tsp. canola oil, divided
- 2 tsp. lime juice
- ½ tsp. ground cumin
- ½ tsp. salt, divided
- ¼ tsp. pepper, divided
- 2 tilapia fillets (6 oz. each)
- ½ medium ripe avocado, peeled and sliced

1. Place the first 4 ingredients in a bowl; toss with 2 tsp. oil, lime juice, cumin, ¼ tsp. salt and ⅛ tsp. pepper. Refrigerate until serving.
2. Pat fillets dry with paper towels; sprinkle with the remaining salt and pepper. In a large nonstick skillet, heat remaining 2 tsp. oil over medium-high heat; cook tilapia until fish just begins to flake easily with a fork, 3-4 minutes per side. Top with slaw and avocado.
1 serving: 293 cal., 16g fat (2g sat. fat), 83mg chol., 663mg sod., 6g carb. (1g sugars, 3g fiber), 33g pro. **Diabetic exchanges:** 5 lean meat, 3 fat, 1 vegetable.

GREEK BROWN & WILD RICE BOWLS

This fresh rice dish tastes like the Mediterranean in a bowl! It's short on ingredients but packs in so much flavor. For a hand-held version, leave out the rice and tuck the rest of the ingredients in a pita pocket.
—Darla Andrews, Boerne, TX

TAKES: 15 MIN. • **MAKES:** 2 SERVINGS

- 1 pkg. (8½ oz.) ready-to-serve whole grain brown and wild rice medley
- ¼ cup Greek vinaigrette, divided
- ½ medium ripe avocado, peeled and sliced
- ¾ cup cherry tomatoes, halved
- ¼ cup crumbled feta cheese
- ¼ cup pitted Greek olives, sliced
  Minced fresh parsley, optional

In a microwave-safe bowl, combine the rice mix and 2 Tbsp. vinaigrette. Cover and cook on high until heated through, about 2 minutes. Divide between 2 bowls. Top with avocado, tomatoes, cheese, olives, remaining dressing and, if desired, parsley.
1 serving: 433 cal., 25g fat (4g sat. fat), 8mg chol., 1355mg sod., 44g carb. (3g sugars, 6g fiber), 8g pro.

HEALTH TIP

These otherwise healthy bowls are high in sodium because of the prepared rice, dressing, feta cheese and Greek olives. Cut the salt by preparing the rice from scratch and using a simple oil-and-vinegar salad dressing.

4 oz. uncooked angel hair pasta
¼ cup plus 1 Tbsp. chopped fresh parsley, divided
2 large garlic cloves, minced
¼ to ½ tsp. crushed red pepper flakes
¼ tsp. salt
2 Tbsp. grapeseed oil

1. Pat shrimp and scallops dry; sprinkle with seafood seasoning.
2. In a small skillet, melt 1 Tbsp. butter over medium heat. Cook and stir mushrooms about 3 minutes. Add peas; cook until vegetables are tender, about 3-4 minutes. Remove. Add shallots and 1 Tbsp. butter; cook and stir until shallots start to soften, 1-2 minutes. Stir in the wine; reduce heat to medium-low and simmer, uncovered, until ready to serve.
3. Meanwhile, in a large saucepan, cook pasta according to package directions; drain, reserving ½ cup pasta water. Return pasta to pan. Over low heat, stir in ¼ cup parsley, garlic, red pepper flakes, salt, mushroom mixture and remaining 1 Tbsp. butter, adding enough reserved pasta water to moisten.
4. In a large skillet, heat the oil over medium-high heat. Add scallops and shrimp; sear until scallops are golden brown and firm and shrimp turn pink, about 2-3 minutes on each side. Combine with pasta and sauce; sprinkle with remaining 1 Tbsp. parsley.
1 serving: 733 cal., 35g fat (13g sat. fat), 210mg chol., 1263mg sod., 56g carb. (3g sugars, 3g fiber), 47g pro.

TEST KITCHEN TIP

It is never a bad idea to rinse scallops in cold water prior to cooking. Pat them dry with a paper towel before proceeding with the recipe.

SAUTEED SCALLOPS & SHRIMP PASTA

I created this tempting seafood pasta for my wife. If you don't like spice, skip the red pepper flakes.
—George Levinthal, Goleta, CA

TAKES: 30 MIN. • **MAKES:** 2 SERVINGS

8 uncooked shrimp (16-20 per lb.), peeled and deveined
6 sea scallops (about 12 oz.)
½ tsp. seafood seasoning
3 Tbsp. unsalted butter, divided
1½ cups (about 3 to 4 oz.) small fresh mushrooms, halved
½ cup frozen peas, thawed
¼ cup finely chopped shallots
⅓ cup white wine or chicken broth

PERSONAL MARGHERITA PIZZAS

This family-friendly supper is simplicity at its finest. Fresh mozzarella and a sprinkling of basil give these little pies Italian flair.
—Jerry Gulley, Pleasant Prairie, WI

TAKES: 25 MIN. • **MAKES:** 3 SERVINGS

- 1 pkg. (6½ oz.) pizza crust mix
- ½ tsp. dried oregano
- ¾ cup pizza sauce
- 6 oz. fresh mozzarella cheese, thinly sliced
- ¼ cup thinly sliced fresh basil leaves

1. Preheat oven to 425°. Prepare pizza dough according to package directions, adding oregano before mixing. Divide into 3 portions.
2. Pat each portion of dough into an 8-in. circle on greased baking sheets. Bake until edges are lightly browned, 8-10 minutes.
3. Spread each crust with ¼ cup pizza sauce to within ½ in. of edge. Top with mozzarella cheese. Bake until crust is golden and cheese is melted, 5-10 minutes longer. Sprinkle with basil.

1 pizza: 407 cal., 15g fat (8g sat. fat), 45mg chol., 675mg sod., 48g carb. (7g sugars, 3g fiber), 18g pro.

COMFORTING TUNA CASSEROLE

My mother gave me the recipe for this classic casserole many years ago. Sometimes I use sliced stuffed olives instead of pimientos.
—Dorothy Coleman, Hobe Sound, FL

PREP: 15 MIN. • **BAKE:** 20 MIN.
MAKES: 2 SERVINGS

- 1¾ cups uncooked wide egg noodles
- 6 tsp. reduced-fat butter, divided
- 4 tsp. all-purpose flour
- ¼ tsp. salt
  Dash pepper
- ¾ cup 2% milk
- 3 oz. reduced-fat cream cheese
- 1 pouch (2½ oz.) albacore white tuna in water
- 2 Tbsp. diced pimientos
- 2 tsp. minced chives
- 2 slices Muenster cheese (¾ oz. each)
- 2 Tbsp. soft bread crumbs

1. Cook egg noodles according to package directions. Meanwhile, in a small saucepan over medium heat, melt 5 tsp. butter. Stir in the flour, salt and pepper until blended; gradually add the milk. Bring to a boil over medium heat; cook and stir 1-2 minutes or until thickened. Reduce heat to medium-low; add the cream cheese, tuna, pimientos and chives. Cook and stir until the cheese is melted.
2. Drain noodles. Spread ¼ cup tuna mixture into a 3-cup baking dish coated with cooking spray. Layer with half of the noodles, ½ cup tuna mixture and 1 slice of cheese. Repeat layers.
3. Microwave the remaining 1 tsp. butter on high, stirring every 30 seconds; stir in bread crumbs. Sprinkle over top of casserole. Bake, uncovered, at 350° for 20-25 minutes or until bubbly.

1½ cups: 493 cal., 26g fat (15g sat. fat), 118mg chol., 941mg sod., 37g carb. (7g sugars, 2g fiber), 28g pro.

TEST KITCHEN TIP

To make soft bread crumbs, tear bread into pieces and place in a food processor or blender. Cover and pulse until crumbs form. One slice of bread yields ½ to ¾ cup crumbs.

TILAPIA WITH JASMINE RICE

This tender, full-flavored tilapia with fragrant jasmine rice is absolutely to die for.
—Shirl Parsons, Cape Carteret, NC

TAKES: 25 MIN. • **MAKES:** 2 SERVINGS

- ¾ cup water
- ½ cup uncooked jasmine rice
- 1½ tsp. butter
- ¼ tsp. ground cumin
- ¼ tsp. seafood seasoning
- ¼ tsp. pepper
- ⅛ tsp. salt
- 2 tilapia fillets (6 oz. each)
- ¼ cup Italian salad dressing

1. In a small saucepan, combine water, rice and butter; bring to a boil. Reduce heat; simmer, covered, until liquid is absorbed and rice is tender, 15-20 minutes.
2. Meanwhile, mix the seasonings; sprinkle over the tilapia. In a large skillet, heat salad dressing over medium heat until hot. Add fillets; cook until fish just begins to flake easily with a fork, 3-4 minutes per side. Serve with rice.

1 fillet with ¾ cup rice: 412 cal., 9g fat (3g sat. fat), 90mg chol., 615mg sod., 42g carb. (2g sugars, 1g fiber), 36g pro. **Diabetic exchanges:** 4 lean meat, 3 starch, ½ fat.

SLOW-COOKER VEGGIE LASAGNA

This veggie-licious alternative to traditional lasagna makes use of slow-cooker convenience. I suggest using chunky spaghetti sauce.
—Laura Davister, Little Suamico, WI

PREP: 25 MIN. • **COOK:** 3½ HOURS
MAKES: 2 SERVINGS

- ½ cup shredded part-skim mozzarella cheese
- 3 Tbsp. 1% cottage cheese
- 2 Tbsp. grated Parmesan cheese
- 2 Tbsp. egg substitute
- ½ tsp. Italian seasoning
- ⅛ tsp. garlic powder
- ¾ cup meatless spaghetti sauce
- ½ cup sliced zucchini
- 2 no-cook lasagna noodles
- 4 cups fresh baby spinach
- ½ cup sliced fresh mushrooms

1. Cut two 18x3-in. strips of heavy-duty foil; crisscross so they resemble an X. Place strips on bottom and up sides of a 1½-qt. slow cooker. Coat the strips with cooking spray.
2. In a small bowl, combine the first 6 ingredients. Spread 1 Tbsp. of spaghetti sauce on the bottom of prepared slow cooker. Top with half of the zucchini and a third of the cheese mixture.
3. Break noodles into 1-in. pieces; sprinkle half of the the noodles over the cheese mixture. Spread with 1 Tbsp. sauce. Top with half of the spinach and half of the mushrooms. Repeat layers. Top with remaining cheese mixture and sauce.
4. Cover and cook on low until noodles are tender, 3½-4 hours.

1 piece: 259 cal., 8g fat (4g sat. fat), 23mg chol., 859mg sod., 29g carb. (9g sugars, 4g fiber), 19g pro. **Diabetic exchanges:** 2 lean meat, 2 medium-fat meat, 1½ starch, 1 vegetable, ½ fat.

BALSAMIC-SALMON SPINACH SALAD

This spinach salad is really healthy and super fast. It's an absolute cinch to make after a long day.
—Karen Schlyter, Calgary, AB

TAKES: 20 MIN. • **MAKES:** 2 SERVINGS

- 1 **salmon fillet (6 oz.)**
- 2 **Tbsp. balsamic vinaigrette, divided**
- 3 **cups fresh baby spinach**
- ¼ **cup cubed avocado**
- 1 **Tbsp. chopped walnuts, toasted**
- 1 **Tbsp. sunflower kernels, toasted**
- 1 **Tbsp. dried cranberries**

1. Drizzle the salmon with 1 Tbsp. vinaigrette. Place on a broiler pan coated with cooking spray. Broil 3-4 in. from heat 10-15 minutes or until fish flakes easily with a fork. Cut salmon into 2 pieces.
2. Meanwhile, in a large bowl, toss the spinach with remaining 1 Tbsp. of vinaigrette. Divide spinach between 2 plates. Top with salmon, avocado, walnuts, sunflower kernels and cranberries.

1 salad: 265 cal., 18g fat (3g sat. fat), 43mg chol., 261mg sod., 10g carb. (4g sugars, 3g fiber), 18g pro. **Diabetic exchanges:** 2 medium-fat meat, 2 fat, 1 vegetable.

SEARED SCALLOPS WITH CITRUS HERB SAUCE

Be sure to pat the raw scallops with a paper towel to remove any excess moisture. This helps create perfectly browned and flavorful scallops.
—April Lane, Greeneville, TN

TAKES: 20 MIN. • **MAKES:** 2 SERVINGS

- ¾ **lb. sea scallops**
- ¼ **tsp. salt**
- ¼ **tsp. pepper**
- ⅛ **tsp. paprika**
- 3 **Tbsp. butter, divided**
- 1 **garlic clove, minced**
- 2 **Tbsp. dry sherry or chicken broth**
- 1 **Tbsp. lemon juice**
- ⅛ **tsp. minced fresh oregano**
- ⅛ **tsp. minced fresh tarragon**

1. Pat scallops dry with paper towels; sprinkle with salt, pepper and paprika. In a large skillet, heat 2 Tbsp. butter over medium-high heat. Add the scallops; sear for 1-2 minutes on each side or until golden brown and firm. Remove from the skillet; keep warm.
2. Wipe skillet clean if necessary. Saute garlic in remaining 1 Tbsp. butter until tender; stir in sherry. Cook until the liquid is almost evaporated; stir in the remaining ingredients. Serve with scallops.

3 scallops with 1½ tsp. sauce: 314 cal., 18g fat (11g sat. fat), 101mg chol., 691mg sod., 6g carb. (0 sugars, 0 fiber), 29g pro.

DID YOU KNOW?

A member of the bivalve mollusk family, scallops are commonly found in 2 groups: the sea scallop, yielding 10-20 per pound, and the much smaller bay scallop, which yield between 60 and 90 per pound. Scallops are usually available shucked, sold fresh or frozen and range in color from pale beige to creamy pink. Scallops can be broiled, grilled, pan-fried or deep-fried and cook in a matter of minutes.

FRESH CORN & TOMATO FETTUCCINE

This recipe combines delicious whole wheat pasta with the best of fresh garden produce. It's tossed with heart-healthy olive oil, and a little feta cheese gives it bite.
—Angela Spengler, Niceville, FL

TAKES: 30 MIN. • **MAKES:** 4 SERVINGS

- 8 oz. uncooked whole wheat fettuccine
- 2 medium ears sweet corn, husked
- 2 tsp. plus 2 Tbsp. olive oil, divided
- ½ cup chopped sweet red pepper
- 4 green onions, chopped
- 2 medium tomatoes, chopped
- ½ tsp. salt
- ½ tsp. pepper
- 1 cup crumbled feta cheese
- 2 Tbsp. minced fresh parsley

1. In a Dutch oven, cook fettuccine according to package directions, adding corn during last 8 minutes of cooking.
2. Meanwhile, in a small skillet, heat 2 tsp. oil over medium-high heat. Add red pepper and green onions; cook and stir until tender.
3. Drain pasta and corn; transfer pasta to a large bowl. Cool corn slightly; cut corn from cob and add to pasta. Add tomatoes, salt, pepper, the remaining 2 Tbsp. oil and the pepper mixture; toss to combine. Sprinkle with cheese and parsley.

2 cups: 527 cal., 17g fat (5g sat. fat), 84mg chol., 1051mg sod., 75g carb. (7g sugars, 9g fiber), 21g pro.

COCONUT CURRY SHRIMP

Here's a shrimp dish with sweet coconut milk, complemented by the spiciness of curry. Jasmine rice makes a fragrant bed for the sumptuous stir-fry.
—Cindy Romberg, Mississauga, ON

TAKES: 25 MIN. • **MAKES:** 3 SERVINGS

- ⅔ cup coconut milk
- 1 Tbsp. fish sauce
- 1½ tsp. curry powder
- 1 tsp. brown sugar
- ¼ tsp. salt
- ¼ tsp. pepper
- 1 lb. uncooked large shrimp, peeled and deveined
- 1 medium sweet red pepper, finely chopped
- 2 green onions, chopped
- ¼ cup minced fresh cilantro
  Hot cooked jasmine rice
  Lime wedges

1. In a small bowl, combine first 6 ingredients. In a large skillet or wok, stir-fry the shrimp in 2 Tbsp. coconut milk mixture until shrimp turn pink. Remove and keep warm.
2. Add red pepper, green onions and remaining coconut milk mixture to pan. Bring to a boil; cook and stir for 3-4 minutes or until vegetables are crisp-tender. Add the shrimp and cilantro; heat through. Serve with rice and lime wedges.

1 cup: 256 cal., 13g fat (10g sat. fat), 184mg chol., 841mg sod., 8g carb. (4g sugars, 2g fiber), 27g pro.

DID YOU KNOW?

Curry powder is a blend of many different ground spices used to replicate the individual spices combined in the cuisine of India. It imparts a distinctive flavor and rich golden color to recipes and can be found in both mild and spicy versions.

GINGER SALMON WITH GREEN BEANS

I developed this flavor-packed dinner for a busy friend who wants to eat clean with little fuss.
—Nicole Stevens, Charleston, SC

TAKES: 30 MIN. • **MAKES:** 2 SERVINGS

- ¼ cup lemon juice
- 2 Tbsp. rice vinegar
- 3 garlic cloves, minced
- 2 tsp. minced fresh gingerroot
- 2 tsp. honey
- ⅛ tsp. salt
- ⅛ tsp. pepper
- 2 salmon fillets (4 oz. each)
- 1 medium lemon, thinly sliced

GREEN BEANS
- ¾ lb. fresh green beans, trimmed
- 2 Tbsp. water
- 2 tsp. olive oil
- ½ cup finely chopped onion
- 3 garlic cloves, minced
- ⅛ tsp. salt

1. Preheat oven to 325°. Mix first 7 ingredients.
2. Place each salmon fillet on an 18x12-in. piece of heavy-duty foil; fold up edges of foil to create a rim around the fish. Spoon lemon juice mixture over salmon; top with the lemon slices. Carefully fold the foil around fish, sealing tightly.
3. Place packets in a 15x10x1-in. pan. Bake 15-20 minutes or until the fish just begins to flake easily with a fork. Open foil carefully to allow steam to escape.
4. Meanwhile, place beans, water and oil in a large skillet; bring to a boil. Reduce the heat; simmer, covered, for 5 minutes. Stir in remaining ingredients; cook, uncovered, until the beans are crisp-tender, stirring occasionally. Serve with salmon.

1 serving: 357 cal., 15g fat (3g sat. fat), 57mg chol., 607mg sod., 35g carb. (18g sugars, 8g fiber), 24g pro.
Diabetic exchanges: 3 lean meat, 1 starch, 1 vegetable, 1 fat.

TEST KITCHEN TIP

The green beans make this a meal-in-one lifesaver. Round out the menu with some brown rice, red potatoes or a few slices of crusty bread.

AIR-FRYER SCALLOPS

I never liked seafood until my husband urged me to try scallops, and now I love them. With the crunchy breading, my air-fryer scallops are the best you'll ever have.
—Martina Preston, Willow Grove, PA

TAKES: 25 MIN. • **MAKES:** 2 SERVINGS

- 1 **large egg**
- ⅓ **cup mashed potato flakes**
- ⅓ **cup seasoned bread crumbs**
- ⅛ **tsp. salt**
- ⅛ **tsp. pepper**
- 6 **sea scallops (about ¾ lb.), patted dry**
- 2 **Tbsp. all-purpose flour Butter-flavored cooking spray**

1. Preheat air fryer to 400°. In a shallow bowl, lightly beat egg. In another bowl, toss potato flakes, bread crumbs, salt and pepper. In a third bowl, toss scallops with flour to coat lightly. Dip in egg, then in potato mixture, patting to adhere.
2. Arrange scallops in a single layer on greased tray in air-fryer basket; spritz with cooking spray. Cook until golden brown, 3-4 minutes. Turn; spritz with cooking spray. Cook until the breading is golden brown and scallops are firm and opaque, 3-4 minutes longer.

3 scallops: 298 cal., 5g fat (1g sat. fat), 134mg chol., 1138mg sod., 33g carb. (2g sugars, 2g fiber), 28g pro.

TUNA TACOS WITH MANGO-PINEAPPLE SALSA

This tastes amazing! Plus, it's quick, fresh and healthy.
—Sunee James, Altadena, CA

PREP: 25 MIN. • **GRILL:** 10 MIN.
MAKES: 2 SERVINGS

- ½ **cup chopped peeled mango**
- ½ **cup cubed avocado**
- ⅓ **cup cubed fresh pineapple**
- 4½ **tsp. chopped seeded jalapeno pepper**

DRESSING

- 3 **Tbsp. sour cream**
- 1 **Tbsp. lime juice**
- 1 **Tbsp. light coconut milk**
- ¼ **tsp. ground ginger**
  Dash salt
  Dash paprika

TUNA

- 2 **tuna steaks (6 oz. each)**
- 1 **Tbsp. lime juice**
- ¼ **tsp. salt**
- ¼ **tsp. pepper**
- 4 **corn tortillas (6 in.)**

1. In a small bowl, combine the mango, avocado, pineapple and jalapeno. Chill until serving.
2. In a bowl, combine the dressing ingredients. Chill until serving.
3. Brush the tuna with lime juice; sprinkle with salt and pepper. For medium-rare, grill tuna, covered, over high heat on a lightly oiled grill rack or broil 3-4 in. from heat for 3-4 minutes on each side or until slightly pink in the center.
4. Cut tuna into bite-size pieces. Spoon salsa on tortillas; top with tuna and dressing.

Note: Wear disposable gloves when cutting hot peppers; the oils can burn skin. Avoid touching your face.
2 tacos: 456 cal., 13g fat (5g sat. fat), 92mg chol., 528mg sod., 40g carb. (11g sugars, 6g fiber), 45g pro.
Diabetic exchanges: 5 lean meat, 2 starch, 1½ fat, ½ fruit.

DID YOU KNOW?

Coconut milk is a sweet milky white liquid high in oil derived from the meat of a mature coconut. In the United States, coconut milk is usually purchased in cans and used in both savory and sweet dishes.

SALADS

Keep the huge serving bowls in the cupboard—no supersize
salads here! These reduced recipes make it a snap to toss
together a refreshing side or even a leafy-green entree.

SPECIAL FRUIT SALAD

Dress up a sweet fruit salad with a creamy drizzle of citrusy flavor.
—Alice Orton, Big Bear Lake, CA

PREP: 10 MIN. + CHILLING
MAKES: 2 SERVINGS

- 1 snack-sized cup (4 oz.) pineapple tidbits
- 1/3 cup chopped apple
- 1/3 cup cubed cantaloupe
- 10 green grapes, halved
- 6 fresh strawberries, quartered
- 1 medium kiwifruit, peeled and sliced

DRESSING

- 2 Tbsp. mayonnaise
- 2 Tbsp. sour cream
- 1½ tsp. sugar
- 1 tsp. orange juice
- ¼ tsp. lemon juice
- ¼ tsp. grated lemon or orange zest

1. Drain pineapple, reserving 1 tsp. juice. In a salad bowl, combine the pineapple, apple, cantaloupe, grapes, strawberries and kiwi.
2. In a small bowl, combine the dressing ingredients; add the 1 tsp. reserved pineapple juice and mix well. Refrigerate fruit and dressing until chilled.
3. Just before serving, pour the dressing over fruit and toss to coat.
1 cup: 136 cal., 2g fat (1g sat. fat), 7mg chol., 140mg sod., 28g carb. (22g sugars, 4g fiber), 3g pro.

THAI SHRIMP SALAD

This distinctive salad blends grilled shrimp, a lean source of protein, with the low-calorie crunch of cucumber and onion. It's tossed and dressed with classic Thai flavors—sesame, cilantro, lime and refreshing mint.
—Annette Traverso, San Rafael, CA

PREP: 25 MIN. • **GRILL:** 10 MIN.
MAKES: 2 SERVINGS

- 2 Tbsp. lime juice
- 1 Tbsp. sesame oil
- 1 Tbsp. reduced-sodium soy sauce
- 1½ tsp. sesame seeds, toasted
- 1½ tsp. minced fresh mint
- 1½ tsp. minced fresh cilantro

- Dash crushed red pepper flakes
- ½ lb. uncooked large shrimp, peeled and deveined
- ⅛ tsp. salt
- ⅛ tsp. pepper
- ½ large sweet onion, sliced
- ½ medium cucumber, peeled and sliced
- 2 cups torn leaf lettuce

1. Combine the first 7 ingredients; set aside. Sprinkle shrimp with salt and pepper; thread onto 2 metal or soaked wooden skewers.
2. Place the skewers on a lightly oiled grill rack; grill, covered, over medium heat (or broil 4 in. from the heat) until shrimp turn pink, 2-4 minutes.
3. Stir the dressing; add the shrimp, onion and cucumber. Toss to coat. Divide lettuce between 2 salad plates; top with shrimp mixture and serve immediately.
1 serving: 212 cal., 9g fat (1g sat. fat), 138mg chol., 614mg sod., 11g carb. (4g sugars, 3g fiber), 21g pro. **Diabetic exchanges:** 3 lean meat, 2 vegetable, 1½ fat.

CRANBERRY-SESAME SPINACH SALAD

For a feast or any occasion, we love this snappy fall salad that balances sweet and sour with a great crunch from almonds and sesame seeds.
—Stephanie Smoley, Rochester, MN

TAKES: 25 MIN. • **MAKES:** 2 SERVINGS

- 1 tsp. butter
- 2 Tbsp. slivered almonds
- 2½ cups fresh baby spinach
- 2 Tbsp. dried cranberries

DRESSING
- 2 Tbsp. canola oil
- 1 Tbsp. sugar
- 1 Tbsp. cider vinegar
- 2 tsp. toasted sesame seeds
- ½ tsp. dried minced onion
- ½ tsp. poppy seeds
- ⅛ tsp. salt
  Dash paprika

1. In a small skillet, melt butter over medium heat. Add the almonds; cook and stir until lightly browned. Remove from heat.
2. Place spinach and cranberries in a medium bowl. In a small bowl, whisk dressing ingredients until blended. Add to salad and toss to coat. Divide between 2 bowls. Sprinkle with toasted almonds. Serve immediately.

1¼ cups: 257 cal., 21g fat (3g sat. fat), 5mg chol., 207mg sod., 16g carb. (12g sugars, 3g fiber), 3g pro.

NUTTY GREEN SALAD

If you're looking for a deliciously different summery salad, you'll definitely want to try this light curry-orange dressing!
—Barbara Robbins, Chandler, AZ

TAKES: 10 MIN. • **MAKES:** 2 SERVINGS

- 2 cups spring mix salad greens
- 1 medium carrot, shredded
- 8 pecan halves, chopped

CURRY CITRUS DRESSING
- 2 Tbsp. orange juice
- 2 tsp. canola oil
- 1 tsp. balsamic vinegar
- ¼ tsp. curry powder
  Dash salt
  Dash pepper

In a bowl, combine salad greens, carrot and pecans. In a jar with a tight-fitting lid, combine the dressing ingredients; shake well. Drizzle over salad and toss to coat.
1 serving: 112 cal., 9g fat (1g sat. fat), 0 chol., 99mg sod., 8g carb. (4g sugars, 3g fiber), 2g pro. **Diabetic exchanges:** 1½ vegetable, 1½ fat.

BLACK-EYED PEA SALAD

This is my little spin on plain boiled black-eyed peas. I like to "eat the rainbow," so I add lots of color with yellow corn, purplish onion and bright red tomatoes.
—Susan Hinton, Apex, NC

PREP: 5 MIN. • **COOK:** 45 MIN.
MAKES: 2 SERVINGS

- 1 cup frozen black-eyed peas
- 1 cup fresh or frozen corn, thawed
- 2 Tbsp. finely chopped red onion
- 4½ tsp. cider vinegar
- 1 tsp. olive oil
- ½ tsp. Dijon mustard
- ¼ tsp. sugar
- ¼ tsp. salt
- ¼ tsp. pepper
  Tomato slices, optional

1. Cook peas according to package directions; drain. In a salad bowl, combine the peas, corn and onion.
2. In a small bowl, whisk vinegar, oil, mustard, sugar, salt and pepper. Pour over vegetables and toss to coat. Serve warm or chilled, with tomato slices if desired.
¾ cup: 205 cal., 4g fat (1g sat. fat), 0 chol., 343mg sod., 37g carb. (6g sugars, 6g fiber), 10g pro.

BALSAMIC TOSSED SALAD

You can toss this tasty salad together in 10 minutes flat. Just drizzle bottled dressing over the colorful blend of greens, tomato and peppers, add a quick sprinkle of cheese and serve!
—*Taste of Home* Test Kitchen

TAKES: 10 MIN. • **MAKES:** 2 SERVINGS

2 cups torn mixed salad greens
1 plum tomato, cut into wedges
½ cup chopped sweet yellow pepper
2 Tbsp. balsamic vinaigrette
2 Tbsp. shredded Asiago cheese

In a small serving bowl, combine the salad greens, tomato and yellow pepper. Drizzle with vinaigrette and toss to coat. Sprinkle with cheese.
1 cup: 72 cal., 4g fat (1g sat. fat), 4mg chol., 169mg sod., 7g carb. (3g sugars, 2g fiber), 4g pro. **Diabetic exchanges:** 1 vegetable, 1 fat.

RHUBARB-STRAWBERRY GELATIN MOLDS

A neighbor with a very large, beautiful rhubarb and strawberry patch gave me one of her favorite recipes. It quickly became one of my favorites as well!
—Janice Wiebelt, Hartville, OH

PREP: 15 MIN. + CHILLING
MAKES: 2 SERVINGS

1 cup diced fresh or frozen rhubarb
¼ cup water
1 Tbsp. sugar
3 Tbsp. plus 1 tsp. strawberry gelatin
¼ cup sliced fresh strawberries
¼ cup orange juice
¼ tsp. grated orange zest
   Whipped cream, optional

1. In a small saucepan over medium heat, bring the rhubarb, water and sugar to a boil. Reduce heat; simmer, uncovered, for 3-5 minutes or until rhubarb is tender. Remove from the heat; stir in gelatin until dissolved. Add the strawberries, orange juice and zest.
2. Divide between two 4-in. mini fluted pans coated with cooking spray; refrigerate for 4 hours or until firm.
3. Just before serving, invert molds onto serving plates; garnish with whipped cream if desired.
1 serving: 143 cal., 0 fat (0 sat. fat), 0 chol., 56mg sod., 34g carb. (31g sugars, 2g fiber), 3g pro. **Diabetic exchanges:** 1½ starch, ½ fruit.

DID YOU KNOW?

Wet the surface of a plate before inverting a gelatin mold onto it; this lets the gelatin slide and makes it easier to center. Blot excess moisture with a paper towel.

QUICK MACARONI SALAD

You can't go wrong with this time-tested winner. It's a staple at parties and potlucks, but here it is scaled down for small households.
—Carma Blosser, Livermore, CO

TAKES: 20 MIN. + CHILLING
MAKES: 2 SERVINGS

- ¾ cup uncooked elbow macaroni
- ⅓ cup frozen peas
- ⅓ cup cubed cheddar cheese
- ¼ cup mayonnaise
- 3 Tbsp. chopped celery
- 1 tsp. finely chopped onion
- 1 tsp. diced pimientos
- 1 tsp. finely chopped green pepper
- ⅛ tsp. salt

1. Cook macaroni according to package directions, adding peas during last 2 minutes of cooking. Drain and rinse pasta and peas in cold water.
2. In a small bowl, combine the remaining ingredients. Stir in the macaroni and peas. Chill until serving.
1 cup: 276 cal., 15g fat (4g sat. fat), 24mg chol., 544mg sod., 28g carb. (4g sugars, 2g fiber), 10g pro.

TRAIL MIX APPLE SALAD

I created this salad as a way to make use of the many wonderful apple varieties available in the fall. It's also a great way to add healthy nuts and seeds to your diet.
—Melissa Boyle, Duluth, MN

TAKES: 20 MIN. • **MAKES:** 2 SERVINGS

- 1 medium apple, coarsely chopped
- ¾ tsp. lemon juice
- 2 Tbsp. chopped walnuts
- 1 Tbsp. sunflower kernels
- 1 Tbsp. dried cranberries
- 2 tsp. honey
- 1 tsp. flaxseed
- ⅛ tsp. ground cinnamon

In a small bowl, combine the apple and lemon juice. Add remaining ingredients; toss to coat. Chill until serving.
¾ cup: 151 cal., 7g fat (1g sat. fat), 0 chol., 19mg sod., 21g carb. (16g sugars, 3g fiber), 3g pro. **Diabetic exchanges:** 1 starch, 1 fat, ½ fruit.

SUNFLOWER BROCCOLI SALAD

This salad is so refreshing—we always make sure to get every last bit from the bowl.
—Marilyn Newcomer, Sun City, CA

PREP: 20 MIN. + CHILLING
MAKES: 2 SERVINGS

- 2 cups fresh broccoli florets
- 2 bacon strips, cooked and crumbled
- 1 green onion, chopped
- 3 Tbsp. raisins
- 1 Tbsp. sunflower kernels

DRESSING

- ⅓ cup mayonnaise
- 4 tsp. sugar
- 2 tsp. white vinegar

In a bowl, combine the broccoli, bacon, onion, raisins and sunflower kernels. In a small bowl, combine the dressing ingredients; stir until smooth. Pour dressing over the broccoli mixture and toss gently. Cover and refrigerate for at least 2 hours before serving, stirring occasionally.

1 cup: 290 cal., 19g fat (3g sat. fat), 19mg chol., 464mg sod., 27g carb. (21g sugars, 3g fiber), 6g pro.

NICOISE SALAD

This garden-fresh salad is a feast for the eyes as well as the palate. Add some crusty bread, and you have a mouthwatering meal.
—Marla Fogderud, Mason, MI

PREP: 40 MIN. + COOLING
MAKES: 2 SERVINGS

- ⅓ cup olive oil
- 3 Tbsp. white wine vinegar
- 1½ tsp. Dijon mustard
- ⅛ tsp. each salt, onion powder and pepper

SALAD

- 2 small red potatoes
- ½ cup cut fresh green beans
- 3½ cups torn Bibb lettuce
- ½ cup cherry tomatoes, halved
- 10 Greek olives, pitted and halved
- 2 hard-boiled large eggs, quartered
- 1 can (5 oz.) albacore white tuna in water, drained and flaked

1. In a small bowl, whisk the oil, vinegar, mustard, salt, onion powder and pepper; set aside.
2. Place the potatoes in a small saucepan and cover with water. Bring to a boil. Reduce heat; simmer, covered, until tender, 15-20 minutes. Drain and cool; cut into quarters.
3. Place beans in another saucepan and cover with water. Bring to a boil. Cover and cook until crisp-tender, 3-5 minutes; drain and rinse in cold water.
4. Divide lettuce between 2 salad plates; top with potatoes, beans, tomatoes, olives, eggs and tuna. Drizzle with dressing.

1 serving: 613 cal., 49g fat (8g sat. fat), 242mg chol., 886mg sod., 18g carb. (3g sugars, 3g fiber), 26g pro.

RADISH & GARBANZO BEAN SALAD

This recipe came about when we had a surprise visit from relatives. I didn't have time to get to the grocery store so I worked with what I had on hand—a can of chickpeas and fresh produce from my garden.
—Grace Struthers, Calgary, AB

PREP: 15 MIN. + CHILLING
MAKES: 3 SERVINGS

- 1   can (15 oz.) garbanzo beans or chickpeas, rinsed and drained
- 6   radishes, halved and thinly sliced
- ¼   cup chopped red onion
- 2   Tbsp. minced fresh parsley
- ¼   cup prepared Italian salad dressing

In a small bowl, combine the beans, radishes, onion and parsley. Drizzle with dressing; toss to coat. Cover and refrigerate for at least 1 hour before serving.
¾ cup: 211 cal., 10g fat (1g sat. fat), 0 chol., 525mg sod., 25g carb. (5g sugars, 6g fiber), 6g pro.

KIDNEY BEAN SALAD

My daughter's friend made this as a side dish, but it's hearty enough to enjoy as a light lunch or even a dinner entree.
—Zelma McKinney, Amarillo, TX

TAKES: 15 MIN. • **MAKES:** 2 SERVINGS

- 1   can (16 oz.) kidney beans, rinsed and drained
- 2   hard-boiled large eggs, chopped
- ½   cup sliced celery
- 1   small onion, chopped
- ¼   cup mayonnaise
- ¼   cup dill pickle relish
- ½   tsp. pepper
- ¼   tsp. salt
     Leaf lettuce, optional

In a bowl, combine all ingredients except the lettuce; stir until coated. Refrigerate until serving. Serve in a lettuce-lined bowl if desired.
1½ cups: 532 cal., 28g fat (5g sat. fat), 222mg chol., 1227mg sod., 51g carb. (16g sugars, 13g fiber), 21g pro.

TURKEY SPINACH SALAD WITH MAPLE DRESSING

My husband and I love to hike in New England. We always bring some Vermont maple syrup home with us to extend the vacation spirit. This recipe reminds us of those lovely days.
—Jessica Gerschitz, Jericho, NY

TAKES: 15 MIN. • **MAKES:** 2 SERVINGS

- 6   oz. fresh baby spinach (about 7 cups)
- ¼   lb. sliced deli smoked turkey, cut into strips
- ⅔   cup sliced baby portobello mushrooms
- 1   hard-boiled large egg, chopped
- ⅓   cup sliced red onion
- ¼   cup walnut halves
- ¼   cup dried cranberries
- 4½ tsp. olive oil
- 1   Tbsp. maple syrup
- 1½ tsp. finely chopped shallot
- 1½ tsp. red wine vinegar
- 1½ tsp. Dijon mustard
- 1   small garlic clove, minced

In a large salad bowl, combine the first 7 ingredients. In a small bowl, whisk the remaining ingredients. Drizzle over salad; toss to coat.
3½ cups: 387 cal., 22g fat (3g sat. fat), 126mg chol., 617mg sod., 30g carb. (18g sugars, 4g fiber), 21g pro.

1½ tsp. lemon juice
¾ tsp. lime juice
⅛ to ¼ tsp. garlic powder
⅛ tsp. salt
⅛ tsp. pepper
1 medium ripe avocado, peeled and cubed
½ cup cubed tomato
¼ cup chopped red onion

In a bowl, combine lemon juice, lime juice, garlic powder, salt and pepper. Add remaining ingredients; toss gently to coat. Refrigerate for 30 minutes before serving.

1 cup: 173 cal., 15g fat (2g sat. fat), 0 chol., 163mg sod., 11g carb. (3g sugars, 5g fiber), 3g pro. **Diabetic exchanges:** 3 fat, 1 vegetable.

SWEETHEART SLAW

I named this salad "sweetheart slaw" because of the sweet fruit and the fact that all the sweethearts in my life love it! It's a colorful refresher with a delicious blend of flavors.
—Debby Mountjoy, Houston, TX

TAKES: 10 MIN. • **MAKES:** 2 SERVINGS

1½ cups shredded red cabbage
½ cup chopped peeled mango
⅓ cup chopped sweet red pepper
¼ cup sliced fresh strawberries
3 Tbsp. balsamic vinegar
4½ tsp. olive oil
4½ tsp. honey

In a serving bowl, combine the cabbage, mango, pepper and strawberries. In a small bowl, whisk the vinegar, oil and honey. Drizzle over cabbage mixture; toss to coat. Chill until serving.

1 cup: 209 cal., 11g fat (1g sat. fat), 0 chol., 23mg sod., 31g carb. (26g sugars, 3g fiber), 1g pro.

EASY TOMATO AVOCADO SALAD

I came up with this recipe one day when avocados were on sale at the market. It's quick to assemble and makes a nice change of pace from lettuce salads.
—Pamela Raybon, Edna, TX

PREP: 20 MIN. + CHILLING
MAKES: 2 SERVINGS

MEATLESS TACO SALAD

This colorful entree combines popular taco ingredients—minus the ground beef. And you won't miss the meat at all! I top each serving with a creamy guacamole dressing, crunchy corn chips and shredded cheese.
—Kimberly Dray, Pflugerville, TX

TAKES: 20 MIN. • **MAKES:** 2 SERVINGS

- ⅓ cup guacamole
- ¼ cup sour cream
- 1 Tbsp. prepared Italian salad dressing
- 1 Tbsp. chopped green onions
- 2 Tbsp. chopped green pepper
- ¼ tsp. pepper
- ¼ tsp. chili powder
- 3 cups shredded lettuce
- 8 cherry tomatoes, halved
- ½ cup canned kidney beans, rinsed and drained
- ¼ cup sliced ripe olives
- ½ cup crushed corn chips
- ½ cup shredded cheddar cheese

1. In a small bowl, combine the first 7 ingredients; set aside. In a large bowl, combine lettuce, tomatoes, beans and olives.
2. Arrange lettuce mixture on 2 serving plates; top with the guacamole mixture. Sprinkle with corn chips and cheese.
1 serving: 486 cal., 33g fat (12g sat. fat), 35mg chol., 849mg sod., 34g carb. (7g sugars, 9g fiber), 16g pro.

GARDEN CHICKPEA SALAD

Looking for something different on a hot summer's day? This refreshing salad makes a terrific cold side dish or even an entree.
—Sally Sibthorpe, Shelby Township, MI

TAKES: 25 MIN. • **MAKES:** 2 SERVINGS

- ½ tsp. cumin seeds
- ¼ cup chopped tomato
- ¼ cup lemon juice
- ¼ cup olive oil
- 1 garlic clove, minced
- ¼ tsp. salt
- ¼ tsp. cayenne pepper

SALAD
- ¾ cup canned chickpeas or garbanzo beans, rinsed and drained
- 1 medium carrot, julienned
- 1 small zucchini, julienned
- 2 green onions, thinly sliced
- ½ cup coarsely chopped fresh parsley
- ¼ cup thinly sliced radishes
- ¼ cup crumbled feta cheese
- 3 Tbsp. chopped walnuts
- 3 cups spring mix salad greens

1. For dressing, in a dry small skillet, toast cumin seeds over medium heat until aromatic, stirring frequently. Transfer to a small bowl. Stir in the tomato, lemon juice, oil, garlic, salt and cayenne pepper.
2. In a bowl, combine chickpeas, carrot, zucchini, green onions, parsley, radishes, cheese and walnuts. Stir in ⅓ cup dressing.
3. To serve, divide greens between 2 plates; top with chickpea mixture. Drizzle with remaining dressing.
1 serving: 492 cal., 38g fat (6g sat. fat), 8mg chol., 619mg sod., 30g carb. (7g sugars, 9g fiber), 12g pro.

WATERMELON-BLUEBERRY SALAD

People love the distinctive combination of flavors in the dressing that tops the fresh fruit in this salad. It's so refreshing on a hot summer evening.
—Jenni Sharp, Milwaukee, WI

TAKES: 5 MIN. + CHILLING
MAKES: 2 SERVINGS

- 1   Tbsp. honey
- ¾ tsp. lemon juice
- ½ tsp. minced fresh mint
- 1   cup seeded chopped watermelon
- ½ cup fresh blueberries

In a small bowl, combine the honey, lemon juice and mint. Add watermelon and blueberries; toss gently to coat. Chill until serving.
¾ cup: 78 cal., 0 fat (0 sat. fat), 0 chol., 2mg sod., 20g carb. (17g sugars, 1g fiber), 1g pro. **Diabetic exchanges:** 1 fruit, ½ starch.

SPINACH SALAD WITH HOT BACON DRESSING

After having a salad like this at a restaurant years ago, I came up with this recipe. It is especially good when the spinach comes right from the garden to the table.
—Wanda Cover, Mediapolis, IA

TAKES: 25 MIN. • **MAKES:** 2 SERVINGS

- 2   cups fresh baby spinach, torn
- 2   hard-boiled large eggs, sliced
- 4   cherry tomatoes, halved
- 3   medium fresh mushrooms, sliced
- ¼ cup salad croutons
- 6   pitted ripe olives, halved
- 3   slices red onion, halved

DRESSING
- 4   bacon strips, diced
- 1   Tbsp. chopped onion
- 2   Tbsp. sugar
- 2   Tbsp. ketchup
- 1   Tbsp. red wine vinegar
- 1   Tbsp. Worcestershire sauce

1. Divide the spinach between 2 plates. Arrange the eggs, tomatoes, mushrooms, croutons, olives and red onion over top.
2. In a small skillet, cook bacon over medium heat until crisp. Using a slotted spoon, remove to paper towels; drain, reserving 2 Tbsp. drippings. Saute onion in reserved drippings until tender.
3. Stir in sugar, ketchup, vinegar and Worcestershire sauce. Bring to a boil. Reduce heat; simmer, uncovered, until thickened, 1-2 minutes.
4. Sprinkle bacon over salads; drizzle with dressing.
1⅓ cups: 367 cal., 21g fat (6g sat. fat), 238mg chol., 1178mg sod., 29g carb. (21g sugars, 2g fiber), 17g pro.

CRUNCHY ASIAN COLESLAW

This flavor-packed twist on traditional creamy coleslaw is a perfect complement to Asian-themed meals. The light, tangy vinaigrette enhances the fresh veggies.
—Erin Chilcoat, Central Islip, NY

PREP: 15 MIN. + CHILLING
MAKES: 2 SERVINGS

- 1 cup shredded Chinese or napa cabbage
- ½ cup sliced water chestnuts, chopped
- ½ small zucchini, julienned
- 2 Tbsp. chopped green pepper
- 4½ tsp. rice vinegar
- 1 tsp. sugar
- 1 tsp. sesame seeds, toasted
- 1 tsp. reduced-sodium soy sauce
- ½ tsp. sesame oil
  Dash crushed red pepper flakes

In a small bowl, combine the cabbage, water chestnuts, zucchini and green pepper. In another small bowl, whisk the remaining ingredients. Drizzle over salad; toss to coat. Refrigerate for at least 1 hour.

1 cup: 65 cal., 2g fat (0 sat. fat), 0 chol., 120mg sod., 11g carb. (5g sugars, 2g fiber), 2g pro. **Diabetic exchanges:** 2 vegetable.

COUSCOUS TABBOULEH WITH FRESH MINT & FETA

Using couscous instead of bulgur for tabbouleh really speeds up the process of making this colorful salad. Other quick-cooking grains, such as barley, also work well.
—Elodie Rosinovsky, Brighton, MA

TAKES: 20 MIN. • **MAKES:** 3 SERVINGS

- ¾ cup water
- ½ cup uncooked couscous
- 1 can (15 oz.) garbanzo beans or chickpeas, rinsed and drained
- 1 large tomato, chopped
- ½ English cucumber, halved and thinly sliced
- 3 Tbsp. lemon juice
- 2 tsp. grated lemon zest
- 2 tsp. olive oil
- 2 tsp. minced fresh mint
- 2 tsp. minced fresh parsley
- ¼ tsp. salt
- ⅛ tsp. pepper
- ¾ cup crumbled feta cheese
  Lemon wedges, optional

1. In a small saucepan, bring water to a boil. Stir in couscous. Remove from the heat; cover and let stand for 5-8 minutes or until water is absorbed. Fluff with a fork.
2. In a large bowl, combine the beans, tomato and cucumber. In a small bowl, whisk the lemon juice, lemon zest, oil, mint, parsley, salt and pepper. Drizzle over chickpea mixture. Add couscous; toss to combine. Sprinkle with cheese. Serve immediately or refrigerate until chilled. If desired, serve with lemon wedges.

1⅔ cups: 362 cal., 11g fat (3g sat. fat), 15mg chol., 657mg sod., 52g carb. (7g sugars, 9g fiber), 15g pro.

HEALTH TIP

Make this refreshing main-dish salad gluten-free by replacing the couscous with 1½ cups of cooked quinoa.

In a serving bowl, combine the vinegar, honey, oil, soy sauce, salt and pepper. Add cucumber and red pepper; stir to coat. Cover and refrigerate for at least 30 minutes, stirring occasionally. Garnish with sesame seeds.

¾ cup: 34 cal., 1g fat (0 sat. fat), 0 chol., 101mg sod., 7g carb. (4g sugars, 1g fiber), 1g pro. **Diabetic exchanges:** 1 vegetable.

SIMPLE LETTUCE SALAD

I grew up on a farm and most of our food came right from the garden. My mother often fixed this salad—we especially enjoyed it in the spring, when early leaf lettuce appeared. After a long winter of cooked vegetables, this was a real treat!
—Susan Davis, Vale, NC

TAKES: 10 MIN. • **MAKES:** 2 SERVINGS

- 2   **cups torn leaf lettuce**
- 1   **hard-boiled large egg, chopped**
- 1   **green onion, sliced**
- 2   **Tbsp. mayonnaise**
- 1   **tsp. cider vinegar**
- ⅛   **tsp. pepper**

In a salad bowl, combine lettuce, egg and onion. In a small bowl, whisk the mayonnaise, vinegar and pepper. Pour over salad and toss to coat.

1 cup: 150 cal., 14g fat (2g sat. fat), 111mg chol., 123mg sod., 3g carb. (1g sugars, 1g fiber), 4g pro.

TEST KITCHEN TIP

In Thailand, cucumber salad is often made with chiles and chopped peanuts. If you like a bit of spice in your salad, try adding thin slices of serrano pepper or another hot chile, or add some red pepper flakes to the marinade.

ASIAN CUCUMBER SALAD

This colorful cucumber dish makes a simple, cool side when we have stir-fry for dinner.
—Tari Ambler, Shorewood, IL

PREP: 15 MIN. + CHILLING
MAKES: 2 SERVINGS

- 4½ **tsp. rice vinegar**
- ½   **tsp. honey**
- ¼   **tsp. sesame oil**
- ¼   **tsp. reduced-sodium soy sauce**
      Dash salt and pepper
- ½   **large cucumber, julienned**
- ½   **medium sweet red pepper, julienned**
      Black and white sesame seeds

HEARTY ASIAN LETTUCE SALAD

This meatless version of a restaurant favorite packs 13 grams of protein and is bursting with juicy flavor.
—Taste of Home Test Kitchen

TAKES: 20 MIN. • **MAKES:** 2 SERVINGS

- 1 cup ready-to-serve brown rice
- 1 cup frozen shelled edamame
- 3 cups spring mix salad greens
- ¼ cup reduced-fat sesame ginger salad dressing
- 1 medium navel orange, peeled and sectioned
- 4 radishes, sliced
- 2 Tbsp. sliced almonds, toasted

1. Prepare rice and edamame according to package directions.
2. In a large bowl, combine the salad greens, rice and edamame. Drizzle with salad dressing and toss to coat.
3. Divide salad mixture between 2 plates; top with orange segments, radishes and almonds.
1 serving: 329 cal., 10g fat (1g sat. fat), 0 chol., 430mg sod., 44g carb. (12g sugars, 7g fiber), 13g pro.

CHOCOLATE PEAR & CHERRY SALAD

It's fun to come up with new ways to use the ingredients we love. I developed a chocolate vinaigrette, knowing how well it would play with stone fruit, the peppery bite of arugula, and the deep acidic sweetness of balsamic. There are tons of other options that can go with this vinaigrette, so feel free to play!
—Ryan Christie, Pacheco, CA

PREP: 25 MIN. + CHILLING
BAKE: 15 MIN.
MAKES: 2 SERVINGS

- ¾ cup cut french-style green beans
- 3 Tbsp. olive oil, divided
- ⅛ tsp. salt
- ⅛ tsp. pepper
- ¼ cup balsamic vinegar
- 1 oz. dark chocolate candy bar, chopped
- 1 Tbsp. red wine vinegar

- 4 cups fresh arugula
- 1 medium pear, peeled and cut into ½-in. cubes
- ½ cup frozen pitted sweet cherries, thawed and halved
- ¼ cup dried cranberries
- 3 Tbsp. coarsely chopped pecans
- 1 Tbsp. minced dried apricots
- 2 tsp. thinly sliced fresh mint leaves

1. Heat oven to 350°. In an 8-in. square baking dish, toss beans with 1 Tbsp. olive oil, salt and pepper. Roast until tender, 12-15 minutes. Remove from oven. Toss with balsamic vinegar; refrigerate, covered, 1½-2 hours.
2. Meanwhile, in a microwave, melt chocolate; stir until smooth. Pulse the melted chocolate, red wine vinegar and the remaining 2 Tbsp. olive oil in a blender until smooth.

3. Divide the arugula evenly between 2 salad bowls. Drizzle with the chocolate vinaigrette. Top with pears, cherries, cranberries and beans; sprinkle with pecans, apricots and mint leaves.
1 serving: 511 cal., 33g fat (6g sat. fat), 2mg chol., 166mg sod., 62g carb. (47g sugars, 8g fiber), 4g pro.

SIDE DISHES

Rounding out your meal with a small but scrumptious side is easier than you may think. Rely on these doubly delightful veggies, pasta dishes and more!

SPICY HONEY MUSTARD GREEN BEANS

I love fresh beans, but I was getting tired of just steaming and eating them plain. So I whipped up this easy honey-mustard version as a simple side dish.
—Carol Traupman-Carr, Breinigsville, PA

TAKES: 20 MIN. • **MAKES:** 2 SERVINGS

- ½ lb. fresh green beans, trimmed
- ¼ cup thinly sliced red onion
- 2 Tbsp. spicy brown mustard
- 2 Tbsp. honey
- 1 Tbsp. snipped fresh dill or 1 tsp. dill weed

1. In a large saucepan, bring 6 cups water to a boil. Add beans; cook, uncovered, just until crisp-tender, 3-4 minutes. Drain beans and immediately drop into ice water. Drain and pat dry; transfer to a small bowl.
2. In another bowl, combine onion, mustard, honey and dill. Pour over beans; toss to coat.

1 serving: 122 cal., 0 fat (0 sat. fat), 0 chol., 159mg sod., 27g carb. (21g sugars, 4g fiber), 2g pro.

GARLIC MASHED POTATOES

I like to infuse mashed potatoes with the subtle taste of garlic, making them a welcome addition to most any meal.
—Myra Innes, Auburn, KS

TAKES: 25 MIN. • **MAKES:** 2 SERVINGS

- 2 medium potatoes, peeled and cut into ½-in. cubes
- 5 garlic cloves, peeled and halved
- ¾ tsp. salt, divided
- 2 Tbsp. butter, softened
- 2 to 3 Tbsp. heavy whipping cream

1. Place the potatoes, garlic and ¼ tsp. salt in a small saucepan; cover with water. Bring to a boil. Reduce heat; cover and simmer 10 minutes or until potatoes are tender. Drain.

2. In a small bowl, mash the potatoes and garlic. Add butter, cream and remaining salt; beat until smooth.

¾ cup: 288 cal., 17g fat (11g sat. fat), 47mg chol., 986mg sod., 32g carb. (3g sugars, 2g fiber), 4g pro.

PARMESAN HERBED NOODLES

Looking for a quick side dish that goes well with all kinds of meats? Try this recipe for tender, tasty noodles. For a colorful variation, sometimes I add slightly cooked red and green pepper strips and a quarter cup of peas. Feel free to toss in your own add-ins to customize this for your own tastes.
—Denise Elder, Hanover, ON

TAKES: 20 MIN. • **MAKES:** 2 SERVINGS

- 1½ cups uncooked wide egg noodles
- 2 Tbsp. shredded Parmesan cheese
- 1 Tbsp. butter
- 1 Tbsp. olive oil
- 2 tsp. minced fresh basil or ½ tsp. dried basil
- ½ tsp. minced fresh thyme or ⅛ tsp. dried thyme
- 1 garlic clove, minced
- ¼ tsp. salt

In a small saucepan, cook noodles according to package directions; drain. Add remaining ingredients and toss to coat.

1 cup: 243 cal., 15g fat (6g sat. fat), 46mg chol., 444mg sod., 21g carb. (1g sugars, 1g fiber), 6g pro.

SPINACH RICE

I like to serve this Greek-style dish alongside steak with mushrooms. It makes an elegant meal that can be doubled for guests.
—Jeanette Cakouros, Brunswick, ME

TAKES: 20 MIN. • **MAKES:** 2 SERVINGS

- 2 Tbsp. olive oil
- ½ cup chopped onion
- ¾ cup water
- 1 Tbsp. dried parsley flakes
- ¼ to ½ tsp. salt
- ⅛ tsp. pepper
- ½ cup uncooked instant rice
- 2 cups fresh baby spinach

1. In a saucepan, heat oil over medium-high heat; cook and stir onion until tender. Stir in water, parsley, salt and pepper; bring to a boil. Stir in rice; top with spinach.
2. Cover; remove from heat. Let stand until the rice is tender, 7-10 minutes. Stir to combine.
¾ cup: 235 cal., 14g fat (2g sat. fat), 0 chol., 326mg sod., 25g carb. (2g sugars, 2g fiber), 3g pro.
Diabetic exchanges: 3 fat, 1½ starch, 1 vegetable.

CHEDDAR BASIL CAULIFLOWER

If you grow your own basil, you'll want to save some for a side of flavorful, versatile cauliflower. I love how this dish not only warms you up in winter but also is delicious in summer made with garden-fresh produce.
—David Harper, Clackamas, OR

TAKES: 20 MIN. • **MAKES:** 2 SERVINGS

- 2½ cups small fresh cauliflowerets
- 1 Tbsp. white wine or water
- 1½ tsp. minced fresh basil or ½ tsp. dried basil
- 1 tsp. water
- 1 tsp. canola oil
- ½ tsp. sugar
- ¼ tsp. salt
- ⅓ cup shredded cheddar cheese

In a small saucepan, combine the first 7 ingredients. Cover and cook over medium heat until cauliflower is tender, 10-12 minutes, stirring once. Transfer to a small serving bowl; sprinkle with cheese.
¾ cup: 128 cal., 8g fat (4g sat. fat), 20mg chol., 446mg sod., 8g carb. (4g sugars, 3g fiber), 6g pro.
Diabetic exchanges: 1 vegetable, 1 fat, ½ fat-free milk.

GARLIC CRESCENT ROLLS

These delicious rolls can embellish a dinner and only take a minute with convenient refrigerator rolls. You can create new flavor combinations to complement your menu.
—Pat Habiger, Spearville, KS

TAKES: 20 MIN. • **MAKES:** 2 SERVINGS

- 1 pkg. (4 oz.) refrigerated crescent rolls
- 2 tsp. grated Parmesan cheese
- ¼ to ½ tsp. garlic powder
- 1 large egg, beaten
- ½ tsp. sesame and/or poppy seeds

1. Separate the crescent dough into 4 triangles. Sprinkle with Parmesan cheese and then the garlic powder. Beginning at the wide end, roll up dough triangles. Place with point down on a greased baking sheet.
2. Brush with egg; sprinkle with sesame and/or poppy seeds. Bake at 375° for 11-13 minutes or until golden brown. Serve warm.
2 rolls: 272 cal., 15g fat (4g sat. fat), 108mg chol., 508mg sod., 23g carb. (4g sugars, 0 fiber), 8g pro.

SQUASH RIBBONS

Steamed and seasoned, these pretty vegetable ribbons will dress up your dinner plate. Strips of yellow summer squash and zucchini are easy to cut using a vegetable peeler or even a cheese slicer.
—Taste of Home Test Kitchen

TAKES: 15 MIN. • **MAKES:** 2 SERVINGS

- 1 **small yellow summer squash**
- 1 **small zucchini**
- 1 **Tbsp. butter, melted**
- ¼ **tsp. onion powder**
- ¼ **tsp. dried rosemary, crushed**
- ⅛ **tsp. salt**
- ⅛ **tsp. dried thyme**
- ⅛ **tsp. pepper**

1. With a vegetable peeler or metal cheese slicer, cut very thin slices down the length of each squash, making long ribbons. Place in a steamer basket; place basket in a saucepan over 1 in. boiling water. Cover; steam until squash is tender, 2-3 minutes.
2. In a small bowl, combine the butter, onion powder, rosemary, salt, thyme and pepper. Add squash and toss to coat.

¾ cup: 80 cal., 6g fat (4g sat. fat), 15mg chol., 206mg sod., 5g carb. (4g sugars, 2g fiber), 2g pro. **Diabetic exchanges:** 1½ fat, 1 vegetable.

STUFFED RED PEPPERS

Tired of tuna-filled tomatoes and rice-stuffed green peppers? Try this vibrant alternative. Lemon zest and mint enhance the filling.
—Kitty Jones, Chicago, IL

PREP: 40 MIN. • **BAKE:** 55 MIN.
MAKES: 2 SERVINGS

- ¼ **cup uncooked millet, rinsed and drained**
- ¾ **cup vegetable broth**
- 2 **medium sweet red peppers**
- ⅓ **cup frozen corn, thawed**
- ¼ **cup finely chopped onion**
- 3 **Tbsp. finely chopped celery**
- 2 **Tbsp. chopped walnuts**
- 1 **green onion, finely chopped**
- 1½ **tsp. chopped fresh mint or ½ tsp. dried mint flakes**
- 1 **tsp. grated lemon zest**
- ¾ **tsp. fresh chopped oregano or ¼ tsp. dried oregano**
- 1 **small garlic clove, minced**
- ¼ **tsp. salt**
- ⅛ **tsp. pepper**
- 1 **Tbsp. olive oil**

1. In a saucepan, bring the millet and broth to a boil. Reduce heat; simmer, covered, until millet is tender and broth is absorbed, 30-35 minutes. Transfer to a large bowl and cool.
2. Meanwhile, cut tops off peppers and remove the seeds. In a large saucepan, cook peppers in boiling water for 3-5 minutes. Drain and rinse in cold water; set aside.
3. With a fork, fluff cooled millet. Add the corn, onion, celery, nuts, green onion and seasonings; blend well. Spoon into sweet peppers. Drizzle with oil. Place peppers in a baking dish coated with cooking spray. Cover and bake at 350° for 55-60 minutes or until tender.

1 stuffed pepper: 278 cal., 13g fat (2g sat. fat), 0 chol., 666mg sod., 37g carb. (8g sugars, 7g fiber), 7g pro.

SCENTED RICE IN BAKED PUMPKIN

This easy, delicious and healthy side is a showpiece that always delights. You can use grain, squash, fruits and nuts to suit your taste.
—Lynn Heisel, Jackson, MO

PREP: 30 MIN. • **BAKE:** 35 MIN.
MAKES: 2 SERVINGS

- 1 small pie pumpkin (about 2 lbs.)
- 1 Tbsp. olive oil
- ½ cup uncooked brown rice
- 1 cup water
- ¼ cup coarsely chopped pecans, toasted
- 3 dried apricots, chopped
- 2 Tbsp. raisins
- ¼ tsp. salt
- ¼ tsp. curry powder
- ⅛ tsp. ground cinnamon
- ⅛ tsp. ground cardamom, optional
- ⅛ tsp. ground cumin

1. Wash pumpkin and cut it into 6 wedges. Remove loose fibers and seeds from the inside, and discard seeds or save them for toasting. Brush wedges with oil. Place on ungreased 15x10x1-in. baking sheet. Bake at 400° until tender, 35-40 minutes.
2. Meanwhile, in a small saucepan, bring the rice and water to a boil. Reduce heat; cover and simmer until liquid is absorbed and rice is tender, 20-25 minutes. Stir in the chopped pecans, apricots, raisins, salt, curry powder, cinnamon and, if desired, cardamom.

3. Set 4 of the pumpkin wedges aside for another use. Sprinkle cumin onto remaining 2 wedges; top with the rice mixture.
1 serving: 389 cal., 15g fat (2g sat. fat), 0 chol., 309mg sod., 62g carb. (13g sugars, 5g fiber), 7g pro.

TEST KITCHEN TIP

Use the 4 leftover roasted pie-pumpkin wedges any way you would use cooked winter squash. Puree for soup, mash for a side dish, or simply cube and stir into a stuffing or pilaf.

MICROWAVED POULTRY DRESSING

Homemade stuffing in just 15 minutes? You bet! This easy microwaved recipe is lower in sodium than packaged mixes.
—Evelyn Clark, Sauk City, WI

TAKES: 15 MIN. • **MAKES:** 2 SERVINGS

- 1 large egg
- ½ cup 2% milk
- 2 Tbsp. chopped celery
- 1 Tbsp. chopped onion
- ½ tsp. poultry seasoning
- ¼ tsp. rubbed sage
- ⅛ tsp. salt
  Dash pepper
- 1¾ cups unseasoned stuffing cubes

1. In a microwave-safe dish, beat egg and milk. Stir in the celery, onion and seasonings. Add the stuffing cubes; mix well. Let stand for 5 minutes.
2. Cover and microwave on high for 1 minute; stir. Cook 1 minute longer; stir. Cook 30 seconds longer or until heated through.
½ cup: 236 cal., 5g fat (2g sat. fat), 111mg chol., 578mg sod., 38g carb. (6g sugars, 3g fiber), 11g pro.

ORANGE ROSEMARY CARROTS

Our whole family loves rosemary, and I grow it in my garden every year, along with carrots. This is a delicious recipe to use them both together.
—Arlene Butler, Ogden, UT

TAKES: 30 MIN. • **MAKES:** 2 SERVINGS

- 1 Tbsp. butter
- 1 Tbsp. finely chopped shallot or red onion
- 1 garlic clove, minced
- 3 medium carrots, cut into ½-in. slices
- 1 Tbsp. brown sugar
- 1 Tbsp. water
- 1 Tbsp. thawed orange juice concentrate
- ½ tsp. minced fresh rosemary
- ⅛ tsp. salt
- ⅛ tsp. pepper
  Minced fresh parsley, optional

1. In a small saucepan, melt butter over medium-high heat. Add the shallot; cook and stir until tender, 2-3 minutes. Add the garlic; cook 1 minute longer.
2. Stir in carrots. Add brown sugar, water, orange juice concentrate, rosemary, salt and pepper. Reduce heat to medium-low. Cook, covered, until the carrots are crisp-tender, 15-20 minutes. Uncover and cook until the liquid is reduced by half, 1-2 minutes. If desired, sprinkle with fresh parsley.
¾ cup: 133 cal., 6g fat (4g sat. fat), 15mg chol., 260mg sod., 20g carb. (14g sugars, 3g fiber), 1g pro.

DID YOU KNOW?

Carrots come in a variety of colors, including white, yellow and even deep shades of purple.

PEA POD CARROT MEDLEY

We grow pea pods, and I wanted to use them in something other than stir-fries. This fit the bill! I have taken it to church potlucks and received compliments on its pretty orange glaze and fresh taste.
—Josie Smith, Winamac, IN

TAKES: 25 MIN. • **MAKES:** 2 SERVINGS

- 2 medium carrots, sliced
- 2 cups fresh sugar snap peas, trimmed
- 1 tsp. cornstarch
- ½ tsp. grated orange zest
- ⅓ cup orange juice
- 2 tsp. reduced-sodium soy sauce
- ¼ tsp. salt

1. Place sliced carrots and enough water to cover in a small saucepan; bring to a boil. Reduce heat and simmer, covered, 5 minutes. Add peas; simmer, covered, until peas are crisp-tender, 2-3 minutes. Drain and remove vegetables from pan; set aside.

2. In same pan, mix remaining ingredients until cornstarch is dissolved; bring to boil. Cook and stir until thickened, 1-2 minutes. Add vegetables; toss to coat.

1 cup: 119 cal., 1g fat (0 sat. fat), 0 chol., 535mg sod., 23g carb. (12g sugars, 6g fiber), 6g pro.
Diabetic exchanges: 2 vegetable, ½ fruit.

OREGANO GARLIC BREAD

I discovered this special sourdough bread at a local grocery store, where they had samples. My husband is Italian and can't get enough garlic flavor in whatever I cook.
—Sarah Vasques, Milford, NH

TAKES: 15 MIN. • **MAKES:** 2 SERVINGS

- 2 slices sourdough bread
- 2 Tbsp. butter, softened
- 1 tsp. dried oregano
- ½ tsp. garlic powder

Preheat oven to 400°. Spread bread with butter; sprinkle with oregano and garlic powder. Place on an ungreased baking sheet. Bake until golden brown, 8-10 minutes.
1 piece: 198 cal., 12g fat (7g sat. fat), 30mg chol., 289mg sod., 19g carb. (1g sugars, 1g fiber), 4g pro.

CREAMY BOW TIE PASTA

Add a little zip to your meal with this saucy pasta dish. It's an excellent accompaniment to almost any meat or seafood.
—Kathy Kittell, Lenexa, KS

TAKES: 25 MIN. • **MAKES:** 2 SERVINGS

- 1 cup uncooked bow tie pasta
- 1½ tsp. butter
- 2¼ tsp. olive oil
- 1½ tsp. all-purpose flour
- ½ tsp. minced garlic
    Dash salt
    Dash dried basil
    Dash crushed red pepper flakes
- 3 Tbsp. 2% milk
- 2 Tbsp. chicken broth
- 1 Tbsp. water
- 2 Tbsp. shredded Parmesan cheese
- 1 Tbsp. sour cream

1. Cook pasta according to package directions. Meanwhile, in a small saucepan, melt butter. Stir in the oil, flour, garlic and seasonings until blended. Gradually add the milk, broth and water. Bring to a boil; cook and stir until slightly thickened, about 2 minutes.

2. Remove from the heat; stir in cheese and sour cream. Drain pasta; toss with sauce.

¾ cup: 196 cal., 12g fat (5g sat. fat), 19mg chol., 252mg sod., 17g carb. (2g sugars, 1g fiber), 6g pro.

⅔ cup sliced fresh shiitake mushrooms
2 Tbsp. chopped onion
1 small garlic clove, minced
⅓ cup uncooked arborio rice
Dash pepper
¼ cup white wine or ¼ cup additional reduced-sodium chicken broth
¼ cup grated Parmesan cheese
1 tsp. minced fresh sage

1. Place cubed squash in a greased 9-in. square baking pan. Add 1 tsp. oil and salt; toss to coat. Roast, uncovered, at 350° until squash is tender, 25-30 minutes, stirring occasionally.
2. Meanwhile, in a small saucepan, heat the broth and keep it warm. In a small skillet, cook and stir the mushrooms, onion and garlic in remaining 1 tsp. oil until tender, 3-4 minutes. Add rice and pepper; cook and stir 2-3 minutes. Reduce heat; stir in wine. Cook and stir until all liquid is absorbed.
3. Add heated broth, ¼ cup at a time, stirring constantly. Allow liquid to absorb between additions. Cook just until the risotto is creamy and the rice is almost tender, about 20 minutes.
4. Stir in cheese until melted. Add roasted squash and minced sage. Serve immediately.
¾ cup: 282 cal., 9g fat (3g sat. fat), 12mg chol., 567mg sod., 40g carb. (3g sugars, 3g fiber), 10g pro.

TEST KITCHEN TIP

If you add the cheese to risotto too early, the heat can cause it to "break," which is when fat separates out of a sauce. This can lead to a greasy and granular dish.

SHIITAKE & BUTTERNUT RISOTTO

I like to think of this recipe as a labor of love. The risotto requires a bit of extra attention, but once you take your first bite you'll know it was worth the effort.
—Stephanie Campbell, Elk Grove, CA

PREP: 25 MIN. • **COOK:** 25 MIN.
MAKES: 2 SERVINGS

1 cup cubed peeled butternut squash
2 tsp. olive oil, divided
Dash salt
1¼ cups reduced-sodium chicken broth

ZUCCHINI FRIES

I often make these fries for my husband and myself, especially when our garden is full of zucchini. The cornmeal coating gives them a nice crunch.
—Sarah Gottschalk, Richmond, IN

TAKES: 30 MIN. • **MAKES:** 2 SERVINGS

- 2   small zucchini
- 1   large egg white
- ¼   cup all-purpose flour
- 3   Tbsp. cornmeal
- ½   tsp. each salt, chili powder, garlic powder, paprika and pepper
  Cooking spray
  Marinara or spaghetti sauce, warmed

1. Cut the zucchini into strips of about 3x½x½-in. In a shallow bowl, whisk egg white. In another shallow bowl, combine flour, cornmeal and seasonings. Dip zucchini in egg white, then roll in flour mixture.
2. Place zucchini on a baking sheet coated with cooking spray. Spray zucchini with additional cooking spray. Bake at 425° until golden brown, 18-22 minutes, turning once. Serve with marinara sauce.

1 serving: 98 cal., 1g fat (0 sat. fat), 0 chol., 414mg sod., 19g carb. (3g sugars, 3g fiber), 5g pro. **Diabetic exchanges:** 1 starch, 1 vegetable.

TWICE-BAKED BREAKFAST POTATOES

A leftover baked potato was the inspiration for this impromptu meal. The bacon and sausage combo make it a hearty breakfast dish, but it can be a filling lunch or dinner as well.
—William Brock, Amelia, OH

PREP: 30 MIN. • **BAKE:** 15 MIN.
MAKES: 2 SERVINGS

- 1   large baking potato
- ¾   tsp. butter
- 1   large egg, beaten
- 3   oz. bulk pork sausage
- 1   Tbsp. sour cream
- 2   bacon strips, cooked and crumbled
- 3   Tbsp. shredded cheddar cheese, divided
- 2   Tbsp. minced chives, divided
- ¾   tsp. minced fresh parsley
- ⅛   tsp. salt
- ⅛   tsp. pepper
  Additional sour cream, optional

1. Scrub and pierce potato; place on a microwave-safe plate. Microwave, uncovered, on high until potato is tender, 15-17 minutes, turning once.
2. Meanwhile, in a large skillet, melt the butter over medium-high heat. Add egg; cook and stir until set. Remove and set aside. In the same skillet, cook the sausage over medium heat until no longer pink; drain and set aside.
3. When potato is cool enough to handle, cut in half lengthwise. Scoop out pulp, leaving thin shells. In a large bowl, mash the pulp with sour cream. Stir in bacon, 2 Tbsp. cheese, 1 Tbsp. chives, parsley, salt, pepper, egg and sausage. Spoon into the potato shells.
4. Place on a baking sheet. Bake, uncovered, at 375° until heated through, 12-15 minutes. Sprinkle with remaining cheese and chives. Serve with additional sour cream if desired.

1 stuffed-potato half: 375 cal., 19g fat (9g sat. fat), 149mg chol., 590mg sod., 35g carb. (4g sugars, 3g fiber), 15g pro.

TENDER BISCUITS

These quick and easy rolls are low in fat but not in flavor. They'll dress up any weeknight meal.
—Ane Burke, Bella Vista, AR

TAKES: 30 MIN. • **MAKES:** 2 BISCUITS

- ⅓ cup self-rising flour
- 1 Tbsp. grated Parmesan cheese
- ⅛ tsp. garlic salt
- 3 Tbsp. reduced-fat cream cheese
- 3 Tbsp. fat-free milk
- 1 Tbsp. fat-free plain yogurt

1. In a small bowl, combine flour, Parmesan and garlic salt. Cut in the cream cheese until mixture resembles coarse crumbs. Stir in the milk and the yogurt just until moistened.
2. Drop by scant ⅓ cupfuls about 2 in. apart onto a baking sheet coated with cooking spray. Bake at 400° for 12-15 minutes or until golden brown. Serve warm.

1 biscuit: 142 cal., 5g fat (4g sat. fat), 18mg chol., 497mg sod., 17g carb. (2g sugars, 0 fiber), 6g pro. **Diabetic exchanges:** 1 starch, 1 fat.

SAUTEED CORN WITH CHEDDAR

My husband likes only this kind of corn, so I make it about once a week. It's so easy that anyone can make it in a jiffy!
—Sarah Cope, Dundee, NY

TAKES: 10 MIN. • **MAKES:** 2 SERVINGS

- 1½ cups frozen corn, thawed
- ⅛ tsp. salt
- ⅛ tsp. pepper
- 1 Tbsp. butter
- ¾ cup shredded cheddar cheese

In a small skillet, saute corn, salt and pepper in butter until tender. Stir in cheese.

¾ cup: 309 cal., 19g fat (13g sat. fat), 60mg chol., 447mg sod., 27g carb. (2g sugars, 3g fiber), 13g pro.

TANGY BAKED BEANS

Different, delicious and sized exactly right for two people, this easy, breezy, home-style side dish is sure to please.
—Dean Copeland, Ochlocknee, GA

PREP: 10 MIN. • **BAKE:** 25 MIN. **MAKES:** 2 SERVINGS

- 2 bacon strips, cut into 1-in. pieces
- 2 Tbsp. strong brewed coffee
- 4 tsp. brown sugar
- 1 tsp. cider vinegar
- ¼ tsp. ground mustard
- ⅛ tsp. salt
- 1 can (8.3 oz.) baked beans, undrained
- ½ cup chopped onion

1. In a small skillet, cook bacon over medium heat until partially cooked but not crisp. Drain bacon on paper towels. Meanwhile, in a saucepan, combine the coffee, brown sugar, vinegar, mustard and salt. Bring to a boil; cook and stir for 2-3 minutes or until sugar is dissolved. Stir in beans and onion.
2. Divide the bean mixture between two 6-oz. ramekins or custard cups coated with cooking spray. Top with bacon. Bake at 350° until bubbly, 25-30 minutes.

½ cup: 213 cal., 5g fat (2g sat. fat), 14mg chol., 741mg sod., 36g carb. (19g sugars, 7g fiber), 9g pro. **Diabetic exchanges:** 2 starch, 1 vegetable, ½ lean meat.

RAINBOW HASH

This hash combines sweet potato, carrot, purple potato and kale for a dish that earns its colorful name!.
—Courtney Stultz, Weir, KS

TAKES: 30 MIN. • **MAKES:** 2 SERVINGS

- 2 Tbsp. olive or coconut oil
- 1 medium sweet potato, peeled and cubed
- 1 medium purple potato, peeled and cubed
- 1 large carrot, peeled and cubed
- ½ tsp. dried oregano
- ½ tsp. dried basil
- ½ tsp. sea salt
- ½ tsp. pepper
- 2 cups coarsely chopped fresh kale or spinach
- 1 small garlic clove, minced

1. In a large skillet, heat oil over medium heat. Add sweet potato, purple potato, carrot, oregano, basil, sea salt and pepper; cook and stir until vegetables are tender, 10-12 minutes.
2. Add kale and garlic; continue cooking until vegetables are lightly browned and the kale is tender, 2-4 minutes.

1 cup: 304 cal., 14g fat (2g sat. fat), 0 chol., 523mg sod., 43g carb. (12g sugars, 5g fiber), 4g pro.

CREAMY TWICE-BAKED POTATOES

With a yummy cream cheese filling, these rich, delicious potatoes are sure winners. They seem fancy but are not tricky to make.
—Linda Wheeler, Harrisburg, PA

PREP: 1¼ HOURS • **BAKE:** 20 MIN.
MAKES: 2 SERVINGS

- 2 medium baking potatoes
- 2 Tbsp. butter, softened
- 1 Tbsp. 2% milk
- ¼ tsp. salt
- 3 oz. cream cheese, cubed
- 2 Tbsp. sour cream
  Paprika
  Optional: Minced fresh parsley and green onions

1. Preheat oven to 350°. Pierce potatoes and bake on a baking sheet until tender, about 1 hour. When cool enough to handle, cut a thin slice off the top of each potato and discard. Scoop out pulp, leaving a thin shell.
2. In a small bowl, mash the pulp with butter, milk and salt. Stir in cream cheese and sour cream. Spoon into potato shells. Sprinkle with paprika.
3. Place on a baking sheet. Bake, uncovered, until filling is heated through and tops are golden brown, 20-25 minutes. If desired, sprinkle with parsley and green onions.

1 serving: 452 cal., 29g fat (18g sat. fat), 88mg chol., 561mg sod., 40g carb. (5g sugars, 3g fiber), 8g pro.

DID YOU KNOW?

Russet potatoes are often considered the best baking potatoes due to their ability to hold their shape as well as the light, fluffy interior they offer.

MASHED CAULIFLOWER

This side dish is lower in carbs than mashed potatoes but just as flavorful and satisfying. It makes an enticing addition to any table. Try chopped green onions for a festive garnish.
—Tina Martini, Sparks, NV

TAKES: 25 MIN. • **MAKES:** 3 SERVINGS

1 medium head cauliflower, broken into florets
½ cup shredded Swiss cheese
1 Tbsp. butter
¾ tsp. salt
¼ tsp. pepper
⅛ tsp. garlic powder
2 to 3 Tbsp. 2% milk

1. In a large saucepan, bring 1 in. water to a boil. Add cauliflower; cook, covered, until very tender, 8-12 minutes. Drain.
2. Mash cauliflower, adding cheese, butter, seasonings and enough milk to reach desired consistency.
¾ cup: 160 cal., 10g fat (6g sat. fat), 28mg chol., 718mg sod., 11g carb. (4g sugars, 4g fiber), 9g pro.

SWEET PEAS PARMA

This is a simple side with delicious Italian flavors. Peas get dressed up for dinner with just a few easy additions.
—Jill Anderson, Sleepy Eye, MN

TAKES: 20 MIN. • **MAKES:** 2 SERVINGS

1¾ cups frozen peas
2 thin slices prosciutto or deli ham, coarsely chopped
½ tsp. minced garlic
1½ tsp. olive oil
1½ tsp. butter
1 small tomato, seeded and chopped
⅛ tsp. salt
Dash pepper

1. Place peas in a steamer basket; place basket in a large saucepan over 1 in. of water. Bring to a boil; cover; steam 4 minutes.
2. Meanwhile, in a large skillet, cook prosciutto and garlic in oil and butter over medium heat until prosciutto is crisp. Add the tomato, salt and pepper; heat through. Stir in the peas.
¾ cup: 192 cal., 9g fat (3g sat. fat), 20mg chol., 584mg sod., 19g carb. (8g sugars, 7g fiber), 11g pro.
Diabetic exchanges: 1 starch, 1 lean meat, 1 fat.

GINGER FRIED RICE

For variety and color, I like to combine at least two types of vegetables. This is a flexible dish, limited only by what's in the fridge and your imagination.
—Becky Matheny, Strasburg, VA

TAKES: 25 MIN. • **MAKES:** 2 SERVINGS

2 tsp. canola oil, divided
1 large egg, lightly beaten
¼ cup chopped sweet red pepper
1 Tbsp. chopped green onion
1 garlic clove, minced
1 cup cold cooked instant rice
¼ cup cubed cooked chicken
1 to 2 Tbsp. soy sauce
½ tsp. ground ginger
1 Tbsp. shredded carrot

1. In a large skillet, heat 1 tsp. oil over medium-high heat. Pour egg into skillet. As the egg sets, lift edges, letting uncooked portion flow underneath. When the egg is completely cooked, remove to plate. Set aside.
2. In same skillet, cook and stir pepper and onion in remaining 1 tsp. oil until tender. Add garlic; cook for 1 minute longer. Stir in the rice, chicken, soy sauce and ginger. Chop egg into small pieces; stir into skillet and heat through. Garnish with carrot.
¾ cup: 223 cal., 9g fat (2g sat. fat), 121mg chol., 517mg sod., 23g carb. (1g sugars, 1g fiber), 11g pro.

NO-COOK CRANBERRY RELISH

This tangy relish pairs well with turkey, chicken or ham—and it makes a plate look so pretty!

—Eleanor Slimak, Chicago, IL

PREP: 5 MIN. + CHILLING
MAKES: 1 SERVING

- ½ cup fresh or frozen cranberries
- ¼ medium orange, peeled
- 1 Tbsp. sugar

In a blender, combine all of the ingredients; cover and process until coarsely chopped. Cover and chill for 30 minutes or until ready to serve.

1 serving: 81 cal., 0 fat (0 sat. fat), 0 chol., 1mg sod., 21g carb. (18g sugars, 2g fiber), 0 pro.

PRONTO VEGETARIAN PEPPERS

In the summer I love to serve these peppers with salad and a roll. At the end of summer, I freeze them for the cold months when the cost of produce is high. For a hot meal on a cold day, try them with a side of warm pasta tossed in olive oil.

—Renee Hollobaugh, Altoona, PA

TAKES: 25 MIN. • **MAKES:** 2 SERVINGS

- 2 large sweet red peppers
- 1 cup canned stewed tomatoes
- ⅓ cup instant brown rice
- 2 Tbsp. hot water
- ¾ cup canned kidney beans, rinsed and drained
- ½ cup frozen corn, thawed
- 2 green onions, thinly sliced
- ⅛ tsp. crushed red pepper flakes
- ½ cup shredded part-skim mozzarella cheese
- 1 Tbsp. grated Parmesan cheese

1. Cut peppers in half lengthwise; remove seeds. Place peppers in an ungreased shallow microwave-safe dish. Cover and microwave on high until tender, 3-4 minutes.
2. Combine the tomatoes, rice and water in a small microwave-safe bowl. Cover and microwave on high 5-6 minutes or until rice is tender. Stir in the beans, corn, onions and pepper flakes; spoon into peppers.
3. Sprinkle with both the cheeses. Microwave, uncovered, until heated through, 3-4 minutes.

2 stuffed pepper halves: 341 cal., 7g fat (3g sat. fat), 19mg chol., 556mg sod., 56g carb. (16g sugars, 11g fiber), 19g pro.

TEST KITCHEN TIP

Want to add meat to this recipe? Stir some cooked chicken, pork or beef into the rice-bean mixture before filling the peppers. Try it with last night's taco meat, too.

LEMON ROASTED RED POTATOES

Lemon juice and thyme give these potatoes fabulous flavor. They go well with just about any main course.
—Sally Sue Campbell, Greenville, TN

PREP: 10 MIN. • **BAKE:** 40 MIN.
MAKES: 2 SERVINGS

- 2 Tbsp. lemon juice
- 4 tsp. olive oil
- ½ tsp. dried thyme
- ½ tsp. garlic salt
- ⅛ tsp. pepper
- 6 small red potatoes (about ¾ lb.), quartered

Preheat oven to 450°. In a medium bowl, combine the lemon juice, oil, thyme, garlic salt and pepper. Add potatoes; toss to coat. Place in a greased 8-in. square baking dish. Bake, uncovered, until the potatoes are tender, about 40 minutes, stirring occasionally.

1 serving: 173 cal., 9g fat (0 sat. fat), 0 chol., 335mg sod., 22g carb. (0 sugars, 0 fiber), 2g pro. **Diabetic exchanges:** 2 fat, 1 starch.

MACARONI & CHEESE

This is one of those dishes that our family calls a "Mama recipe." My own mother rarely consulted a cookbook, so when asked for a recipe, she could only estimate. I make it for two, but it can easily be doubled.
—Betty Allen, East Point, GA

PREP: 10 MIN. • **BAKE:** 30 MIN.
MAKES: 2 SERVINGS

- 1½ cups cooked elbow macaroni
- 1 cup shredded sharp cheddar cheese
- ½ cup 2% milk
- 1 large egg, lightly beaten
- ½ tsp. salt
- 1 Tbsp. butter

Preheat oven to 350°. In a medium bowl, combine macaroni, cheese, milk, egg and salt; mix well. Pour into a greased 1-qt. shallow baking dish; dot top with the butter. Bake, uncovered, 30-35 minutes, or until a knife inserted in the center comes out clean.

1½ cups: 447 cal., 27g fat (18g sat. fat), 190mg chol., 1050mg sod., 30g carb. (4g sugars, 1g fiber), 21g pro.

HOMEMADE CHUNKY APPLESAUCE

Applesauce is so easy to make—so forget buying it in the grocery store. This one has such delicious flavor and is sure to be a favorite.
—Deborah Amrine, Fort Myers, FL

PREP: 10 MIN. • **COOK:** 30 MIN.
MAKES: 2 SERVINGS

- 3 cups chopped peeled tart apples (about 1 lb.)
- 3 Tbsp. brown sugar
- ¼ tsp. ground cinnamon
- ¾ tsp. vanilla extract

1. In a small saucepan, combine apples, brown sugar and cinnamon. Cover and cook over medium-low heat, stirring occasionally, until apples are tender, 30-40 minutes.
2. Remove from heat; add vanilla. Mash until applesauce reaches the desired consistency. Can be served warm or chilled.

½ cup: 176 cal., 1g fat (0 sat. fat), 0 chol., 8mg sod., 45g carb. (40g sugars, 3g fiber), 0 pro.

AMBER'S SOURDOUGH STUFFING

All my kids and grandkids absolutely love this stuffing, but especially my daughter-in-law, Amber. I usually make a big batch at Thanksgiving so I'll have leftovers for my husband. Otherwise, you can use this recipe if you'd like to make a smaller batch for two.
—Kathy Katz, Ocala, FL

PREP: 20 MIN. • **BAKE:** 20 MIN.
MAKES: 2 SERVINGS

  1 Tbsp. olive oil
⅓ cup sliced fresh mushrooms
⅓ cup chopped celery
⅓ cup finely chopped carrot
⅓ cup finely chopped onion
2½ cups cubed sourdough bread
½ tsp. poultry seasoning
¼ tsp. salt
⅛ tsp. pepper
  2 Tbsp. beaten egg
½ to ¾ cup chicken broth

1. Preheat oven to 350°. In a large skillet, heat oil over medium-high heat. Add the mushrooms, celery, carrot and onion; cook and stir until tender.
2. Transfer to a large bowl. Add bread cubes and seasonings; toss to combine. Stir in egg and enough broth to reach desired moistness.
3. Transfer mixture to 2 greased 10-oz. ramekins or a 1-qt. baking dish. Bake 20-25 minutes or until the top is lightly browned and a thermometer reads 160°.
1 serving: 228 cal., 10g fat (2g sat. fat), 58mg chol., 806mg sod., 28g carb. (5g sugars, 3g fiber), 7g pro.

SWEET-SOUR RED CABBAGE

The first time I bought a red cabbage, I didn't quite know what to do with it, but after some experimenting, I came up with this recipe. It has now become my fall comfort food. This side dish is compatible with a variety of meat entrees, but I especially like it with a pork roast or chops.
—Karen Gorman, Gunnison, CO

TAKES: 25 MIN. • **MAKES:** 2 SERVINGS

  2 Tbsp. cider vinegar
  1 Tbsp. brown sugar
¼ tsp. caraway seeds
¼ tsp. celery seed
  2 cups shredded red cabbage
½ cup thinly sliced onion
    Salt and pepper to taste

1. In a small bowl, combine the vinegar, brown sugar, caraway seeds and celery seeds; set aside. Place the cabbage and onion in a saucepan; add a small amount of water. Cover; steam until tender, about 15 minutes.
2. Add vinegar mixture; toss to coat. Season with salt and pepper. Serve cabbage warm.
1 serving: 60 cal., 0 fat (0 sat. fat), 0 chol., 12mg sod., 15g carb. (12g sugars, 2g fiber), 1g pro. **Diabetic exchanges:** 1 vegetable, ½ starch.

TEST KITCHEN TIP

Caraway seeds are a traditional part of many German dishes such as this one. If you don't have them on hand or you're simply not a fan, feel free to leave them out.

1 Tbsp. olive oil
2 medium sweet potatoes
 (about 1¼ lbs.), peeled and
 cut into ½-in.-thick strips
1 Tbsp. apricot preserves
¼ tsp. salt
3 Tbsp. crumbled blue cheese

In a large skillet, heat the oil over medium heat. Add sweet potatoes and cook until tender and lightly browned, turning occasionally, 12-15 minutes. Add the preserves, stirring to coat; sprinkle with salt. Top with cheese.

1 serving: 246 cal., 11g fat (3g sat. fat), 9mg chol., 487mg sod., 34g carb. (15g sugars, 3g fiber), 5g pro.

RICE PASTA

My friend shared this recipe with me several years ago. It is a good side dish that complements chicken, pork and beef. It's a big hit whenever I serve it.
—Anne Jones, Pinehurst, NC

PREP: 5 MIN. • **COOK:** 30 MIN.
MAKES: 2 SERVINGS

2 Tbsp. butter
½ cup uncooked long grain rice
¼ cup uncooked egg noodles
 or vermicelli, broken into
 small pieces
1⅓ cups chicken broth

In a small saucepan, melt butter. Add rice and noodles; cook and stir for 3-4 minutes or until lightly browned. Stir in broth. Bring to a boil. Reduce heat; cover and simmer for 20-25 minutes or until the rice is tender and the broth is absorbed.

1 cup: 297 cal., 12g fat (7g sat. fat), 37mg chol., 737mg sod., 41g carb. (1g sugars, 1g fiber), 5g pro.

SWEET POTATO FRIES WITH BLUE CHEESE

I hated sweet potatoes when I was a child—mostly because they came out of a can. When I learned of their many health benefits, I began trying fresh sweet potatoes with my husband. Now we enjoy them fried and topped with cinnamon sugar or cayenne pepper. We've also discovered how awesome they are with blue cheese.
—Katrina Krumm, Apple Valley, MN

TAKES: 25 MIN. • **MAKES:** 2 SERVINGS

WHITE BEANS & SPINACH

This skillet side is a variation of one I learned from my Italian mother. I have prepared spinach like this for years, especially since my children really like it this way!
—Lucia Johnson, Massena, NY

TAKES: 10 MIN. • **MAKES:** 2 SERVINGS

- 2 Tbsp. water
- 2 garlic cloves, minced
- 8 cups fresh spinach
   (about 6 oz.)
- ¾ cup canned cannellini beans,
   rinsed and drained
- ⅛ tsp. salt
   Dash cayenne pepper
   Dash ground nutmeg

Place water, garlic and spinach in a large skillet. Cook, covered, over medium heat 2-3 minutes or just until tender, stirring occasionally. Stir in the remaining ingredients and heat through.

½ cup: 116 cal., 1g fat (0 sat. fat), 0 chol., 561mg sod., 21g carb. (1g sugars, 7g fiber), 7g pro.
Diabetic exchanges: 1½ starch.

ROASTED CORN & GARLIC RICE

I usually roast quite a few ears of corn when they are on sale and freeze what I don't use at that time. This is a great side dish to go with a fish fry, barbecue or almost any summer meal. It's a constant at my house.
—Marilyn Rodriguez, Sparks, NV

PREP: 40 MIN. • **COOK:** 20 MIN.
MAKES: 2 SERVINGS

- 2 ears sweet corn in husks
- 1 to 2 garlic cloves, peeled
- 1¼ tsp. olive oil, divided
- ½ cup uncooked long grain rice
- 1 cup chicken broth
- 1 bay leaf
- ⅛ tsp. salt
   Dash pepper

1. Preheat oven to 400°. Carefully peel back corn husks to within 1 in. of bottom; remove silk. Rewrap corn in husks. Place garlic cloves on a piece of heavy-duty foil; drizzle with ¼ tsp. oil. Fold the foil around the garlic and seal tightly.
2. Place corn and garlic on a baking sheet. Bake for 30 minutes.
3. Remove the corn; bake the garlic 5-10 minutes longer or until it is softened. Remove garlic from foil and place in a small bowl; let cool; mash with fork. When corn is cool enough to handle, cut the kernels from the cobs with a sharp knife.
4. In a small saucepan, heat the remaining 1 tsp. oil over medium heat. Add the rice; cook and stir 2 minutes. Gradually add broth, bay leaf, salt, pepper and roasted garlic. Bring to a boil. Reduce heat; cover and simmer 12-13 minutes or until heated through.
5. Stir in roasted corn; cook, covered, until the rice is tender, 7-10 minutes longer. Discard the bay leaf.

1 cup: 327 cal., 5g fat (1g sat. fat), 3mg chol., 662mg sod., 65g carb. (5g sugars, 5g fiber), 9g pro.

APRICOT-GINGER ACORN SQUASH

It's a real treat digging into this tender baked squash with its buttery apricot sauce. The natural fruit preserves add sweetness, and ginger makes it savory without loading on unwanted calories.
—Trisha Kruse, Eagle, ID

PREP: 10 MIN. • **BAKE:** 1 HOUR
MAKES: 2 SERVINGS

- 1 small acorn squash
- 2 Tbsp. apricot preserves
- 4 tsp. butter, melted
- 1½ tsp. reduced-sodium soy sauce
- ¼ tsp. ground ginger
- ¼ tsp. pepper

1. Preheat oven to 350°. Cut squash lengthwise in half; remove seeds. Cut a thin slice from the squash bottoms to level if desired. Place in a greased 11x7-in. baking dish, cut side up.
2. Mix remaining ingredients; spoon over the squash. Bake, covered, for 45 minutes.
3. Uncover and bake until tender, 15-20 minutes longer.
½ squash: 234 cal., 8g fat (5g sat. fat), 20mg chol., 221mg sod., 43g carb. (15g sugars, 4g fiber), 3g pro.

BAKED MUSHROOM RICE PILAF

My husband, Steve, and I were experimenting one night, tossing together things we both like, and we created this recipe. It's a wonderful side dish that turns out moist and flavorful every time.
—Marianne Bauman, Modesto, CA

PREP: 10 MIN. • **BAKE:** 55 MIN.
MAKES: 2 SERVINGS

- 1 cup chicken broth
- 1 can (4 oz.) mushroom stems and pieces, drained and coarsely chopped
- ¼ cup uncooked long grain rice
- ¼ cup uncooked wild rice
- 2 Tbsp. sliced almonds, toasted

Preheat oven to 350°. Place the first 4 ingredients in a 3-cup baking dish coated with cooking spray. Bake, covered, until liquid is absorbed and the rice is tender, 55-60 minutes. Just before serving, sprinkle the pilaf with the almonds.
¾ cup: 225 cal., 4g fat (0 sat. fat), 0 chol., 674mg sod., 40g carb. (1g sugars, 3g fiber), 8g pro.

THAI-STYLE GREEN BEANS

Two for Thai, anyone? Peanut butter, soy sauce and ginger flavor this quick and fabulous dish.
—Candace McMenamin, Lexington, SC

TAKES: 20 MIN. • **MAKES:** 2 SERVINGS

- 1 Tbsp. reduced-sodium soy sauce
- 1 Tbsp. hoisin sauce
- 1 Tbsp. creamy peanut butter
- ⅛ tsp. crushed red pepper flakes
- 1 Tbsp. chopped shallot
- 1 tsp. minced fresh gingerroot
- 1 Tbsp. canola oil
- ½ lb. fresh green beans, trimmed
  Optional: Minced fresh cilantro and chopped dry roasted peanuts

1. In a small bowl, combine the soy sauce, hoisin sauce, peanut butter and red pepper flakes; set aside.
2. In a small skillet, cook and stir the shallot and ginger in oil over medium heat for 2 minutes or until shallot is crisp-tender. Add green beans; cook and stir until beans are crisp-tender, about 3 minutes. Add sauce; toss to coat. Sprinkle with cilantro and peanuts if desired.
1 cup: 168 cal., 12g fat (1g sat. fat), 0 chol., 476mg sod., 14g carb. (3g sugars, 4g fiber), 5g pro.

DESSERTS

Love a luscious finale after a hearty meal? Whether served at a celebration or a cozy night in, the sweet delights in this chapter fit perfectly at any table for two.

LAYERED CHOCOLATE PUDDING DESSERT

This layered dessert is cool, creamy, chocolaty and a winner with everyone who tries it. What's not to like?
—Carma Blosser, Livermore, CO

PREP: 30 MIN. + COOLING
MAKES: 2 SERVINGS

- ⅓ cup all-purpose flour
- 3 Tbsp. chopped pecans
- 3 Tbsp. butter, melted
- 3 oz. cream cheese, softened
- ⅓ cup confectioners' sugar
- 1 cup whipped topping, divided
- ⅔ cup cold 2% milk
- 3 Tbsp. instant chocolate pudding mix

1. Preheat oven to 350°. In a small bowl, combine the flour, pecans and butter; press into 2 ungreased 8-oz. ramekins or custard cups. Bake until crust is lightly browned, 10-12 minutes. Cool on a wire rack.
2. In a small bowl, beat cream cheese and confectioners' sugar until smooth; fold in ½ cup whipped topping. Spread over crust.
3. In a small bowl, whisk milk and pudding mix for 2 minutes. Let stand until soft-set, about 2 minutes. Spread over the cream cheese mixture. Spread with the remaining ½ cup whipped topping. Chill until serving.

1 dessert: 584 cal., 33g fat (19g sat. fat), 52mg chol., 264mg sod., 66g carb. (40g sugars, 2g fiber), 6g pro.

BANANAS FOSTER SUNDAES

I have wonderful memories of eating Bananas Foster in New Orleans, and as a dietitian, I wanted to find a healthier version. I combined the best of two recipes and added my own tweaks to create this southern treat. And with this version, it's the perfect dessert for two!
—Lisa Varner, El Paso, TX

TAKES: 15 MIN. • **MAKES:** 2 SERVINGS

- 1 tsp. butter
- 1 Tbsp. brown sugar
- 1 tsp. orange juice
- ⅛ tsp. ground cinnamon
- ⅛ tsp. ground nutmeg
- 1 large banana, sliced
- 2 tsp. chopped pecans, toasted
- ⅛ tsp. rum extract
- 1 cup reduced-fat vanilla ice cream

In a large nonstick skillet, melt butter over medium-low heat. Stir in the brown sugar, orange juice, cinnamon and nutmeg until blended. Add banana and pecans; cook until banana is glazed and slightly softened, stirring lightly, 2-3 minutes. Remove from the heat; stir in extract. Serve with ice cream.

1 sundae: 259 cal., 8g fat (4g sat. fat), 26mg chol., 74mg sod., 45g carb. (32g sugars, 2g fiber), 5g pro.

BAKED APPLE SURPRISE

This sweet-savory recipe is a favorite. Use Brie instead of blue cheese if you like things creamier. My tip? Bake the apples in a muffin tin so they won't roll around.
—Jessica Levinson, Nyack, NY

PREP: 10 MIN. • **BAKE:** 35 MIN.
MAKES: 2 SERVINGS

- 2 medium apples
- 2 Tbsp. crumbled blue cheese, divided
- 2 Tbsp. quick-cooking oats
- 2 Tbsp. bran flakes
- 1 Tbsp. golden raisins
- 1 Tbsp. raisins
- 1 Tbsp. brown sugar

1. Preheat oven to 350°. Cut apples in half lengthwise; remove cores. Place in an ungreased 8-in. square baking dish. Place 1 tsp. of blue cheese into each apple half.
2. In a small bowl, combine oats, bran flakes, golden raisins, raisins and brown sugar; spoon into the apples. Top with the remaining 2 tsp. cheese. Bake, uncovered, until tender, 35-40 minutes.

2 filled apple halves: 181 cal., 3g fat (2g sat. fat), 6mg chol., 141mg sod., 39g carb. (27g sugars, 5g fiber), 3g pro.

RASPBERRY SORBET

You won't believe that you made this refreshing, fruity sorbet yourself! We came up with this healthy freezer fare that will satisfy even your sweetest tooth.
—*Taste of Home* Test Kitchen

PREP: 5 MIN. + FREEZING
MAKES: 2 SERVINGS

- 4½ **tsp. lemon juice**
- 1¼ **cups fresh or frozen unsweetened raspberries**
- ¾ **cup confectioners' sugar**

1. In a food processor, combine all ingredients; cover and process until smooth. Pour into 2 dessert dishes. Freeze, covered, for 1 hour or until edges begin to firm.
2. Stir and return to freezer. Freeze 1½ hours longer or until firm. Remove from the freezer 15 minutes before serving. If desired, garnish with raspberries.
½ cup: 216 cal., 0 fat (0 sat. fat), 0 chol., 1mg sod., 55g carb. (46g sugars, 5g fiber), 1g pro.

MINTY BAKED ALASKA

I've made this dessert on special occasions for my husband and me. He just loves it. It's so simple, but it looks and tastes like you spent all day in the kitchen. Crushed peppermint candy adds a special taste and decorative touch.
—Brenda Mast, Clearwater, FL

TAKES: 30 MIN. • **MAKES:** 2 SERVINGS

- 2 **large egg whites**
- ¼ **cup sugar**
- ¼ **tsp. cream of tartar**
- ¼ **tsp. vanilla extract**
  Dash salt
- 1 **Tbsp. crushed peppermint candy**
- 2 **individual round sponge cakes**
- ⅔ **cup mint chocolate chip ice cream**

1. In a heatproof bowl of a stand mixer, whisk egg whites, sugar and cream of tartar until blended. Place over simmering water in a large saucepan over medium heat. Whisking constantly, heat mixture until a thermometer reads 160°, 4-5 minutes. Remove from heat; add vanilla and salt. With the whisk attachment of the stand mixer, beat on high speed until stiff, glossy peaks form and the meringue has slightly cooled, 7-9 minutes. Fold in peppermint candy.
2. Preheat broiler. Place sponge cakes on an ungreased, foil-lined baking sheet and top each with ⅓ cup ice cream. Immediately spread meringue over ice cream and cake, sealing it to the foil on the sheet. Broil 8 in. from heat until lightly browned, 3-5 minutes. Serve immediately.
1 baked Alaska: 326 cal., 9g fat (5g sat. fat), 44mg chol., 333mg sod., 54g carb. (46g sugars, 0 fiber), 6g pro.

DID YOU KNOW?

Older eggs produce fluffier meringue than fresh. To test your eggs, submerge them in water. If they stand on their end (and don't float!), they're perfect for meringue.

PUMPKIN PIE SMOOTHIE

As an after-dinner treat, an afternoon snack or even for breakfast, this delicious drink lets you have your pie and drink it, too!
—Alisa Christensen, Rancho Santa Margarita, CA

TAKES: 10 MIN. • **MAKES:** 2 SERVINGS

- 1 carton (5.3 oz.) fat-free plain Greek yogurt
- ½ cup 2% milk
- 2 Tbsp. maple syrup
- ¼ tsp. ground cinnamon or pumpkin pie spice
- 2 tsp. almond butter or peanut butter
- ⅔ cup canned pumpkin
- 1 cup ice cubes
- 1 Tbsp. granola

Place the first 7 ingredients in a blender; process until blended. Pour into glasses; top with granola.
1¼ cups: 197 cal., 5g fat (1g sat. fat), 5mg chol., 79mg sod., 30g carb. (21g sugars, 4g fiber), 12g pro. **Diabetic exchanges:** 2 starch, 1 fat.

MAPLE CREME BRULEE

The slow cooker is the perfect way to cook a classic creme brulee. The crunchy brown sugar topping is wonderful, and the custard is smooth and creamy. You can create the burnt sugar topping either with a kitchen torch or under the broiler.
—*Taste of Home* Test Kitchen

PREP: 20 MIN.
COOK: 2 HOURS + CHILLING
MAKES: 3 SERVINGS

- 1⅓ cups heavy whipping cream
- 3 large egg yolks
- ½ cup packed brown sugar
- ¼ tsp. ground cinnamon
- ½ tsp. maple flavoring
- TOPPING
- 1½ tsp. sugar
- 1½ tsp. brown sugar

1. In a small saucepan, heat cream until bubbles form around the side of the pan. In a small bowl, whisk the egg yolks, brown sugar and cinnamon. Remove cream from the heat; stir a small amount of cream into the egg mixture. Return all to the pan; stir constantly. Stir in the maple flavoring.
2. Transfer to three 6-oz. ramekins or custard cups. Place in a 6-qt. slow cooker; add 1 in. of boiling water around the ramekins. Cook, covered, on high 2 to 2½ hours or until centers are just set (mixture will jiggle).
3. Carefully remove ramekins from slow cooker; cool for 10 minutes. Refrigerate, covered, for at least 4 hours.
4. For topping, combine sugars and sprinkle over the ramekins. Hold a kitchen torch about 2 in. above the custard surface; rotate slowly until sugar is evenly caramelized. Serve immediately.
5. If broiling the custards, preheat broiler and place ramekins on a baking sheet; let stand at room temperature for 15 minutes. Broil 8 in. from heat until the sugar is caramelized, 3-5 minutes. Refrigerate until firm, 1-2 hours.
1 creme brulee: 578 cal., 44g fat (26g sat. fat), 350mg chol., 63mg sod., 44g carb. (40g sugars, 0 fiber), 5g pro.

COCOA MERINGUES WITH BERRIES

Meringues can be a challenge to make on a humid day, but if you can't make them, you can often buy them at your favorite bakery. Add this sweet sauce, and you're all set!
—Raymonde Bourgeois, Swastika, ON

PREP: 20 MIN.
BAKE: 50 MIN. + STANDING
MAKES: 2 SERVINGS

- 1 **large egg white**
- ⅛ **tsp. cream of tartar**
  Dash salt
- 3 **Tbsp. sugar, divided**
- 1 **Tbsp. baking cocoa**
- ¼ **tsp. vanilla extract**
- 2 **Tbsp. finely chopped bittersweet chocolate**

BERRY SAUCE
- 2 **Tbsp. sugar**
- 1 **tsp. cornstarch**
- 2 **Tbsp. orange juice**
- 1 **Tbsp. water**
- ½ **cup fresh or frozen blueberries, thawed**
- ½ **cup fresh or frozen raspberries, thawed**
  Grated orange zest, optional

1. Place egg white in a small bowl; let stand at room temperature for 30 minutes.

2. Preheat oven to 275°. Add cream of tartar and salt to the egg white; beat on medium speed until soft peaks form. Gradually beat in 2 Tbsp. sugar.

3. Combine cocoa and remaining 1 Tbsp. sugar; add to meringue with vanilla. Beat on high until stiff glossy peaks form and sugar is dissolved. Fold in chopped chocolate.

4. Drop 2 mounds of meringue onto a parchment-lined baking sheet. Shape into 3-in. cups with the back of a spoon. Bake until set and dry, 50-60 minutes. Turn oven off; leave meringues in oven for 1 hour.

5. In a small saucepan, combine sugar, cornstarch, orange juice and water. Bring to a boil; cook and stir 1 minute or until thickened. Remove from heat; stir in berries. Cool to room temperature. Spoon into meringues. If desired, top with grated orange zest.

1 meringue with ½ cup sauce:
215 cal., 4g fat (2g sat. fat), 0 chol., 102mg sod., 46g carb. (41g sugars, 3g fiber), 3g pro.

CHOCOLATE TURTLE CHEESECAKE

I always get compliments when I whip up this rich little cheesecake. With layers of caramel, chocolate and vanilla, it's an instant classic.
—Erin Byrd, Springfield, MO

PREP: 20 MIN.
BAKE: 20 MIN. + CHILLING
MAKES: 2 SERVINGS

- ⅓ cup crushed vanilla wafers (about 10 wafers)
- 4   tsp. butter, melted
- 4   oz. cream cheese, softened
- 2   Tbsp. sugar
- ½   tsp. vanilla extract
- 2   Tbsp. beaten egg, room temperature
- 2   Tbsp. hot fudge ice cream topping, warmed
- 3   Tbsp. hot caramel ice cream topping

1. Preheat oven to 350°. In a small bowl, combine wafer crumbs and butter. Press onto the bottom and ½ in. up the side of a greased 4-in. springform pan.
2. In a small bowl, beat the cream cheese, sugar and vanilla until smooth. Add egg; beat on low speed just until combined. Spread half the batter into the crust. Stir fudge topping into the remaining batter; gently spread over cream cheese layer. Place pan on a baking sheet.
3. Bake until center is almost set, 20-25 minutes. Cool on a wire rack for 10 minutes. Carefully run a knife around the edge of pan to loosen; cool 1 hour longer.
4. Refrigerate overnight. Remove side of pan. Drizzle caramel topping over cheesecake.

½ cheesecake: 554 cal., 34g fat (18g sat. fat), 137mg chol., 462mg sod., 58g carb. (48g sugars, 1g fiber), 7g pro.

CONTEST-WINNING EASY TIRAMISU

Sweet little servings of tiramisu, dusted with a whisper of cocoa, end any meal on a high note. What a fun use for pudding snack cups!
—Betty Claycomb, Alverton, PA

TAKES: 10 MIN. • **MAKES:** 2 SERVINGS

- 14 vanilla wafers, divided
- 1   tsp. instant coffee granules
- 2   Tbsp. hot water
- 2   snack-size cups (3½ oz. each) vanilla pudding
- ¼   cup whipped topping
- 1   tsp. baking cocoa

1. Set aside 4 vanilla wafers; coarsely crush the remaining 10 wafers. Divide wafer crumbs between 2 dessert dishes.
2. In a small bowl, dissolve coffee granules in hot water. Drizzle over the wafer crumbs. Spoon pudding into the dessert dishes. Top with whipped topping; sprinkle with cocoa. Garnish with the reserved vanilla wafers.

1 tiramisu: 267 cal., 9g fat (4g sat. fat), 4mg chol., 219mg sod., 41g carb. (28g sugars, 1g fiber), 3g pro.

DID YOU KNOW?

The literal translation of *tiramisu* from the Italian is "pick me up." A classic tiramisu chills for up to 24 hours; this easy version is the definition of a quick "pick me up!"

APPLE CRISP

Delicious with ice cream or whipped topping, this apple crisp is always welcome at our table. We especially like it served warm. I make this year-round, but it's tastiest in the fall with newly harvested apples.
—Patricia Gross, Etna Green, IN

PREP: 10 MIN. • **BAKE:** 45 MIN.
MAKES: 2 SERVINGS

- 1 **large tart apple, peeled and sliced**
- 1 **Tbsp. lemon juice**
- 2 **Tbsp. brown sugar**
- 2 **Tbsp. quick-cooking oats**
- 2 **Tbsp. butter, melted**
  Dash ground cinnamon
  Optional: Whipped cream or vanilla ice cream

1. Preheat oven to 350°. Place cut apples in an ungreased 2-cup baking dish; sprinkle with lemon juice. Combine the brown sugar, oats, butter and cinnamon; sprinkle over the apples.
2. Bake, covered, for 30 minutes. Uncover; bake until apples are tender, about 15 minutes longer. If desired, serve with whipped cream or ice cream.
1 serving: 217 cal., 12g fat (7g sat. fat), 31mg chol., 121mg sod., 29g carb. (23g sugars, 2g fiber), 1g pro.

SEMISWEET CHOCOLATE MOUSSE

A friend shared this rich, velvety mousse recipe with me. I love to cook and have tons of recipes, but this one is a favorite. Best of all, it's easy to make.
—Judy Spencer, San Diego, CA

PREP: 20 MIN. + CHILLING
MAKES: 2 SERVINGS

- ¼ **cup semisweet chocolate chips**
- 1 **Tbsp. water**
- 1 **large egg yolk, lightly beaten**
- 1½ **tsp. vanilla extract**
- ½ **cup heavy whipping cream**
- 1 **Tbsp. sugar**
  Optional: Whipped cream and raspberries

1. In a small saucepan, melt chocolate chips with water; stir until smooth. Stir a small amount of the hot chocolate mixture into the egg yolk; return all to the pan, stirring constantly. Cook and stir for 2 minutes or until slightly thickened. Remove from heat; stir in vanilla. Quickly transfer mixture to a small bowl. Stir occasionally until completely cooled.
2. In a small bowl, beat whipping cream until it begins to thicken. Add sugar; beat until soft peaks form. Fold into cooled chocolate mixture.
3. Refrigerate, covered, for at least 2 hours. If desired, garnish with whipped cream and raspberries.
1 cup: 367 cal., 31g fat (18g sat. fat), 188mg chol., 29mg sod., 21g carb. (20g sugars, 1g fiber), 3g pro.

TEST KITCHEN TIP

If your mousse isn't fluffy, your cream may not have been whipped enough when you folded it into the chocolate mixture. Also, if the chocolate mixture is warm, it can deflate the whipped cream. To revive your mousse, whisk it in a bowl with a large whip. Make big, exaggerated circles to work air into the mousse. If that fails, try fold in some more whipped cream.

1 cup all-purpose flour
¼ tsp. salt
⅓ cup shortening
3 Tbsp. ice water
2 medium baking apples
3 Tbsp. sugar
½ tsp. ground cinnamon
1 Tbsp. half-and-half cream

SAUCE

⅓ cup sugar
2 Tbsp. Red Hots or ¼ tsp. ground cinnamon
½ tsp. cornstarch
⅔ cup water
1 Tbsp. butter
  Additional half-and-half cream, optional

1. Preheat oven to 400°. In a bowl, combine flour and salt. Cut in shortening until mixture resembles coarse crumbs. With a fork, stir in water until dough forms a ball. Roll out on a floured surface to a 14x7-in. rectangle; cut crust in half.
2. Peel and core apples; place an apple on each square of crust. Combine sugar and cinnamon; spoon into apples. Moisten edges of crust with water and gather around apples; pinch seams to seal.
3. Place the dumplings in an ungreased 9x5-in. loaf pan or a shallow 1½-qt. baking dish. Brush with cream.
4. In a small saucepan, combine the sugar, Red Hots, cornstarch, water and butter. Bring to a boil over medium-low heat, stirring frequently; boil for 2 minutes. Pour between dumplings.
5. Bake until the crust is golden brown and the apples are tender, 35-45 minutes. Serve warm, with cream if desired.

1 dumpling: 906 cal., 39g fat (12g sat. fat), 19mg chol., 346mg sod., 132g carb. (76g sugars, 4g fiber), 7g pro.

CINNAMON APPLE DUMPLINGS

When Mom made pies to feed the crew during the wheat harvest, she always had plenty of dough left over, so she treated us to apple dumplings. I've carried on this tradition in my own family. My husband and I enjoy this dessert even when I'm not baking pies!
—Marie Hattrup, Sonoma, CA

PREP: 20 MIN. • **BAKE:** 35 MIN.
MAKES: 2 SERVINGS

PEANUT BUTTER COOKIE IN A MUG

This cookie in a mug is perfect for when you have a craving but don't want to make an entire batch of cookies. So quick and easy!
—Rashanda Cobbins, Milwaukee, WI

PREP: 10 MIN. • **COOK:** 2 MIN.
MAKES: 1 SERVING

- 1 Tbsp. butter, softened
- 3 Tbsp. creamy peanut butter
- 3 Tbsp. sugar
- 1 large egg yolk
- ¼ cup all-purpose flour
- 3 Tbsp. 2% milk
- ⅛ tsp. vanilla extract
- 1 Tbsp. chopped unsalted peanuts

1. Spray a 12-oz. mug with cooking spray. Add butter; microwave on high until melted, about 10 seconds. Stir in peanut butter and sugar until combined. Add egg yolk; stir in flour. Add milk and vanilla extract. Top with peanuts.
2. Microwave on high until set, 1 to 1½ minutes. Serve immediately.

1 cookie: 782 cal., 46g fat (15g sat. fat), 219mg chol., 327mg sod., 77g carb. (46g sugars, 4g fiber), 20g pro.

INDIVIDUAL FLANS

I'm a long-time empty nester and am always on the lookout for special desserts sized for two. This rich, comforting custard is smooth, easy and just right for my husband and me!
—Lee Bremson, Kansas City, MO

TAKES: 30 MIN.+ STANDING
MAKES: 2 SERVINGS

- 2 Tbsp. sweetened shredded coconut
- 2 tsp. caramel ice cream topping
- 1 large egg
- 1 large egg yolk
- ¾ cup half-and-half cream
- 3 Tbsp. sugar
- ¼ tsp. vanilla extract
  Pinch ground allspice

1. Divide the coconut between 2 ungreased 6-oz. ramekins or custard cups. Drizzle with caramel topping. In a small bowl, whisk the remaining ingredients; pour into ramekins.
2. Place a steamer rack inside a large skillet. Pour water into skillet until it comes almost to the top of the rack. Place ramekins on rack. Bring to a boil; cover and steam until a knife inserted 1 in. from the edge comes out clean, 10-12 minutes.
3. Remove the ramekins to a wire rack; let stand for 10 minutes. Carefully run a knife around the edge of each ramekin. Unmold each flan onto a dessert plate; serve warm.

1 flan: 307 cal., 16g fat (9g sat. fat), 258mg chol., 119mg sod., 30g carb. (28g sugars, 0 fiber), 8g pro.

DID YOU KNOW?

Flan dates back to the days of the Roman empire, when it was often a savory dish. The Romans created a sweet version using honey, and the Spanish later adapted it to use caramelized sugar.

CINNAMON-RAISIN BREAD PUDDING

This rich bread pudding recipe goes together in minutes and delivers plenty of old-fashioned cinnamon flavor.
—Edna Hoffman, Hebron, IN

PREP: 5 MIN. • **BAKE:** 35 MIN.
MAKES: 2 SERVINGS

- 1 cup cubed cinnamon-raisin bread
- 1 large egg
- ⅔ cup 2% milk
- 3 Tbsp. brown sugar
- 1 Tbsp. butter, melted
- ½ tsp. ground cinnamon
- ¼ tsp. ground nutmeg
  Dash salt
- ⅓ cup raisins

1. Preheat oven to 350°. Place bread cubes in a greased 2-cup baking dish. In a small bowl, whisk the egg, milk, brown sugar, butter, cinnamon, nutmeg and salt until blended. Stir in raisins. Pour over bread; let stand for 15 minutes or until bread is softened.
2. Bake until a knife inserted in the center comes out clean, 35-40 minutes. Serve warm.

1 serving: 337 cal., 11g fat (6g sat. fat), 133mg chol., 260mg sod., 54g carb. (42g sugars, 3g fiber), 9g pro.

CHILLY SNOW DAY FLOATS

On your next snow day, pass out these frothy floats. It's easy to make just as many as you need. Cream soda works with the peppermint ice cream, too.
—Julianne Schnuck, Milwaukee, WI

TAKES: 10 MIN. • **MAKES:** 2 SERVINGS

- ½ cup lemon-lime soda
- 1 cup peppermint ice cream
- ½ cup whipped cream
  Peppermint candy, optional

Pour half of the lemon-lime soda into each of 2 glasses; add ice cream. Top with whipped cream. If desired, sprinkle with peppermint candy. Serve immediately with straws and spoons.

1 float: 248 cal., 15g fat (9g sat. fat), 44mg chol., 59mg sod., 27g carb. (19g sugars, 0 fiber), 3g pro.

FROSTED WALNUT BROWNIE PIE

Dessert isn't just for when the house is full— so I downsized a favorite family recipe to create this chocolaty treat.
—Mary Jo Amos, Noel, MO

PREP: 15 MIN. • **BAKE:** 20 MIN. + COOLING
MAKES: 4 SERVINGS

- ¼ cup butter, softened
- ½ cup sugar
- 1 large egg, room temperature
- ½ tsp. vanilla extract
- ¼ cup all-purpose flour
- 3 Tbsp. baking cocoa
- ¼ cup chopped walnuts
FROSTING
- ½ cup confectioners' sugar
- 1 Tbsp. baking cocoa
- 2½ tsp. 2% milk

1. Preheat oven to 350°. Cream the butter and sugar until light and fluffy, 5-7 minutes. Beat in egg and vanilla. Combine flour and cocoa; gradually add to the creamed mixture. Stir in walnuts.
2. Coat a 6-in. round springform pan with cooking spray and dust with sugar; add the batter. Place pan on a baking sheet. Bake for 20-25 minutes or until a toothpick inserted in the center comes out clean. Cool on a wire rack.
3. Remove side of pan. In a small bowl, combine frosting ingredients. Spread over pie.

1 piece: 368 cal., 18g fat (8g sat. fat), 84mg chol., 134mg sod., 50g carb. (39g sugars, 2g fiber), 5g pro.

CREAMY BUTTERSCOTCH PUDDING

One day when I had a craving for something homemade, I tried from-scratch pudding. It's so much better than the store-bought kind!
—EMR, tasteofhome.com

PREP: 10 MIN.
COOK: 10 MIN. + CHILLING
MAKES: 2 SERVINGS

- ¼ cup packed brown sugar
- 1 Tbsp. plus 1 tsp. cornstarch
  Dash salt
- 1 cup fat-free milk
- 1 large egg yolk, lightly beaten
- 1½ tsp. butter
- ¾ tsp. vanilla extract
- 2 Pirouette cookies, optional

1. In a small saucepan, combine the brown sugar, cornstarch and salt. Add milk and egg yolk; stir until smooth. Cook and stir over medium heat until the mixture comes to a boil. Cook and stir until thickened, 1-2 minutes longer.
2. Remove from the heat; stir in butter and vanilla. Cool to room temperature, stirring several times. Pour into 2 individual dessert dishes. Refrigerate, covered, until chilled, 1-2 hours. If desired, serve with Pirouette cookies.
½ cup: 217 cal., 5g fat (2g sat. fat), 111mg chol., 157mg sod., 38g carb. (33g sugars, 0 fiber), 5g pro.

MUD PIES

Inspired by recipes that use premade individual pie crusts and ice cream, I created this combination. I love that it doesn't require any baking.
—Cassandra Gourley, Williams, AZ

TAKES: 10 MIN. • **MAKES:** 2 SERVINGS

- ⅓ cup Nutella
- 2 individual graham cracker tart shells
- 1 cup coffee ice cream
  Whipped cream and chocolate-covered coffee beans

Spoon Nutella into tart shells. Top each with ice cream; garnish with whipped cream and coffee beans. Serve immediately.
1 pie: 499 cal., 29g fat (8g sat. fat), 26mg chol., 197mg sod., 59g carb. (47g sugars, 2g fiber), 7g pro.

CONTEST-WINNING STRAWBERRY PRETZEL DESSERT

I love the sweet-salty flavor of this pretty layered dessert. Sliced strawberries and gelatin top a smooth cream cheese filling and crispy pretzel crust. I think it's best when eaten within a day of being made.
—Wendy Weaver, Leetonia, OH

PREP: 15 MIN. + CHILLING
MAKES: 2 SERVINGS

- ⅓ cup crushed pretzels
- 2 Tbsp. butter, softened
- 2 oz. cream cheese, softened
- ¼ cup sugar
- ¾ cup whipped topping
- 2 Tbsp. plus 1½ tsp. strawberry gelatin
- ½ cup boiling water
- 1 cup sliced fresh strawberries
  Optional: Whipped topping and pretzel twists

1. Preheat oven to 375°. In a large bowl, combine pretzels and butter. Press onto the bottom of 2 greased 10-oz. custard cups. Bake until set, 6-8 minutes. Cool on a wire rack.
2. In a small bowl, combine the cream cheese and sugar until smooth. Fold in whipped topping. Spoon over crust. Refrigerate for 30 minutes.
3. Meanwhile, in a small bowl, dissolve gelatin in boiling water. Refrigerate, covered, 20 minutes or until slightly thickened. Fold in strawberries. Carefully spoon over the filling. Refrigerate, covered, at least 3 hours. If desired, top with whipped topping and pretzel twist.
1 dessert: 516 cal., 27g fat (18g sat. fat), 62mg chol., 458mg sod., 64g carb. (47g sugars, 2g fiber), 6g pro.

THIN MINT MILK SHAKE

Stick a sleeve of those yummy chocolate-mint Girl Scout cookies in the freezer and save them to use for creamy milk shakes. They go over big with kids and adults alike.
—Shauna Sever, Oak Park, IL

TAKES: 5 MIN. • **MAKES:** 2 SERVINGS

- 3 Tbsp. creme de menthe or 3 Tbsp. 2% milk plus a dash of peppermint extract
- 1¼ to 1½ cups vanilla ice cream
- 7 Girl Scout Thin Mint cookies Green food coloring, optional

Place all ingredients in a blender in order listed; cover and process until blended. Serve immediately.

⅔ cup: 363 cal., 12g fat (7g sat. fat), 36mg chol., 70mg sod., 49g carb. (47g sugars, 1g fiber), 3g pro.

STRAWBERRY CREAM PUFFS

My whole family loves to cook; this came from a collection of family recipes handed down through several generations. These cream puffs were a favorite for holidays, but they are good anytime. This is a nice departure from strawberry shortcake.
—Suzette Jury, Keene, CA

PREP: 30 MIN. + CHILLING
BAKE: 25 MIN. + COOLING
MAKES: 3 SERVINGS

- ¼ cup water
- 2 Tbsp. butter
- ¼ tsp. sugar
  Dash salt
- ¼ cup all-purpose flour
- 1 large egg, room temperature

FILLING
- 1¼ cups sliced fresh strawberries
- 3 tsp. sugar, divided
- ½ cup heavy whipping cream
- ¼ tsp. confectioners' sugar
  Additional sliced fresh strawberries, optional

1. Preheat oven to 400°. In a small saucepan, bring the water, butter, sugar and salt to a boil. Add flour all at once and stir until a smooth ball forms. Remove from heat; let stand for 5 minutes. Add egg and beat well. Continue beating until mixture is smooth and shiny. Drop by rounded tablespoonfuls 3 in. apart onto a greased baking sheet.
2. Bake for 25-30 minutes or until golden brown. Remove to a wire rack. Immediately split puffs open; remove tops and set aside. Discard soft dough from inside. Cool puffs.
3. For filling, in a small bowl, combine strawberries and 2 tsp. sugar. Cover and refrigerate for 30 minutes.
4. In a small bowl, beat cream and the remaining 1 tsp. sugar until stiff peaks form. Fold in the strawberry mixture.
5. Fill the cream puffs just before serving. Sprinkle with confectioners' sugar. Garnish with additional strawberries if desired.
1 serving: 311 cal., 24g fat (14g sat. fat), 145mg chol., 142mg sod., 21g carb. (9g sugars, 2g fiber), 5g pro.

MALTED CHOCOLATE CHEESECAKE

With an impressive presentation and a scrumptious, classic malt flavor, this small-scale dessert will make anyone feel special.
—Anna Ginsberg, Chicago, IL

PREP: 30 MIN.
BAKE: 40 MIN. + COOLING
MAKES: 2 SERVINGS

- 4 portions refrigerated ready-to-bake sugar cookie dough
- 4 oz. cream cheese, softened
- ½ cup dark chocolate chips, melted
- 2 Tbsp. sugar
- 1 large egg white, room temperature
- ½ tsp. vanilla extract

TOPPING
- 4½ tsp. cream cheese, softened
- 2 tsp. sugar
- 1 tsp. malted milk powder
- 1 tsp. baking cocoa
- ⅔ cup whipped topping
- 1 Tbsp. chocolate syrup

1. Preheat oven to 325°. Line a 5¾x3x2-in. loaf pan with foil. Press cookie dough onto bottom of pan. Bake for 15-20 minutes or until golden brown. Cool on a wire rack.
2. In a small bowl, beat the cream cheese, melted chocolate and sugar until smooth. Add egg white; beat on low speed just until combined. Stir in vanilla. Pour over crust.
3. Place loaf pan in a baking pan; add 1 in. of hot water to larger pan. Bake at 325° for 40-45 minutes or until the center is just set and top appears dull.
4. Remove loaf pan from water bath. Cool on a wire rack for 10 minutes. Carefully run a knife around edge of pan to loosen; cool 1 hour longer and then refrigerate overnight.
5. For topping, in a small bowl, beat the cream cheese, sugar, milk powder and baking cocoa until smooth. Fold in whipped topping. Spread over chilled cheesecake. Cover; refrigerate 1 hour longer.
6. Using foil, lift cheesecake out of pan. Cut in half. Drizzle chocolate syrup over each piece. Refrigerate any leftovers.

½ cheesecake: 934 cal., 58g fat (34g sat. fat), 74mg chol., 350mg sod., 92g carb. (68g sugars, 0 fiber), 14g pro.

CHEESECAKE BERRY PARFAITS

The summer berry season is a real treat. This is an easy way to enjoy berries with cheesecake, a refreshing change from traditional pudding and fruit parfaits.
—Patricia Schroedl, Jefferson, WI

TAKES: 15 MIN. • **MAKES:** 2 PARFAITS

- 2 oz. cream cheese, softened
- 4 tsp. sugar
- ⅔ cup whipped topping
- 1½ cups mixed fresh berries
  Additional whipped topping, optional

1. In a small bowl, beat cream cheese and sugar until smooth. Fold in whipped topping.
2. In each of 2 parfait glasses, layer a fourth of the cream cheese mixture and a fourth of the berries. Repeat layers. Top with additional whipped topping if desired. Chill until serving.
1 parfait: 146 cal., 4g fat (4g sat. fat), 0 chol., 1mg sod., 25g carb. (21g sugars, 3g fiber), 1g pro.

STRAWBERRY RHUBARB COBBLER

Full of berries and rhubarb, this pretty cobbler is the perfect finale for a summer dinner for two. Pecans in the topping and the delicious sauce make it extra special.
—Lily Julow, Lawrenceville, GA

PREP: 20 MIN. + STANDING
BAKE: 25 MIN. • **MAKES:** 2 SERVINGS

- 1 cup sliced fresh or frozen rhubarb
- 1 cup sliced fresh strawberries
- ¼ cup sugar
- 1 Tbsp. quick-cooking tapioca
- 1 tsp. lemon juice
  Dash salt

TOPPING
- ⅓ cup all-purpose flour
- ¼ cup chopped pecans
- 3 Tbsp. sugar
- ⅛ tsp. baking powder
  Dash salt
- 2 Tbsp. cold butter
- 1 large egg

SAUCE
- ½ cup vanilla ice cream
- 2¼ tsp. Marsala wine

1. Combine the first 6 ingredients; divide between 2 greased 8-oz. ramekins or custard cups. Let stand 15 minutes.
2. In a small bowl, combine the flour, pecans, sugar, baking powder and salt; cut in butter until mixture resembles coarse crumbs. Stir in egg. Drop by spoonfuls over the fruit mixture; spread evenly.
3. Bake at 375° until filling is bubbly and a toothpick inserted in topping comes out clean, 25-30 minutes.
4. In a microwave-safe bowl, combine ice cream and wine. Cook, uncovered, at 50% power for 1-2 minutes or until heated through; stir until blended. Serve with warm cobbler.
1 cobbler: 619 cal., 29g fat (11g sat. fat), 150mg chol., 318mg sod., 85g carb. (56g sugars, 5g fiber), 9g pro.

CHERRY-CHOCOLATE PUDGY PIE

Here's an ooey-gooey treat that's just right for campfires and cookouts.
—Josh Carter, Birmingham, AL

TAKES: 10 MIN. • **MAKES:** 1 SERVING

- 2 slices white bread
- 3 Tbsp. cherry pie filling
- 1 Tbsp. chopped almonds
- 1 Tbsp. semisweet chocolate chips

1. Place 1 slice of bread in a greased sandwich iron. Spread with pie filling; top with almonds, chocolate chips and the remaining bread slice. Close iron.
2. Cook over a hot campfire until golden brown and heated through, 3-6 minutes, turning occasionally.
1 sandwich: 309 cal., 9g fat (3g sat. fat), 0 chol., 294mg sod., 51g carb. (9g sugars, 3g fiber), 7g pro.

CHERRY CREAM CHEESE TARTS

It may be hard to believe, but just 5 ingredients and a few minutes of preparation result in these delicate and scrumptious tarts!
—Cindi Mitchell, Waring, TX

TAKES: 10 MIN. • **MAKES:** 2 SERVINGS

- 3 oz. cream cheese, softened
- ¼ cup confectioners' sugar
- ⅛ to ¼ tsp. almond or vanilla extract
- 2 individual graham cracker shells
- ¼ cup cherry pie filling

In a small bowl, beat the cream cheese, sugar and extract until smooth. Spoon into shells. Top with pie filling. Refrigerate until ready to serve.

1 tart: 362 cal., 20g fat (10g sat. fat), 43mg chol., 265mg sod., 42g carb. (29g sugars, 1g fiber), 4g pro.

CHOCOLATE PEANUT PARFAITS

This lower-in-fat-and-calories version of a pie recipe I dearly love still tastes great. It's make-ahead handy!
—Lisa Varner, El Paso, TX

PREP: 15 MIN. + CHILLING
MAKES: 2 SERVINGS

- 2 chocolate wafers, crushed
- ¼ cup fat-free sweetened condensed milk
- 2 oz. fat-free cream cheese
- 2 Tbsp. reduced-fat creamy peanut butter
- ¾ tsp. lemon juice
- ½ tsp. vanilla extract
- ¼ cup reduced-fat whipped topping
- 1 tsp. chocolate syrup
- 1 tsp. chopped dry roasted peanuts

Divide crushed wafers between 2 parfait glasses. In a small bowl, beat the milk, cream cheese, peanut butter, lemon juice and vanilla. Fold in whipped topping. Spoon over crushed wafers. Refrigerated, covered, for at least 1 hour. Just before serving, drizzle with syrup and sprinkle with peanuts.

1 serving: 300 cal., 9g fat (3g sat. fat), 9mg chol., 385mg sod., 41g carb. (32g sugars, 1g fiber), 13g pro.

CREAMY RICE PUDDING

I was fortunate to grow up around fabulous cooks. My mother and grandmother taught me to experiment with recipes. We tried a lot of variations on this one; no matter how we embellished it, it was always tasty. It still brings back fond memories.
—Laura German, North Brookfield, MA

TAKES: 25 MIN. • **MAKES:** 2 SERVINGS

- 1 cup cooked long grain rice
- 1 cup whole milk
- 5 tsp. sugar
  Dash salt
- ½ tsp. vanilla extract
  Optional: Whipped cream, sliced almonds, raisins, ground cinnamon and cinnamon stick.

1. In a small heavy saucepan, combine rice, milk, sugar and salt; bring to a boil over medium heat. Reduce heat to maintain a low simmer. Cook, uncovered, until thickened, about 20 minutes, stirring often.

2. Remove from the heat; stir in vanilla. Spoon into serving dishes. Serve warm or cold; serve with desired toppings.

1 serving: 220 cal., 4g fat (3g sat. fat), 17mg chol., 134mg sod., 38g carb. (16g sugars, 0 fiber), 6g pro.

½ tsp. grated orange zest
⅛ tsp. orange extract
   Additional grated orange
   zest, optional

1. Core pears from bottom, leaving stems intact. Peel pears; cut ¼ in. from bottom to level if necessary. Place pears on their sides in a large saucepan. Add water, wine, sugar and vanilla. Bring to a boil. Reduce heat; simmer, covered, turning once, until the pears are almost tender, 35-40 minutes. (For more intense flavor and color, leave fruit in cooking liquid and refrigerate overnight.)
2. Combine the sour cream, confectioners' sugar, orange zest and extract. Refrigerate until serving.
3. Remove pears with a slotted spoon; pat dry and, if warm, cool to room temperature. Discard the cooking liquid. Place pears on dessert plates. Serve with orange cream; if desired, top with additional grated orange zest.
1 pear: 239 cal., 3g fat (2g sat. fat), 10mg chol., 23mg sod., 46g carb. (36g sugars, 5g fiber), 3g pro.

POACHED PEARS WITH ORANGE CREAM

End the meal with a flourish with this easy and elegant dessert. A hint of orange lends just enough sweetness to temper the wine's bold taste.
—Julianne Schnuck, Milwaukee, WI

PREP: 10 MIN.
COOK: 45 MIN. + COOLING
MAKES: 2 SERVINGS

   2 firm medium pears
1½ cups water
   1 cup dry red wine or
      red grape juice
½ cup sugar
   2 tsp. vanilla extract
¼ cup reduced-fat sour cream
   2 tsp. confectioners' sugar

TEST KITCHEN TIP

Using red wine in the poaching liquid produces an intensely flavored, rosy red pear. You can also use a fruity white wine for a pear that is natural looking. Have leftover sparkling wine or Champagne? Use that for a lightly flavored pear.

AIR-FRYER CHOCOLATE BREAD PUDDING

This is a fun dish because the chocolate makes it different from traditional bread pudding recipes. It's a rich, comforting dessert.
—Mildred Sherrer, Fort Worth, TX

PREP: 15 MIN. + STANDING
COOK: 15 MIN. • **MAKES:** 2 SERVINGS

- 2   oz. semisweet chocolate, chopped
- ½   cup half-and-half cream
- ⅔   cup sugar
- ½   cup 2% milk
- 1   large egg, room temperature
- 1   tsp. vanilla extract
- ¼   tsp. salt
- 4   slices day-old bread, crusts removed and cut into cubes (about 3 cups)
      Optional: Confectioners' sugar and whipped cream

1. In a small microwave-safe bowl, melt chocolate; stir until smooth. Stir in cream.
2. In a large bowl, whisk sugar, milk, egg, vanilla and salt. Stir in chocolate mixture. Add bread cubes and toss to coat. Let stand 15 minutes.
3. Preheat air fryer to 325°. Spoon bread mixture into 2 greased 8-oz. ramekins or custard cups. Place on tray in air-fryer basket. Cook until a knife inserted in the center comes out clean, 12-15 minutes.
4. If desired, top with confectioners' sugar and whipped cream.

1 pudding: 729 cal., 22g fat (12g sat. fat), 128mg chol., 674mg sod., 107g carb. (81g sugars, 2g fiber), 14g pro.

PINEAPPLE UPSIDE-DOWN CAKE

Tender, moist and sweet, these luscious but lighter cakes are as special as the person you choose to share them with!
—*Taste of Home* Test Kitchen

PREP: 15 MIN. • **BAKE:** 20 MIN.
MAKES: 2 SERVINGS

- 4   tsp. butter, melted, divided
- 4   tsp. brown sugar
- 2   canned unsweetened pineapple slices
- 2   maraschino cherries
- ⅓   cup all-purpose flour
- 3   Tbsp. sugar
- ½   tsp. baking powder
- ⅛   tsp. salt
      Dash ground nutmeg
- 3   Tbsp. fat-free milk
- ¼   tsp. vanilla extract

1. Preheat oven to 350°. Pour ½ tsp. butter into each of two 10-oz. ramekins or custard cups coated with cooking spray. Sprinkle with brown sugar. Top with a pineapple slice. Place a cherry in the center of each pineapple slice.
2. In a small bowl, combine the flour, sugar, baking powder, salt and nutmeg. Beat in the milk, vanilla and remaining 3 tsp. melted butter just until combined. Spoon over the pineapple.
3. Bake 20-25 minutes or until a toothpick inserted in the center comes out clean. Cool 5 minutes. Run a knife around edges of ramekins; invert onto dessert plates. Serve warm.

1 cake: 290 cal., 8g fat (5g sat. fat), 21mg chol., 318mg sod., 53g carb. (37g sugars, 1g fiber), 3g pro.

LEMON PUDDING CAKE

My husband, Lloyd, loves this cake because it tastes like lemon meringue pie. The cake is no-fuss and makes just enough for the two of us.
—Dawn Fagerstrom, Warren, MN

PREP: 15 MIN. • **BAKE:** 40 MIN.
MAKES: 2 SERVINGS

- 1   large egg, separated, room temperature
- ½   cup sugar
- ⅓   cup whole milk
- 2   Tbsp. all-purpose flour
- 2   Tbsp. lemon juice
- 1   tsp. grated lemon zest
- ⅛   tsp. salt
     Optional: Confectioners' sugar, lemon slices and whipped cream

1. Preheat oven to 325°. In a bowl, beat egg yolk. Add sugar, milk, flour, lemon juice, zest and salt; beat until smooth. Beat egg white until stiff peaks form; gently fold into lemon mixture. Pour into 2 ungreased 6-oz. ramekins or custard cups (ramekins will be very full).
2. Place the ramekins in an 8-in. square baking pan. Pour boiling water into baking pan to a depth of 1 in. Bake until a knife inserted in the center comes out clean and top is golden, 40-45 minutes. If desired, top with confectioners' sugar, lemon slices and whipped cream.

1 cake: 288 cal., 4g fat (2g sat. fat), 112mg chol., 200mg sod., 60g carb. (51g sugars, 0 fiber), 5g pro.

EASY ALMOND JOY CHIA PUDDING

I enjoy making this recipe because it's easy and I can find all of the ingredients at my local market. There is no baking required, and it's served in individual jars for guests. For more flavor, add shredded coconut.
—Ashley Altan, Hanover, MD

PREP: 15 MIN. + CHILLING
MAKES: 2 SERVINGS

- 1   cup refrigerated unsweetened coconut milk
- 4   Tbsp. chia seeds
- 3   Tbsp. maple syrup
- 2   Tbsp. baking cocoa
- ¼   cup dairy-free semisweet chocolate chips
- ¼   cup slivered almonds

1. In a small bowl, mix coconut milk, chia seeds and maple syrup. Remove half of the mixture to a small bowl; stir in cocoa until blended. Refrigerate both plain and chocolate mixtures, covered, until thickened, at least 6 hours.
2. In dessert dishes, layer a fourth each of the white pudding, chocolate pudding, almonds and chocolate chips. Repeat layers. Serve immediately or store in the refrigerator up to 3 days.

Note: This recipe was tested with Enjoy Life semisweet chocolate chips.

1 pudding: 414 cal., 24g fat (8g sat. fat), 0 chol., 7mg sod., 50g carb. (30g sugars, 12g fiber), 9g pro.

QUICK BANANA SPLIT SHORTCAKE

Two delicious desserts combine to create an out-of-this-world treat. I serve my banana split on a layer of tender pound cake. Yum!
—Christi Gillentine, Tulsa, OK

TAKES: 10 MIN. • **MAKES:** 2 SERVINGS

- 4   slices pound cake (½ in. thick) or 2 individual round sponge cakes
- 1   medium firm banana, sliced
- 2   scoops vanilla ice cream
- 2   Tbsp. chocolate syrup

Place a cake slice on each of 2 dessert plates. Top each with banana and ice cream. Drizzle with chocolate syrup. Serve immediately.

1 serving: 468 cal., 19g fat (11g sat. fat), 162mg chol., 305mg sod., 70g carb. (29g sugars, 2g fiber), 7g pro.

SPICED CHOCOLATE MOLTEN CAKES

Take some time to linger over this decadent dessert. There is nothing better than a chocolate cake with a warm melted center.
—Deb Carpenter, Hastings, MI

TAKES: 30 MIN. • **MAKES:** 2 SERVINGS

¼   cup butter, cubed
2   oz. semisweet chocolate, chopped
1½ tsp. dry red wine
½   tsp. vanilla extract
1   large egg, room temperature
2   tsp. egg yolk, room temperature
½   cup confectioners' sugar
3   Tbsp. all-purpose flour
⅛   tsp. ground ginger
⅛   tsp. ground cinnamon
     Additional confectioners' sugar

1. Preheat oven to 425°. In a microwave, melt the butter and chocolate; stir until smooth. Stir in wine and vanilla.
2. In a small bowl, beat the egg, egg yolk and confectioners' sugar until thick and lemon-colored. Beat in the flour, ginger and cinnamon until well blended. Gradually beat in the butter mixture.
3. Transfer batter to 2 greased 6-oz. ramekins or custard cups. Place ramekins on a baking sheet. Bake until a thermometer inserted in the center reads 160° and sides of cakes are set, 10-12 minutes.
4. Remove from the oven and let stand for 1 minute. Run a knife around edges of ramekins; invert onto dessert plates. Dust with additional confectioners' sugar. Serve immediately.
1 cake: 560 cal., 36g fat (21g sat. fat), 234mg chol., 200mg sod., 56g carb. (43g sugars, 2g fiber), 8g pro.

WARM PINEAPPLE SUNDAES WITH RUM SAUCE

Pineapple, rum and sugar are already a flavorful dream together, but adding ginger and butter takes this dessert to another level.
—Jamie Miller, Maple Grove, MN

TAKES: 25 MIN. • **MAKES:** 2 SERVINGS

4   fresh pineapple spears (about 8 oz.)
½   cup packed brown sugar
2   Tbsp. dark rum
¾   tsp. ground ginger
4   tsp. butter, cut into small pieces
2   scoops vanilla ice cream or low-fat frozen yogurt
4   gingersnap cookies, crushed

1. Preheat oven to 425°. Place pineapple in 1-qt. baking dish. In a small bowl, combine the brown sugar, rum and ginger; spoon over the pineapple. Dot with butter.
2. Bake, uncovered, until pineapple is lightly browned and the sauce is bubbly, 8-10 minutes.
3. Place ice cream in 2 dessert dishes; top with pineapple and sauce. Serve immediately with crushed cookies.
1 sundae: 536 cal., 16g fat (10g sat. fat), 49mg chol., 221mg sod., 95g carb. (78g sugars, 2g fiber), 4g pro.

DID YOU KNOW?

The "sundae" is said to have originated in the 19th century as a virtuous Sunday alternative to ice-cream sodas—since carbonated soda was seen as morally dubious.

RECIPE INDEX